The Felonious & Wilful Murder of Edith Jeal: The Brighton Outrage

By Charles James Hayward

Copyright © 2023

Contents:

Introduction		1
Chapter 1:	The Families	3
Chapter 2:	'A Crime of Unspeakable Atrocity'	9
Chapter 3:	'A Mysterious Stranger'	19
Chapter 4:	The Early Career of the Culprit	27
Chapter 5:	Lewes House of Correction and County Gaol	35
Chapter 6:	'Torn to Pieces'	51
Chapter 7:	The Opening of the Inquest	59
Chapter 8:	'The Black Maria'	69
Chapter 9:	'Suffer Little Children to Come Unto me'	75
Chapter 10:	A Letter from the Prisoner	81
Chapter 11:	A Verdict of Wilful Murder and Outrage	85
Chapter 12:	'It may be true, but I hope it is not'	97
Chapter 13:	'What dreadful news it is?'	119
Chapter 14:	Committed for Trial	125
Chapter 15:	'A Neurotic Subject'	131
Chapter 16:	'A Painful Experience'	145
Chapter 17:	'A Half-witted Ignoramus'	155

Chapter 18:	Manitoba Penitentiary	165
Chapter 19:	The Court of Assize	175
Chapter 20:	The Day of Reckoning	181
Chapter 21:	*'A Very Decent Fellow'*	189
Chapter 22:	*'He knew perfectly the charges against him!'*	201
Chapter 23:	*'A Frenzied Man'*	215
Chapter 24:	The Medical Evidence	225
Chapter 25:	*'May the Lord have Mercy on your Soul'*	239
Chapter 26:	*'And for this, petitioners will ever pray'*	253
Chapter 27:	Behind the Scenes	265
Chapter 28:	Arrangements for the Execution	275
Chapter 29:	*'In Life we are Death'*	281
Chapter 30:	The Aftermath	293
Bibliography		297

Dedicated to little
Edith Jeal

15th October 1886 - 10th December 1891

Introduction

Anyone who finds themselves within Brighton cannot fail to appreciate its deep, rich and diverse history. From the Royal Pavilion to the Duke of York's Picture House, the city of Brighton offers a glimpse into most aspects of society's past. Even those without an interest in bygone times cannot help but appreciate Brighton's historical significance.

Today Brighton is a bustling and vibrant city. However, it was only a tiny village when the Saxons landed in the 5th century AD. Over time, the settlement grew, and a prosperous fishing and farming town was established. In 1789, Doctor Richard Russell published 'A *Dissertation on the Use of Sea Water in the Affections of the Glands'*, which promoted bathing in the sea as a treatment for many diseases and illnesses.

In his writings, Doctor Russell promoted Brighton as an excellent place to live after concluding that its waters were far superior to other sites. Consequently, droves of people flocked to the area, keen to drink and bathe in the local waters, and Brighton's population exponentially grew. Some areas of the town became affluent, attracting members of the upper classes, aristocracy and even royalty.

However, as is often the case in such circumstances, many people within the lower classes also moved to the town in search of employment, opportunity and a better quality of life. But after arriving, many people struggled to find work, and in some areas, poverty was rife. As is typical, levels of crime within Brighton increased, and as many historic newspapers reported at the time, theft, pick-pocketing and fraud were prevalent within the town.

These acts low level crimes pale in comparison to other crimes that have been committed within Brighton's borders. Even up to the current day, it has often been the scene of many barbaric and brutal murders. In 1831, John Holloway committed one of Brighton's most infamous murders. After falling in love with his mistress Ann Kennard, he strangled his downtrodden wife. Poor Celia Holloway was then dismembered and with the help of a wheelbarrow, transported and buried at Lovers Walk, Brighton. He was later convicted of the murder and executed at Horsham Gaol.

Other grisly murders have occurred, including the Brighton Trunk Murders in 1934, one of which was attributed to Tony Mancini and led to Brighton being described as the *'Queen of all Slaughtering Places'* due to the murder's cold and savage nature.

Crime fascinates many, and therefore these and many more of Brighton's murders were highly publicised and saturated the newspapers of the time. Consequently, they have survived the passage of time and become modern-day urban legends frequently spoken of by locals. With the recent renewed obsession with true crime, the most infamous cases are recounted in many books and, more recently, crime blogs and podcasts.

However, despite being just as sensational and shocking, some have been wholly forgotten with time. As a true-crime enthusiast and a lifelong Brighton resident, I have spent much of my adult life researching local murders, particularly those that happened long ago. I can still remember the first time I visited Preston Park Cemetery as a child and the unease I experienced as I read Celia Holloway haunting memorial, which hangs on the ancient cemetery's flint wall.

Yet, approximately two years ago, after purchasing a second-hand copy of *Douglas d'Enno's* book *'Foul Deeds and Suspicious Deeds around Brighton'* I became aware of a long-forgotten murder, which happened less than a mile from where I live. The murder relates to the incomprehensible death of five-year-old Edith Jeal in 1891. As I read through the sparse details of the crime, I was shocked and appalled by the nature of her murder and violation and turned to the internet to try and learn more about the crime.

Very little information about the murder was readily available, which I found intriguing. I have questioned how one of the century's most sensational and high-profile murders had simply been forgotten. Since then, I have spent many hours researching the case using local, national and international archives to try and obtain the full facts of Edith's story.

For the first time, little Edith Jeal's murder and the facts surrounding it are recounted within the pages of this book. I hope this book proves of interest to any true crime enthusiasts and, more importantly, revives the memory of poor little Edith Jeal, whose life was cruelly and barbarically taken over a century ago.

Chapter 1: The Families

This story centres upon a district located in the south-easterly corner of Brighton. This area, known as Kemp Town, can be found by travelling approximately two miles east of the Palace Pier. At the name's inception, *'Kemp Town'* referred to a 19th-century residential estate featuring Regency architecture that consisted of Arundel Terrace, Lewes Crescent, Sussex Square, Chichester Terrace, and the Kemp Town enclosures.

The estate's name came from Thomas Read Kemp, who conceived and financed the design. The project's building work started in 1823, and despite the estate's age, it survives today and continues to boast some of the most beautiful symmetry and architecture in Sussex. Since then, the original Kemp Town estate has gone on to share its name with a much broader district, which starts at St James Street and continues east, right up to the Bell Tower to the north of Brighton Marina. It also includes the many roads which branch to the south and the north of the St James Street, Kemp Town's main thoroughfare.

Aside from some small pockets of social housing, today, modern Kemp Town is considered affluent, cosmopolitan and inclusive. But in 1891, it was known for its poverty, deprivation and contained some of the worst housing in Brighton. The Jeal family, the first family involved in this sorrowful tale, lived in this area. The family belonged to the lower classes but were thriving and happy despite their financial woes.

Mr Edward Jeal, the head of the family, was a well-known and respected member of the community. In 1891, the year this story begins, Edward Jeal was 46 years old and had worked as a dairyman for the Sussex Dairy Company for many years. The company operated out of premises at St. George's Place, St. James's Street and East Street, Brighton. Edward Jeal's responsibilities involved delivering milk churns on the back of a horse-drawn cart to various clients and businesses across the town.

Edward lived with his wife, Charlotte Jeal (*née Rogers*), to whom he had married at Nicholas Church on the 24th of April 1871. Charlotte was already heavily pregnant with their first child, Alice at the time of their wedding. Being pregnant out of wedlock was entirely against the accepted norms of the Victorian era and was often viewed by society as scandalous. In many instances, illegitimacy could also lead to legal consequences for the child's parents and this forced woman to hide away from society and in many instances, to give their babies away to regain respectability and employment.

In Charlotte's case, she appears to have given Alice's care to her parents, John and Ann Rogers. According to the censuses, Alice remained in the care of her Grandparents for the duration of her childhood. However, later reports suggest that Alice maintained a close relationship with her parents, despite this informal arrangement.

With Edward being the sole earner and only receiving a small income, the newly married couple must have found their living costs challenging to manage. Nonetheless, by 1881 the family had settled into a small house at 7 Montague Street, Kemp Town. The town authorities would later classify the dwelling as a slum due to its inferior nature and poor sanitation. Consequently, the local authorities demolished the property and the surrounding tenements during the extensive slum clearances in the late 19th century.

The census of 1871 shows that Edward and Charlotte's family grew considerably after Alice's birth, with Edward Jeal Junior in April 1874, John Jeal in 1877, and Emily Jeal in 1879. In the 1880s, Edward and Charlotte Jeal's family continued to expand with the births of Bertram in 1883, Ellen in 1885, Edith in 1886 and Arthur in 1889.

In 1885, the Jeal family suffered their first tragedy with the death of their daughter Ellen, who passed away at the tender age of seven weeks. The Coroner ruled that the cause of death was *'General atrophy, inanition and convulsions for two days*. Although tragic and sad, infant mortality was prevalent in the 19th century. Several infectious diseases were endemic and, on the whole, untreatable.

These diseases affected all classes in the Victorian era. However, factors such as poor sanitation, a limited diet and overcrowding increased the infection rates among the lower classes. After Ellen's death, she was buried with her father's parents James and Ann Rogers, at the Extra-Mural Cemetery at the top of Bear Road in Brighton. Tragically, this was not the only occasion the Jeals had to reopen these graves for one of their children.

By 1891, the Jeal family moved to number 8 Bedford Buildings, just around the corner from Montague Place. The property was described as a comfortable but dilapidated dwelling in significant disrepair. Bedford Buildings and substantial proportions of Montague Street, Crescent Cottages and Somerset Street were demolished in the 1920s to make way for

Warwick Mount and Somerset Point, the two high-rise tower blocks now standing on the site Even though Bedford Buildings no longer exists; the local archives contain both descriptive and photographic records of the tenements.

In 1891, Bedford Buildings was accessed via an archway set into the Stag Inn Public House on the corner of Somerset Street and Upper Bedford Street, Kemp Town. This archway led into a narrow pathway that transversed the Bedford Buildings' tenements which sat on either side. The Stag Inn survived the slum clearances and operated as a public house for many years. Sadly, in 2013 the well-loved inn was demolished to make way for low-rise flats.

Around a ten-minute walk to the east of Bedford Buildings, another family resided. In 1891, the head of this family, George Wood Senior, was 50 years old. He was also the sole earner of the family and generated income as a self-employed Cordwainer, which involved making shoes from leather. He operated his business out of his home at 11 Rock Street, Kemp Town, and regularly advertised in local newspapers.

George Wood Senior resided with his wife Margery Ellen Wood (*née Fuller*), whom he had wed at St Nicholas Church on the 10th of June, 1860. The 1871 tells us that the family initially resided at 14 Liverpool Street, Kemp Town. The pair had their first son George Henry Wood on the 21st of November 1862, followed by Sarah Ann in 1867 and James in 1869. By 1881, the family had resettled at 14 Rifle Butt Road, located close to Black Rock, Brighton. In the subsequent years, George Wood Senior and Margery went on to have four more children, William, John, Florence and Alice.

By the early 1880s, Margery Wood had developed a heart condition. With a large family to care for and failing health, she no longer worked as a *'Charlady'* as she had done in previous years and instead spent her days caring for her family. In 1891, the Wood family moved to 11 Rock Place, which, unbeknownst to them, set in motion the required elements which would lead to the fateful collision with the Jeal family.

Edith, the youngest daughter of Charlotte and Edward Jeal, attended All Souls School in Essex Street, Kemp Town. She was a bright and popular child described as having a promising future ahead of her. In contrast, George Henry Wood, the eldest of Margery and George Wood Senior's children was not so fortunate. The archives tell of a troubled childhood that began with episodes of ill health.

George Henry Wood was considered an extremely sickly child that was hard to nurture and practically impossible to soothe. According to his father, George Henry Wood used to scream and wail for long periods as a baby and was practically inconsolable. By the age of two, his health significantly deteriorated due to an unspecified illness. His worried parents called upon the services of Doctor Harris Ross, a well-known local surgeon and vaccinator who attended the family home and examined the child. To George and Margery Wood's horror, Doctor Ross concluded that George Henry Wood suffered from brain compression and would not survive more than a few weeks. It is unclear if the cause of this condition was congenital or had developed following a disease process.

In any case, George and Margery Wood had limited options available and were forced to wait for their child's inevitable demise. George Henry Wood began suffering from seizures as his condition continued to deteriorate. These fits were later described as severe and worsened as his illness took hold. During these episodes, his father said he would foam at the mouth and gnaw his tongue until it bled. The crying spells increased, and the child displayed a *'vacant manner.'*

Despite their best efforts, George Henry Wood's parents could not bring him out of the trance-like state he appeared to be locked into. Yet, against all odds, George Henry Wood miraculously survived. However, he remained thin and emaciated until he was around nine. After this, his condition improved, and in terms of his health, he experienced a normal childhood. He attended the Belgrave Street Chapel School and received a typical standard education per the Education Act, 1870.

Afterwards, the archives suggest that George Henry Wood received further tuition from Mrs Chamberlain, a housekeeper at 8 Sussex Square, Kemp Town. This additional education was unusual for someone of George Henry Wood's standing. However, despite this privilege, later reports would indicate that his parent's efforts had little impact on his intellectual ability or moral conscience.

George Wood Senior was devoutly religious and had been an elder at the Belgrave Street Chapel for several years. He regularly assisted in the church's activities and donated significant amounts to the church and other good causes, despite his low income and large family. Margery also supported the Belgrave Street Chapel's operations and despite her worsening health, was always to support the church's activities.

Yet despite his parent's religious lifestyle and respectability, it is apparent that George Henry Wood was innately attracted to trouble. He often truanted from school and became involved in anti-social and criminal behaviour. His parents later reported that when he was around ten, George Henry Wood would often leave the family home and not return for hours. He would sometimes stay out all night, which undoubtedly caused his poor parents further anguish. His behaviour continued to deteriorate during his teenage years, which we will revisit in later chapters.

The Wood family were involved in the temperance movement, which many consider a significant cause of social reform. Towards the later part of the 19th century, many Victorians began to view alcohol consumption, particularly amongst the working classes, as immoral and crude. This belief stemmed from an increasing acceptance from the general public that alcohol was linked to many social problems, including crime and violence.

The temperance movement looked to reduce alcohol consumption, which many felt was a wasteful pastime. Its members attended meetings where they would publically take *'the oath'*, which equated to total alcohol abstinence. The temperance campaign was closely aligned with the church, and many within society believed teetotalism was essential for salvation. In December 1891, George Henry Wood had recently taken the abstinence pledge to his parents' satisfaction and probably a relief. However, as we will later find out, how seriously he took the oath of temperance is questionable.

In early December 1891, George Henry Wood was working as a cabman at the goods yard at the rear of Brighton Station. Every day except Sunday, he would rise early, dress in his uniform and walk to Brighton Station. Here, he would work for at least 12 hours before returning home. He had also recently proposed to a respectable young woman called *'Lizzie'*, whose marriage would occur days before Christmas 1891.

After being told of their son's plans, George and Margery Wood must have felt immense relief that their troublesome son had finally decided to settle down. As they cheerfully prepared for their son's upcoming nuptials, they could not have imagined the horror and turmoil their own flesh and blood would unleash upon the local community in the following days.

Chapter 2: *'A Crime of Unspeakable Atrocity'*

Thursday, the 10th of December 1891, began as a typical day in the busy Jeal household. Edward Jeal arose early as he did most days. After eating and dressing he said goodbye to his wife Charlotte he headed off to the Sussex Dairy Company to complete his assigned duties for the day. After her husband left, Charlotte called for her children to get up. After being awoken, 5-year-old Edith Jeal washed and dressed in a '*brown stuff*' dress that she selected herself.

After eating a small breakfast, she said goodbye to her mother and accompanied by her eight-year old brother Bertram, began the short journey to All Souls School at Essex Street, Kemp Town. Edith's school day was uneventful, and she took part in literacy, numeracy, and religious lessons; as dictated by the Brighton and Preston School Board. After completing their studies, the two children returned to Bedford Buildings.

After a brief conversation with her mother, Edith went outside into the small cobbled area between the Bedford Building tenements, and played street games with their her brother and friends. At approximately 4.30 pm, Edward Jeal returned home and called his told Edith and Bertram in for supper and the family sat and ate shrimps together. It is not hard to imagine Edith's lively and excitable chatter as she recalled her day's events as the family ate their meal.

At 8.15 pm, unbeknownst to him, Edward Jeal made a decision that would change his family's lives forever. Charlotte informed him that they had run out of firewood and eggs, and in response, Edward asked Bertram to walk to the local shops to get the items. Earlier that week, Edward Jeal had given Edith a half-penny as pocket money. As is often the case with young children, Edith was extremely eager to spend her pocket money and had been pestering her parents about spending it.

Having overhearing her father and brother's conversation, she began pleading for permission to accompany her brother on his errands. With an appreciation of his young daughter's excitement, Edward Jeal willingly agreed. Today, allowing two small children to venture alone on a dark winter night might appear neglectful and careless. However, it was common for children in the Victorian era, to be given freedom and responsibilities beyond what would be deemed acceptable today.

In any case, Edward gave Bertram a small amount of money and aware of the heavy wind and rain outside, asked his children to wrap up in their warmest clothing. Bertram immediately complied with his father's request. Edith, who was extremely excited, did not and immediately exited the cottage door.

The two children walked onto Upper Bedford Street and made their way northwards towards Mr Trengrove's Grocery Store, where the Jeal family usually shopped. After reaching the shop, the two children quickly noticed that Mr Trengrove's firewood was sodden in the heavy falling rain. Not wanting to disappoint their father, the two children visited Mr Clarke's Fishmongers at 35 Upper Bedford Street which the pair knew occasionally stocked firewood.

When they reached number 35, the two noticed that Mr Clarke had a supply of wood, and after inspecting the bundles, Bertram selected a large sheaf and gave Mr Clarke the necessary money. The two children left the shop and then walked south towards Mr Gravett's Store. Once inside, Edith carefully counted some chestnuts out and handed the shopkeeper her pocket money. Before they left, in a courteous gesture, Bertram removed his cricket cap and passed it to his sister so that she could carry her chestnuts.

After thanking Mr Gravett, the small pair returned to Mr Trengrove's to make their final purchase. However, when they reached the shop, Bertram was hesitant. As a regular customer, he felt embarrassed to enter the store with firewood purchased elsewhere. Not wanting to cause offence, he told his sister to wait outside whilst he entered the store. Edith happily complied and agreed to wait near the door with the bundle of firewood and chestnut-filled cap.

After selecting and paying for a single egg, Bertram returned to the street. He had only been inside the store for a few moments, but to his surprise, he could see Edith anywhere. Not wanting to leave his younger sister unaccounted for, Bertram walked up and down the road, searching and calling out his sister's name. After several minutes of failing to find Edith, Bertram decided to walk home believing she had returned without him.

As Bertram entered the cottage, he asked, *'Where's Edie, Mum?'* His mother replied that she did not know and had not seen her since they had left. Bertram explained to his parents that he had lost sight of his sister outside Mr Trengrove's store and, despite looking in the surrounding area, had not managed to locate her. Initially, Edward and Charlotte were not too concerned by their daughter's disappearance and believed that Edith had met up with her friends. However, as time passed, Edward and Charlotte Jeal became increasingly concerned.

Eventually, Edward Jeal informed his wife that he was going out to look for Edith. He repeatedly walked up and down Upper Bedford Street and stopped several people to ask if they had seen anyone matching Edith's description. No one appeared to have seen anything of his young daughter which only added to Edward's alarm.

At about 9.15 pm, Edward Jeal returned to the family home with hopes that Edith had returned in his absence, but as he entered the cottage wife's tearful wife appearance informed him that she had not. At this point, the panic that Charlotte and Edward must have felt is unimaginable. It was nearly 9.30 pm, and the weather outside continued deteriorating. The temperature had fallen to a few degrees above zero, and although the sparse oil lamps outside had been lit, it was nearly pitch black.

Edward and Charlotte recognised that Edith's disappearance was entirely at odds with her usual behaviour, and both parents understandably began to fear the worst. So, at 9.40 pm, Edward Jeal informed his wife that they could no longer wait and set off for the local police station, which in 1891, was situated at number 2 Freshfield Road. As he entered the main office at the front of the building, Edward Jeal was greeted by the duty constable. Edward Jeal explained the reason for his attendance and gave details of Edith's disappearance. He also volunteered a detailed description of his young daughter.

After carefully documenting Edith's details, the duty constable questioned the anguished father to establish what he thought had happened. Edward Jeal replied, *'We don't know what to think. Her mother is very anxious and thinks someone must have stolen her.'*
The duty constable immediately recognised the situation's seriousness and agreed to assist in the search.

Thirty minutes later, Edward arrived back at Bedford Buildings with P.C. Pelling of the Brighton Constabulary to see if Edith had been located. Tearfully, Charlotte Jeal informed him that she had not. In response, Edward, Charlotte, P.C. Pelling and a neighbour walked up to the grassland surrounding Manor Farm, Manor Hill, and Kemp Town to search for the lost five-year-old.

Shortly before midnight, Charlotte Jeal explained that she would have to return home. However, Edward and the others stayed out the entire night despite the abysmal and stormy weather to continue searching. Early on the 11th of December Edward returned home. Despite concerns for his daughter's wellbeing, Edward knew he could not afford the loss of a day's wages. So, after informing his wife of his intentions, he left for work without changing his clothes.

By the time dawn broke, the stormy and wet weather that had pounded Brighton the night before began to clear, much to the relief of the local police, who had continued searching in the local area. As the community arose, the police knocked on doors and questioned neighbours about Edith's strange disappearance. However, no trace of the child could be found.

Charlotte Jeal, by this point, was hysterical and becoming increasingly concerned for her daughter. She recognised that no small child would have willingly stayed out for an entire night, and as the day drew on, dark thoughts consumed her mind as she contemplated Edith's likely fate. As the day drew on, Charlotte Jeal was overwhelmed with grief and neighbours became concerned about her mental state. At 11 am, Edward and Charlotte's eldest daughter Alice was sent for and shortly after, arrived to comfort her mother, who was said to be *'completely prostrated with grief.'*

Meanwhile, in another area of Kemp Town, Edward Villiers and William Stamford, who were completely unaware of the unfolding tragedy, were beginning their day's work. The pair worked as gardeners for the Brighton Corporation and having been asked to trim the trees in the area, the two arrived at Rock Street with the necessary equipment. At noon, the pair broke for lunch and Edward Villiers found himself in a quandary. He needed to relieve himself but knew no public toilet facilities were in the immediate area.

As he searched his mind for a solution, he remembered a field, around 100 yards eastward from his location, which he knew housed an outdoor water closet. St Mary Girls School owned the domain in question, but it had recently been leased to Arlington House School as a playing field. The field in question was large, square and bordered by a flint wall which varied in height. However, Edward Villiers knew that a wooden gate was set into the south-eastern corner of the wall.

After explaining his position to his colleague William Stamford, Edward Villiers began the short walk to the playing field. When he arrived, he found the access gate was locked, and in a rush to relieve himself, he quickly climbed over the wooden structure to enter the field. Around twelve steps from the gate stood a building initially described as a shed but later renamed a barn due to its immense size and style. The building was a heavy, dull-looking stone structure, which had a slate roof and stored gardening and sporting equipment for Arlington School. The building had no windows and only one door, which opened to the east.

Edward Villiers approached the urinal and noticed the barn door was wide open. He was aware that vagrants and the homeless often loitered in the area, much to the disdain of nearby homeowners, who frequently complained to the Brighton Corporation. Desperate to relieve himself, Edward Villiers was suspicious of the open door and decided to investigate. When he reached the barn, he peered inside but heard and saw nothing. Nonetheless, he cautiously entered the door with concerns about what might be waiting inside.

As he slowly entered the cold, dank building, the lack of natural light hampered his vision and caused his heart to race. Undeterred, he crept further into the building and his eyes slowly adjusted to darkness. Edward Villiers continued to move forward, and as he did so, he spotted something lying on the floor which looked entirely out of place from its surroundings. Edward Villiers froze like a statue, unsure whether the object was a trespassing vagrant or a sleeping tramp.

He scanned the strange mass resting against some cricket nets, but saw no movement and concluded that it must be a bundle of discarded clothing. However, as he continued to scan the mass, he was still unsure and decided to investigate further. He cautiously walked closer towards the anomaly, reached out his hands, and touched the heap with trepidation after pausing. As his hands made contact, he immediately recoiled with shock and horror, having realised that the bundle of clothing was, in fact, a child's body.

Although shaken by his gruesome discovery, Edward Villiers remained at the scene and studied the motionless corpse for several minutes. Despite the lack of light, he noticed extensive bruising on the body's visible parts. His disgust grew as he observed that the little girl's skirt had been thrown over her head, leaving her genitalia completely exposed. As Edward Villiers moved around the scene, he found significant pools of blood in various positions, particularly around its lower half. He also noticed a bundle of firewood and a cap lying on the floor to the right of the upper body and several chestnuts randomly scattered around the body's feet.

Eventually, Edward Villiers' nerves got the better of him. He bolted out of the barn and ran back to Rock Street. He immediately informed him of his gruesome discovery when he reached William Stamford. After a short conversation, the two gardeners returned to the barn. After showing William Stamford the corpse, Edward Villiers told him to remain at the spot and ran off for help. After his colleague had left, William Stamford, who was understandably horrified and unnerved by the scene before him, exited the barn and decided to wait by the field's gate.

Meanwhile, Edward Villiers arrived at Sussex Square. He spotted Police Constable Herbert Pelling, who was patrolling the area, and informed him of his discovery. The two returned to the field and found William Stamford waiting with another unknown man. In Edward Villiers's absence, William Stamford had spotted Doctor Humphrey, a local surgeon in

Chichester Place which bordered the east side of the field. He immediately called out to the Doctor to get his attention and informed him that *'murder had been done!'* The pair forced open the gate, and Doctor Humphrey drove his ambulance car up to the barn doors and waited for help to arrive.

After getting permission from P.C. Pelling, Doctor Humphrey entered the barn and performed a rudimentary inspection of the corpse. After checking for signs of life, Doctor Humphrey concluded that the child was clearly deceased. He noted a range of visible injuries. Afterwards, Constable Pelling also examined the body and concluded that Edith had been strangled. He also spotted serious injuries on the child's genitals, which P.C. Pelling concluded must have been caused by a bladed weapon.

Keen to identify any clues, P.C. Pelling examined the area around the body but could not locate any weapons. He did find a child's cap, several chestnuts, and a pair of knickers close to Edith's legs, which he collected as evidence. Having he examined the crime scene, P.C. Pelling asked Doctor Humphrey to transport the corpse to Freshfield Road. He agreed and the two men carefully carried the small body to the ambulance and drove straight to the police station.

When they arrived, the two men solemnly carried the body to the mortuary at the building's rear and gently placed it on a cold hard marble slab at the centre of the room. P.C. Pelling laid the cap, chestnuts, firewood and a pair of knickers around the body. Finally, he laid a blanket over Edith, exposing only her head.

Victorians were known for having an insatiable appetite for crime. Therefore to increase sales, many newspapers would routinely publish sensational reports about serious or scandalous crimes. The articles often contained gratuitous and graphic details and were saturated with speculation and conjecture. The local Brighton tabloids were no different. This is shown in a report published in the late edition of *The Brighton Argus,* on the 12th of December, which reads as follows:

'The body was found lying just inside the door against the wall. A dark wet stain about the size of a dinner plate - blood - marks where the awful deed was committed. There is nothing else to show that an innocent little girl was murdered there. It is the most deserted part of the town and favoured by the darkness of night and such weather as last night, such a deed could be perpetrated, and no one would be any the wiser. The murderer and his victim must certainly have got over the wall in full view of the houses on the western side of Chichester Place.'

Unusually for the time, this article included a map depicting the location of the murder. As a result, as the late edition made its way into the public domain, many curious and voyeuristic readers flocked to the area and tried to gain access to the barn. An urgent message was sent to Brighton's Chief Constable, James Terry informing him of the murder. It also stated that growing crowds were assembling at the playing field and requested that he urgently send officers to protect the crime scene and to prevent disorder.

Meanwhile, at the Freshfield Road Police Station, the police knew that only one child had been reported as missing. They had taken down Edith Jeal's description the previous night during Edward Jeal's missing person report. After comparing this description to the body, the police quickly concluded that the body was Edith Jeal. Chief Constable Terry, who had travelled to Freshfield Road after hearing of the murder, dispatched P.C. Pelling to Bedford Buildings to inform Edward and Charlotte Jeal of their daughter's demise and to request that they identify the body.

P.C, Pelling agreed and with a heavy heart began walking the short journey to Bedford Buildings. When he reached number 8, he knocked on the shabby door and waited for an answer. Before this visit, it was reported that Charlotte Jeal still clung to the hope that her daughter would be found safe and well. However, as she opened the door, her optimism was shattered by P.C. Pelling's sorrowful expression. After a brief introduction, P.C. Pelling informed Charlotte of the grim discovery. Charlotte Jeal collapsed in a heap and began sobbing uncontrollably.

Edward Jeal, who received a message urging him to return home quickly, arrived at Bedford Buildings a short time after and was given the grim news. After allowing the distraught father a few moments to compose himself, P.C. Pelling asked Edward Jeal to accompany him to Freshfield Road to identify his daughter's body. God only knows what he must have thought when he saw his little daughter's lifeless and ruthlessly abused body lying before him. From her appearance, it was clear that Edith must have experienced horrendous terror and suffering in her final moments. Edward broke down into anguished sobs, and this unimaginable experience went on to haunt Edward for the rest of his life.

After completing the formal identification, Edward Jeal returned home to comfort his wife and other children. Despite the family's suffering, a reporter from *The Brighton Argus,* keen to provide sustenance to the next day's reports, arrived at the Jeal family home to witness their grief. Their account of this visit reads as follows:

'A distressed household -

Bedford buildings open off Upper Bedford Street, halfway up on the right-hand side. You enter it by an arch of masonry over which the place's name is displayed. Only a paved footway runs through it; some houses have walled gardens. The front door of number 8 opens right onto the footpath, the house having no garden.

A representative of the Brighton Argus saw the eldest sister of the murdered child and the only married child of the family. Her married name is Cook, and she resides with her husband at 4 Montague Street, quite close to the old house.

She willingly told all she knew. The poor mother, she said, was sadly prostrated and, during the whole afternoon, had been unconscious because of hysterical fits. The father is a milk carrier in the employ of Mr Pointing, proprietor of the St James Dairy, where also one of the sons assists with the work of the dairy.

Eight children of the family are now living - three girls and five boys. All reside at home save the eldest daughter. Edith was next to the youngest, a little boy of two and a half years.

The little boy Bertie, who accompanied his sister on last night's errand, is a bright, intelligent lad of ten years. Happily, because of his youth, he cannot understand the awful fate of his little sister. He seemed pretty merry tonight, and it is as well that it is so. The father said the whole family is naturally distressed.'

Later that day, Doctor Ross, surgeon to the Brighton Borough Police, carried out a full post-mortem on Edith's violated remains. In the late 19th century, embarrassment and conservativeness meant that those in authority used terms deemed more palatable when describing sexual injuries. Consequently, as Doctor Ross completed the official record, he wrote that Edith had been murdered and was *'grossly outraged'*.

He also documented extensive bruising, which covered vast swathes of Edith's body. In his report, Doctor Ross describes Edith's face as being covered in blood, which he concluded had originated from her nose which appeared *'completely flattened'*. He observed that blood had seeped down the cheeks into Edith's long dark hair, causing it to become sticky and matted. He detailed several abrasions across Edith's forehead and cheeks.

As Doctor Ross lifted Edith's head, he found several bruises on the neck, and as Doctor Humphrey and P.C. Pelling had earlier concluded, he ruled that the cause of death was manual strangulation. Doctor Ross finally examined the child's hands, which were black and dirty, as if she had clawed at the ground as she fought with her attacker. He also detailed Edith's blood-saturated pinafore in his notes.

After the post-mortem, Doctor Ross discussed his findings with Chief Constable Terry. He explained that he believed that Edith's abuser had placed her dress over her head, possibly to hide her face. He confirmed to the police that Edith had died through asphyxia but said that the injuries caused by sexual assault were so severe that they would have also eventually caused death. He explained that he did not believe that a weapon had been used and instead concluded that a *'man's person'* was more likely to be responsible.

The Brighton Borough police now knew a sadistic and violent murderer was on the loose and ramped up their investigation to try and locate the killer. In vast numbers, the police patrolled Kemp Town and questioned everyone they encountered. Over the course of the day, the murder became national news. Edith's violent and gruesome injuries were so horrific that commentators began comparing Edith's murder to other infamous crimes.

The murderous series of Jack the Ripper occurred in London's Whitechapel district and had taken place a mere three years before, and was still fresh in people's minds. The press was fully aware that coverage of the Whitechapel murders had exponentially increased both local and national newspaper sales. Keen to seize on the opportunity, many publications likened Edith's murder to those carried out by Jack the Ripper.

One such report appeared in the Brighton Herald on Saturday, the 13th of December. The report reads as follows:

'A crime of unspeakable atrocity was brought to light in Brighton yesterday, a crime even more indescribably horrible in its circumstances than any of the Whitechapel murders. In the case of the murders in the East end of London, almost all details could be made public. Still, in the case of this lawless and terrible revelation of lust in the east of Brighton, there are facts so horrible that they can never appear before the general public in the columns of a newspaper.'

Chapter 3: *'A Mysterious Stranger.'*

By the early afternoon of the 11th of December 1892, a full-blown murder investigation was underway. In the Victorian era, the police had limited tools and had to rely on old-fashioned police work to solve crimes. Consequently, Chief Constable James Terry sent his entire posse of officers out onto the streets of Kemp Town and ordered that they question anyone they encountered. Initially, they focused on the area close to Edith's disappearance, but as the day drew on, the police enquiry extended to various quarters of the wider districts of the town.

Meanwhile, Brighton's press organisations became aware that Edith's post-mortem was taking place at Freshfield Road. Keen to stay abreast of any developments, representatives from the Brighton's Herald, Argus and Gazette arrived at the police station and congregated around its wooden doors. The police station was a hub of activity, and in anticipation of unofficial titbits, the journalists called out to every constable that entered or exited.

Chief Constable Terry was informed about the waiting press pack, and, to increase the case's publicity, he decided that the press should be briefed. At 1.00 pm, Inspector Jupp, who had been appointed as the senior investigating officer, came out onto Freshfield Road. After a brief introduction, he informed them that a murder investigation had been launched. He assured the waiting journalists that the matter was in hand and explained that he and other detectives were *'making the minutest enquiries.'*

Even at this early stage, the Police understood the importance of public interest in the case. Having interacted with many local residents, they were acutely aware that the Kemp Town community were worried that the murderer would strike again. Rather than alleviating these concerns, Inspector Jupp firmly stated that there would be a significant risk to the public until the murderer was caught. He urged anyone with any information about the crime or perpetrator to contact the police immediately.

Elsewhere, waves of furious and fast-travelling gossip were spreading through the area. As a result, information flooded into the police, and by mid-afternoon, the police received their first credible leads. After hearing of Edith's demise, several people contacted the police to report that a *'mysterious stranger'* had been loitering in the Eastern Road vicinity in the days following the murder. These accounts suggested that this person had offered little girls money to accompany him onto the Sussex Downs north of Kemp Town.

In addition, two young girls aged ten and twelve, were brought to the Freshfield Road Police Station by their mother to make statements. The children's identities are missing from the case files, but both informed the police that a stranger had accosted them the previous night. They explained that the stranger had offered them sixpence to go *'up the hill'* with him. The girl's mother informed the police that the younger of the two agreed to accompany the stranger. She added that the eldest of the two had refused to go and, sensing danger, had bravely informed the man that their mother would be waiting for them.

Despite her elder sister's protestations, the younger of the two, tempted by money, started to accompany the unknown man up the road. Scared for her younger sibling's safety, the older sister sprinted home and informed her mother, who chased after her daughter. She quickly caught up with the pair and thankfully rescued her child.

The family was questioned extensively by the police, but the girls did not know the identity of the individual concerned. However, the two young girls managed to describe the man, who they believed to be a *'seafarer'*. The two also remembered that he had worn a long molten cloth coat and a cheese cutter's hat. As the poor mother listened to her young daughter's recollections, she became extremely distressed. Had it not been for her elder daughter's quick thinking, her youngest child would have likely been seriously harmed.

Further witnesses were identified from the police's house-to-house enquiries. They reported also seeing the same man in the Kemp Town area but described him as being dressed as a *'railway worker'* and stated that he appeared to be intoxicated. These witness reports were relayed to the Freshfield Road Police Station, where they came to the attention of P.C. Pelling, who had been on duty in Lavender Street, Kemp Town, on the night of Edith's disappearance.

He too had encountered a *'railway man'* on the 10th of December, 1891 in Lavender Street, Kemp Town as he was on duty. As the two passed, the railway man turned his head and said, *'Good evening.'* and was swaying as if he was drunk. P.C. Pelling had recognised the man as George Henry Wood, of 11 Rock Street, and had made a mental note of the sighting.

After hearing the various accounts of a drunken railwayman acting suspiciously, P.C. Pelling realised the relevance of this sighting and immediately informed his superiors.

Meanwhile, the investigating officers continued to analyse the numerous statements from the public. From these witness accounts, the police found they could trace the same intoxicated railwayman from Brighton Station, across the town, and right up to the abduction scene. After he was alerted to P.C. Pelling's earlier identification, George Henry Wood quickly became Chief Constable Terry's prime suspect.

At 6 pm on the 11th of December, Chief Constable Terry sent Inspector Jupp to visit the Brighton Station to locate and question George Henry Wood. After he arrived, he quickly found George Henry Wood, his suspect, at work in the goods yard. After introducing himself and explaining the reason for his visit, Inspector Jupp asked George Henry Wood to describe his movements the previous evening. He replied that he had worked till about 8 pm, then visited the Hippodrome Circus at North Road, and remained there all night.

Inspector Jupp asked George Henry Wood if he could name anyone who could corroborate his account. He said he could not but suggested that the doorman might remember him. As the Inspector's questions continued, George Henry Wood struggled to provide credible answers. Eventually, Inspector Jupp arrested George Henry Wood and walked him down to the Brighton Police's headquarters at the town hall for further questioning.

The Brighton Town Hall, still in use today, is located within Bartholomew's Square, a short stone's throw away from the Palace Pier. The structure stands at the site of the Priory of Bartholomew, which French raiders destroyed in June 1514. By the early 1800s, the existing town hall, which stood on the western side of Market Street, had fallen into disrepair. After discussions, the Brighton authorities ordered the construction of a new building.

In 1830, Thomas Cooper, one of Brighton's Commissioners, created designs for the new facility in the Greek revival style and after being given the seal of approval, contractors built the structure between 1830 and 1832 at the cost of £60,000 to the Brighton Corporation. Serendipitously, Thomas Kemp, after whom the Kemp Town Estate was named, supported the project and was asked to lay the first stone as part of an elaborate ceremony.

Although much of Brighton Town Hall's interior and exterior have been preserved, significant portions of the structure has been repeatedly remodelled over the years. Unfortunately, few descriptions of the town hall's layout during 1891 have survived the passage of time. However, when the building opened in 1832, various commentators were critical of its location, design, and layout.

As a result of this public dissatisfaction, several newspaper articles include scathing descriptions of the building. These reports allow us to view the structure and early functions of the building in 1891. One such article appeared in the Brighton Gazette in July 1832. The article reads as follows:

At the north entrance, we find ourselves opposite a blank wall at about 20 paces as soon as we reach the doorway. On the left is the grand staircase, undoubtedly the poorest effort we have ever witnessed. The stairs at the Albion Hotel is superior in every respect. It turns off abruptly and awkwardly, without one imposing feature.

In the entrance are four square columns to support the staircase and the landings above; and here so bad a taste is displayed that it cannot escape proportion with the height to the landing above, so that the columns look, to use a vulgar word, - gawky, tall and ill-proportioned.

Before we ascend the stairs, we want our readers to accompany us to the blank wall already leading to small but very convenient rooms. These are the Clerk's and Surveyor's offices, with no fault to find. They are light, airy and convenient. On the left is a glass door leading to a passage.

Opening his door and turning right, he will find himself in a long narrow dark room. This is the police office. On the right-hand side, after entering this room, is a door which leads to the dungeons below, intended for the confinement of offenders, and to a narrow stone staircase.

Communicating with the long dark room we have described is a double door, which communicates with a tiny space, not capable of holding with any degree of comfort, with about 20 persons seated. This is the room of the Directors and Guardians, a body comprising nearly 40 persons. The offices of the Clerk to the Directors and Guardians and of the Assistant Overseer, adjoining the room of the Directors and Guardians, are comfortable and convenient. At the end of the passage, a door opens to the north at the rear of the grand entrance.

We now proceed upstairs, where two folding doors are at the centre of the landing. These open into the Magistrate's public room, which reaches across the whole building with windows at each end. The benches for the magistrates, desks for the Clerk, attorneys, reporters etc., are very well managed, and the whole room is adapted for the petty sessions, but it needs to be of sufficient width.

As previously stated, Brighton's Town Hall was the site of Brighton's main police station for many years until it was decommissioned in the 1970's. In contrast to the lavish architecture in the upper areas of the building, the police station was located in the town hall's dark and dismal basement. The complex contained the police's primary custody cells and the Chief Constable's offices. Although it is no longer used as a police station, the complex has been preserved and currently functions as a museum.

As you pass the ground floor of the town hall, you reach a steep, narrow, stone staircase which descends into the basement. At the bottom of the stairs, you immediately enter a damp and musty corridor devoid of natural light, which appears almost like a tunnel. On the left are several custody cells which housed prisoners when the police station was operational. These cells have high-domed ceilings, and an arched, bar-covered opening on the back wall allows ventilation into the cell but no natural light.

It was into this subterranean dungeon that Inspector Jupp led George Henry Wood on the evening of the 11th of December. After securing his prisoner in one of the custody cells, Inspector Jupp quickly began arranging an identity parade to see if the growing list of witnesses could identify George Henry Wood as the man they had seen acting suspiciously on the night of Edith's murder.

To complete the line-up, Inspector Jupp went onto the streets surrounding the town hall. He stopped several men with a similar appearance to his suspect and asked them to participate. Once sufficient men were found, the police contacted the witnesses and asked them to attend the town hall. By this time, it was late in the evening, and many of the witnesses, who were young children, were already in bed. Nonetheless, realising the seriousness of the situation, the children's parents agreed and travelled down to the town hall.

The identity parade occurred in the large hall in the northern section of the ground floor. In contrast to modern practices, the children's identities were afforded no protection during the line-up. The police gave each of the children a short time to examine the participants, and afterwards, Inspector Jupp asked them whether the stranger they had encountered on the 10th of December was in the room. Bravely, all the children positively identified George Henry Wood as the individual who had approached them.

After completing the line-up, Inspector Jupp thanked the witnesses and their parents and allowed them to return home. Inspector Jupp escorted George Henry Wood back to the main corridor of the police station. In a stern tone, he formally charged him with the felonious and wilful murder of Edith Jeal and asked if he had any reply. Tellingly he made no response and remained utterly silent, even when asked to remove his clothes for analysis.

Meanwhile, Doctor Ross, who had performed the autopsy on Edith Jeal's body, was asked to attend the police station to examine George Henry Wood. The police wanted him to examine the prisoner's body to see if he had any injuries that could link him to the crime. After the examination, Doctor Ross informed Inspector Jupp that he observed a small bruise on George Henry Wood's penis, which he believed could have been sustained during Edith's sexual assault.

Despite this, the police still believed that some of Edith's injuries may have been caused by a knife. Consequently, Superintendent Carter and Holloway attended George Henry Wood's home at 11 Rock Place. They knocked on the door, and as George Wood Senior answered, they barged into the property and began searching the basement. The reason is not given in the records, but it is apparent that the police chose not to search the rest of the house.

In any case, they found no bladed weapons capable of causing Edith's injuries. However, they did locate and seize various items of clothing they believed George Henry Wood may have worn on the night of the murder. When the search was completed, the inspectors returned to the town hall and passed the seized garments to Inspector Jupp for analysis.

He began by examining a pair of black flap trousers which he noticed had several red stains. He also noticed these areas were damp and concluded they had recently been washed. The shirt and underpants also had red smears and marks in various places. Whilst he could not be sure, he suspected the stains were blood.

After examining his suspect's clothes, Inspector Jupp returned to the Good's Yard to establish George Henry Wood's movements on the previous day. The supervisor informed him that George Henry Wood and a colleague had spent the last day delivering hops to Preston Brewery. He explained that the brewery had been pleased with their work and had offered the two cabmen an amount of beer as a tip. The two men had reportedly accepted the tokens and quickly became drunk.

The supervisor recalled that the two men returned to the goods yard after completing their deliveries. However, as they reached the entrance, the gatekeeper supervisor noticed that George Henry Wood was intoxicated. Concerned for his safety, the supervisor explained that he told George Henry Wood that he was in no fit state for work and ordered that he go home.

Inspector Jupp knew that this evidence was significant. It meant that George Henry Wood began the journey home at a time which would allow him to reach the crime's key locations. He also matched the witnesses' descriptions of a '*drunken railwayman*'. These statements linked him with the various witness statements the police had collected.

Consequently, Inspector Jupp returned to the town hall and informed Chief Constable Terry of his findings. Satisfied that he had the right man in custody, the Chief Constable visited George Henry Wood in his cell and told him that he would appear before the Magistrates the following Monday. He explained that the Magistrate would hear all of the evidence and decide if the case should be committed to the Court of Assize.

Later that evening, Inspector Jupp returned to Rock Street and informed George and Margery Wood that their son had been charged and would remain in custody. The pair were devastated at the news and felt compelled to act. Consequently, on the morning of the 13th of December, George Wood Senior visited the offices of Messrs. Prince and Ayres at 8 Middle Street, Brighton, to retain legal counsel.

Mr Ayres listened to the frantic parents and agreed to take the case. Immediately after they left his offices, Mr Ayres drafted and sent a letter to the town hall to say he would be representing George Henry Wood and would attend the court hearing on the following day.

Chapter 4: The Early Career of the Culprit

So, exactly who was George Henry Wood? As many would later testify, he appeared to his acquaintances to be an honest and hardworking young man who had recently become engaged to be married. Outwardly, he seemed to be a religious man who attended the Belgrave Street Church and was well-known by the congregation. However, as the police began looking into his background, George Henry Wood's apparent honest and respectable character was clearly a sham.

Neighbours and acquaintances were interviewed and informed the police that George Henry Wood meandered from his parent's moralistic and religious lifestyle from a young age. They informed the police that as a child, George Henry Wood often associated with other unruly children who caused problems within the neighbourhood. The police also became aware that George Henry Wood was well known to the Borough Police, hence P.C. Pelling's identification shortly before his arrest. Inspector Jupp began the laborious task of manually reviewing Brighton Police's criminal records and found that George Henry Wood had been imprisoned on two occasions.

On Thursday, the 8th of April 1875, twelve-year-old George Henry Wood was arrested for the first time for committing larceny against John Botting, a baker of 66 St Georges Road, Kemp Town. The baker asked Emma Capp, his assistant, to forward some money to 5 Crescent Place, Brighton. Having numerous other duties to complete, Emma Capp requested the assistance of an errand boy named Robert Greenland and gave him nine pounds to deliver.

The money consisted of a £5 note, four sovereigns, and some silver coins wrapped in brown paper. Robert Greenland immediately set off for Crescent Place. On route, he bumped into George Henry Wood and informed him of his task. Whether or not Robert Greenland was part of the unruly boys that George Henry Wood was associated with is unclear. Still, in any case, George Henry Wood offered to complete the delivery and was given the parcel by Robert Greenland, who had other tasks to complete.

George Henry Wood successfully delivered the parcel. However, when it was opened by its recipient, a sovereign was missing. After checking with Emma Capp, the recipient reported the missing money to the police as theft. After a short investigation, Detective Stanley arrested and interviewed George Henry Wood. Even at this young age, George Henry Wood appeared adept at lying and remained adamant that he had not stolen the money. Instead, he suggested that the package's paper had become torn in his pocket. The police demanded that George Henry Wood return the missing money, to which he replied that he could not find it.

After, Detective Stanley made further enquiries and discovered that George Henry Wood had spent 5 shillings at a local shop shortly before his arrest. George Henry Wood was again questioned but could not explain how he had obtained such a large sum of money. Consequently, he was charged and, later the same day appeared at the Brighton Borough Police Court, which formed a significant part of the Victorian judicial system in England.

Otherwise known as the Petty Sessions, the police court dealt with low-level crimes such as drunkenness, minor theft, and bastardy examinations. The police courts no longer feature in the British judicial system, and their duties have largely been forgotten over time. However, an article published in May 1875 in the *Brighton Gazette* gives a glimpse into the workings of Brighton's police court. The article reads as follows:

'Of the cases tried at the court, there need not be much said here, for it is one of the repulsive sides of human nature, and one never cares to unduly expose the wickedness and frailties of fellowmen. These are the usual batches of drunk and disorderly characters, poor miserable-looking creatures as thoroughly wretched as humanity can look. There are the habitual criminals, hardened, cruel-looking men and women whose beauty has lost its crown of glory amid the dark shadow of vice and crime which veils it.

The poor pitiful little children are growing up to be regular criminals. Still, those who now thank Heaven, many find that their appearance in a police court is the first step in a new and better life of aspiration after higher things and of honest labour to obtain that livelihood (sic), which before there was no prospect of providing except by 'picking and stealing.' There are also - alas that it should be so - the base, brutal animals who come home drunk and thrash their wives, patient, honest, good souls, who, when once they have been stirred, by an act of unusual violence, to bring their lord and master to book before Mr Bigge, have for their only aim how to screen him from the evil consequences of his crime.

This is one of the most painful experiences of police courts and makes one long for the day when the humanising influences of religion and education shall make the institution of marriage rightly understood, even by the debased creatures who now seem to think that all the use of a wife is to earn money for them to spend in drink and to 'come and be kicked.'

But there is also the humorous side to contrast with the tragic portion of police court business. This is generally found to mainly arise from petty assault cases, particularly among young women, and is technically known as neighbour quarrels. As circumstantial evidence, Miss Kinshalee produces a torn dress or a bundle of hair ripped from her head. After a long story, with innumerable 'I sez to her, I sez, sez I', probably winds up with the proof positive 'and Mary Taylor will tell you the same.'

Then there are witnesses called, and Mrs Milligan, the defendant, gives her story and calls her witnesses, the whole being interspersed with plenty of 'I sez to her', 'she sez to me', and interruptions from the various parties concerned, such as 'Oh, you're a false woman', 'you never were there at all', 'Did you see me there?', etc.

The most striking features of these cases are these kinds of women's distinctive capabilities for inventing nasty names and the persevering determination with which they will swear their way through the thickest wall of fact that may stand in their way. It is also a noticeable feature how polite the witnesses are, both men and women, in describing the persons concerned. One will say, 'And this lady had hold of that lady', or 'I see this gentleman and that gentleman a-scuffling, and I sez' - the fact is that both the 'ladies' and 'gentlemen' alluded to are generally the lowest and meanest of human creatures, poor and wretched in both pulse and mind.

It frequently happens that neither party gains victory in these kinds of cases. However, even in that event, the facts of the dispute to the sympathetic ears of Mr Bigge and his brother justices seem to have a calming and soothing influence on the minds of poor people.'

On the 10th of April 1875, George Henry Wood stood in the dock, ready to face the charges laid against him. During the short trial, the Magistrate acknowledged that George Henry Wood had a wealth of good home influences yet, had chosen to take up the companionship of boys described as having a *'loose character.'* The Magistrate also discussed his problematic behaviour, late-night antics and frequent truancy with his father, who was also present in the court.

George Wood Senior was called to give evidence. He informed the Magistrate that he was struggling to control his wayward child. The Magistrate found George Henry Wood guilty and, in an attempt to halt the young boy's criminal ways, sentenced him to seven days of hard labour. This sentence may appear severe to inflict upon a child by today's standards. However, during the Victorian era, there was considerable concern about criminality and society as a whole was keen to prevent it.

As a result, juveniles commonly received prison sentences for what would today be considered low-level crimes. Unfairly, many children from the poorest classes were forced to beg and steal to survive, and with hindsight, many could be excused from their actions. However, in George Henry Wood's case, there was no excuse for his behaviour. Despite the family's lowly means, George Henry Wood had been well cared for, and his father had worked hard to ensure he was adequately provided for.

The archives show that George Henry Wood was impulsive and simply enjoyed misbehaving. It appears that after years of disobedience, his troublemaking ways had finally caught up with him. In addition to a prison term, the judge also ordered that George Henry Wood receive eight strokes of the birch rod. This additional punishment was frequently inflicted on juvenile criminals and involved exposing and whipping a child's bare buttocks.

At the time of George Henry Wood's conviction, there were no rules to dictate the nature of the whip that prisons used. Despite being called *'birching'*, the torturous device could comprise rods originating from various trees and shrubs, such as willow or hazel, the latter of which was considered especially painful compared to others. Prisons selected specific plant species based on length, weight, number of branches, and spines.

Some institutions had multiple versions and selected their weapon of choice depending on the prisoner's age and crime. The birch rod was soaked in water overnight before its use, adding to the pain it inflicted. The archives confirm that George Henry Wood served his sentence at the Lewes House of Correction, which we will revisit later in this story. Shortly after his arrival, prison wardens would have escorted George Henry Wood to the basement punishment cells where prison punishments were carried out.

Whilst there are no surviving records of George Henry Wood's experience, a detailed witness account appeared in the *Pall Mall Gazette* on the 5th of August, 1887, which describes the brutal nature of juvenile birching. The article reads as follows:

'I was once a newspaper reporter in a town not fifty miles from London. At one of the ordinary morning sittings of the borough bench on a particular day, a couple of youngsters about the ages of twelve and thirteen were brought on a charge of theft. They were convicted and

received six strokes with a birch rod each. I immediately slipped around to the chief inspector's corner of the court and asked if he could allow me to be present to witness the birching. 'Oh, yes; we can manage that. Be here at about one o'clock.' Immediately the bench rose, about 12.30, I finished off my police copy as quickly as possible and put my appearance in the charge room at the time stated, where I found the two delinquents crying and their friends waiting for them, apparently in great distress. Who performs the operation?' I whispered to one of the detectives. He replied, 'I do, and I've got a nice old rod in pickle for 'em too,' came back the reply in a tone of very great satisfaction. 'And', continued the officer, 'I'll fetch blood from the young devils this morning. 'Oh, but you ought not to do that?' I suggested. 'Won't I, you'll see,' he sneered and presently returned with the wretched instrument of torture in his hand - the birch. 'How's this? Feel it,' he said, holding out two or three of the twigs of which the delightful article was composed. I complied with the officer's request and felt two or three of the lashes, which were wiry and wet. The brush had been in the pickle for an hour or two since the sentence was pronounced. I was incredibly impressed with the idea that, if such lashes were to be applied to a boy's bare skin with any degree of vigour, birching was a barbarous punishment.' Everybody and everything was ready. The persons present were a magistrate, the chief superintendent of police, a detective who administered the punishment, a couple of constables and me. Of course, the two poor little fellows who were to be so cruelly tortured by both of them, it is hardly necessary to state, were crying bitterly. One of the constables quickly unbuttoned one of the poor little fellows' braces, and his trousers were pulled down to leave his buttocks bare. Almost with lightning rapidity, he was placed on his stomach over the form; one constable at one end held his hands with an iron grasp, and the other took the poor little wretch's legs. Immediately the birch had touched the poor little fellow's skin, the weal's or marks of the lashes were plainly visible, and after two or three strokes had been laid on the culprit's right buttock, it resembled nothing so much as a piece of raw beef. When the whole complement of six strokes had been inflicted, I say it to the disgrace of the nation, and blood was drawn, and, as his comrades viewed the matter, the official who held the birch had proved himself clever fellow; for it is the acme of ambition on the part of the officers who are told to administer punishment to draw blood. The detective with the birch then moved his precious body to the other side of the form and similarly inflicted the remaining six strokes on the tiny culprit's left buttock. The other little boy was put through the same cruel ordeal with precisely identical results. The agony caused to these two poor little mites by such barbarous treatment was simply indescribable, and their unearthly yells, the results of such punishment, are ringing in my ears at this time as plainly as if I were still watching the proceedings in the courtyard of that prison on the occasion of which I write. If the constable who administers the birch fails to draw blood, he is subjected to all the chaff and banter imaginable among his companions. And these are the men who were told off to punish the poor little defenceless mortals who have made a trivial transgression of the laws of their country and who are led to the whipping form like lambs in Her Majesty's name?'

This article shows how traumatic birching would have been to experience. You would have thought that this, along with imprisonment, would have stopped George Henry Wood's defiant ways, and it did - for a short time. After completing his sentence, he returned to Brighton and was released into his parents' care. On the 10th of January 1878, George Henry Wood enlisted in the Navy for ten years following his 15th birthday. It is unclear whether this was his parent's decision or, instead, was officially ordered by the Brighton Authorities following his conviction, as was typical.

In any case, the young nautical recruit was too young for active service and found himself stationed aboard the HMS St Vincent Training Ship, harbouring in Haslar Creek's mouth. The 2612-tonnage vessel was built in Plymouth in 1815 and was described as *'One of the good old wooden three decked sailing vessels, of the victory type, and could carry 102 guns'*.

The Navy had used HMS St Vincent during the Crimean War to transport French troops to the Baltic, but by 1978 it had been many years since she had been in active service. Limited records relating to the HMS St Vincent training ship have survived and therefore there are no records detailing George Henry Wood's service.

However, in 1880, Mr Black M.P was commissioned to carry out a routine expectation on different training ships for boys in the Royal Navy in early 1880. Following his inspection, Mr Black's subsequent report describes the routine and training schedule as satisfactory and includes a description of the daily life and regime the boys on board experienced. His report is as follows:

'Anyone with the good fortune to visit HMS must to the full letter endorse that opinion, everything being conducted on board with perfect discipline, yet without too much rigour. The boy recruits' faces beam with life and health. *At eight bells, the bugle is sounded, and the boys from all parts of the ship tumble down the hatchways to take their seats for dinner. At the command, grace is said by the whole crew in unison.*

Dinner on the day Mr Blake visited consisted of roast beef and baked potatoes with plum pudding to follow. The cleanliness of the vessel was scrupulous from the deck to the hold. All of the 800 recruits are provided with baths located in the ship's bows near the other essential appliances. Most of the child sailors opt to take a bath nearly every day. However, for those that do not, it was made compulsory.

At the stern of the ship is a schoolroom to provide the young men of the boat with an adequate education. The gun drill takes place on the main deck daily, with exactly twenty old-style, muzzle-loading guns, ten on each side. The canteen is below the fourth deck, known as the orlop in the stern most part.

Here only adult men receive their beer and spirits, and this treat is substituted for bread for the younger boys. None of the young sailors is given intoxicating liquors. Towards the evening, cans are broached, and each boy receives his share in a basin, with bread which makes up their supper'.

The Navy offered George Henry Wood much-needed discipline, separation from his undesirable friends and the prospect of a career. With their son safely away from Brighton, George and Margery Wood must have immense relief. Initially, their son appeared to thrive on the ship. The records suggest that he could follow orders and that his conduct on board the vessel was *'very good.'*

However, George Henry Wood's naval career was incredibly short-lived. The archives state that he was discharged as an invalid on the 13th of March 1878, just 63 days after he enlisted. He was said to be suffering from malformation of the chest, scrofula and *'the itch'*, which he caught on board the ship. In later years George Henry Wood would say that he was discharged after falling from the ship's mast, although this account was later disputed and shows his propensity to manipulate events for his own ends.

Nonetheless, in March 1878, George Henry Wood found himself back in Brighton, to his parent's disappointment. In November 1879, he secured employment at Brighton Station as a machinist. However, it took only a short time for George Henry Wood to hang around with his old acquaintances. Presumably, the harsh memories of imprisonment and birching had quickly faded. On the 4th of May 1880, George Henry Wood once again found himself in front of the Brighton Magistrates facing theft charges.

The charges related to a box of five dozen chocolates, valued at 3s 6d. The chocolates were the property of Ann and George Humphrey, who owned a shop at 3 Park Road East (later renamed Queens Park Road), which sold confectionery. On Tuesday, the 6th of April, Ann Humphrey was working in her shop and noticed several missing things and decided to keep a watch from the backroom to see if she could catch the person responsible for the act.

During the afternoon of the 3rd of May, she saw George Henry Wood enter the shop and was seen to take a box of chocolates without paying. Ann immediately came out from the back room and boldly challenged the thief, who wore a railway uniform, but whose name she did not know. Startled by the encounter, George Henry Wood ran straight out of the shop and continued down the road with the chocolates under his arm. Keen to identify the culprit, Ann followed the thief as he made his way down towards the town.

Eventually, Ann's persistence paid off, and she caught up with the thief near the Evershed Candle Factory at the junction of Eastern Road and Montague Place. She snatched the box of chocolates from under George Henry Wood's arm, but he managed to escape. Ann Humphrey reported the incident and the thief's description to the police. Later that day, George Henry Wood was arrested by Detective Rosser at the Brighton Railway Station Works.

Shortly after, he appeared at the Brighton Police Court for the second time, and was without legal representation. The police added a charge related to the theft of 3 lbs of peppermints on a previous occasion. Ann Humphrey was called to the witness box and informed the Magistrate that she was adamant that George Henry Wood had stolen the sweets on the 5th of April. However, when she was pressed, she refused to swear to it. George Henry Wood repeatedly exclaimed that he was innocent and knew nothing of the alleged crimes and was released from the court.

Undeterred, the astute Detective Rosser visited the Brighton Station Works to speak to George Henry Wood's associates. After interviewing various people, he located George Harman, who confirmed George Henry Wood's guilt. This young man would later testify at the police court that George Henry Wood had been offering 12 peppermints for a penny around six weeks before.

The following day, George Henry Wood reappeared at the Brighton Police Court. George Harman appeared as a witness and recounted the story he had given Detective Rosser the previous day. The trial records show George Henry Wood's impulsivity and lack of intelligence for the first time. As George Harman testified, an unremorseful George Henry Wood said, *'Yes, you took many peppermints but refused to pay for them!'* This statement completely contradicted his previous denials and only highlighted his guilt to the court.

Mr Barden, the acting Chief Constable, read George's prior conviction to the court. George Henry Wood initially continued to protest his innocence but eventually pleaded guilty. The stipendiary Magistrate sentenced George Henry Wood to two months imprisonment at Lewes House of Correction, with hard labour upon each charge. To add to his problems, George Henry Wood was dismissed from his employment.

Chapter 5: Lewes Gaol and House of Correction

So having been convicted of larceny for the second time, George Henry Wood once again found himself imprisoned at Lewes, an Assizes town that has housed Sussex's criminals for many years. Initially, criminals were incarcerated at the old convict gaol at the corner of North Street, Lewes. However, by the mid-1800s, the prison had become dilapidated, overcrowded and struggled with poor sanitation.

Concerned about the prison's declining conditions, the local authorities raised the prison's problems at the Sussex Summer Assizes in 1848. The sitting justices listened to the gaol's extensive issues. They concluded the repairs were too vast and costly and ordered Lewes Corporation erecting a new convict gaol as soon as possible.

In recognition of the project's vast scale and cost, a committee was elected to oversee the venture. Land for the new prison was purchased from William Verrall, a local landowner and publican of the White Hart Inn, Lewes. After acquiring the deeds, the committee employed the services of Sir Joshua Jebb, Royal Engineer and British Surveyor General of Convict Prisons, who prepared plans for the new prison. He based his plans on Pentonville Prison, which had received numerous accolades and was considered the *'model prison'* design of the time.

Pentonville has four radiating wings of cells around a central corridor, which cleverly enabled a single warden standing in this hall to see into every convict cell. After approving the design, the committee ordered the prison's construction. The work took place between 1849 and 1852 at an estimated cost of £56,000, a considerable amount of money at the time. However, the committee partially offset this expense by selling the old North Street Gaol to the Admiralty.

At the Midsummer Assizes in 1853, the justices announced that the new prison would be available for the reception of prisoners from the 8th of August that year. Published statistics for 1853 showed that the old North Street Gaol housed 394 prisoners and 52 debtors, many of which originated from Brighton.

When the new gaol opened, the Brighton authorities, whose convict numbers were increasing, agreed to continue paying the Borough of Lewes to house its prisoners. Due to the increasing influx from Brighton, the new prison's 265 cells quickly filled, and overcrowding again became a problem. So, in 1866, a further 132 cells were added at an additional cost of £12,600, raising the total construction costs to nearly £70,000.

Limited archives about Lewes have survived the passage of time. However, the *Croydon Observer* published a lengthy and detailed description of the jail following Percy *'Lefroy'* Mapleton's infamous execution. The article provides a real insight into the prison's layout and regime at the time of George's incarceration. The report reads as follows:

'The appearance of the gaol suggests enjoyment rather than pains and penalties. The building overlooks Brighton Road and the valley, the heights beyond it, and the Downs rise behind its back. The Brighton Downs, Brookside, Newhaven and beyond present a charming view from the drive, separated from the road by a piece of turf and a stone wall leading up to the gate. On either side of the latter, possessing a separate entrance, although joined to the building, with which they communicate by a private entrance, are the official residences of the governor on the right hand and the Chaplain on the left.

A high wall faced like the walls of the building, with grey and black flint edged with red brick, encloses the prison precincts. The extreme length of the prison building is 611 feet, and the width or depth from the front backwards is 414 feet. The main entrance lies in the middle of the facade. There is no mistaking it for anything but a prison gate.

Admission is only granted on production of an order from the Home Office, the number of which, along with the visitor's name, is carefully noted in the prison book by an aged porter opening the gate. His office is the first room visible inside the entrance. On either side is a lodge for one of the warders. Further progress leads across an open yard.

A second gate opens into a passage, 10 feet wide and 74 feet long; on either side are offices for the Visiting Justices, the Governors, the Clerks, and the Chaplain, besides a storeroom and sitting and bedrooms for the warders. After passing an iron grating, you find yourself among the male prisoners, not without discomfort, probably creeping involuntarily over you.

If it is your first visit, the sight of the prison garb, of warders, iron bars, and gates locked by a key, not in your possession is alarming, but you are happy in the thought that it is your own and not Her Majesty's pleasure that has brought you to this uncanny spot.

Triple tiers of cells extend in double rows on either hand, facing a passage. In front of you, a staircase leads up to cells, workshops, the infirmary and the chapel. There is an unmistakable look of restraint about the place, but at the same time, there is no gloom. The building looks light, airy, and almost cheerful. The walls are carefully whitewashed, and everything is kept scrupulously clean. There is life, too, for the convicts are employed in various kinds of work.

You cannot expect them to look happy, for a class of men deprived at the time of civil rights and compelled to move and work, not as they please, but as they are told. Even involuntary occupation exercises beneficial influence both on body and mind and keeps both alike from stagnating, strengthening the frame and preventing the reason from brooding.

The warders or 'officers' on duty watch the prisoner at work or keep guard in the corridor. Whenever you look, they seem vigilant and rigid disciplinarians but also act with humaneness and consideration. Cases of harsh conduct are not heard of in Lewes so far as we know. Now and then, you see a batch of prisoners come in from their exercise, of which they have an hour daily in the open yard to go into their cells or resume their work. You can watch the warder walking behind them and testing each cell door after it is closed to ensure it is locked. Some sly customers have been known to keep the door shut by planting their foot against it to be able to slip out afterwards.

You see other men busy washing, cleaning, or doing other housework under supervision. You notice a difference in their dress. Most wear the ordinary prison garb, drab from head to foot, with a broad arrow mark. Others are clad in a suit of the same cut but different dark, greenish-grey cloth. These are men in Her Majesty's services.

As we have said, the cells are primarily ranged in two rows, and triple tiers and galleries with iron railings run along them. The central hall measuring 39 ½ feet by 28, has an octagonal shape. Corridors branch off in three directions, leaving angle rooms between them, used as day rooms for the trade instructors and the surgeon and rooms for misdemeanants. The corridors to the right and left are 16 feet wide and 126 feet long on either hand, presenting a somewhat striking vista.

The outside length of the male prison is 309 feet. On either side of the main corridors are cells for prisoners of various classes. With few exceptions to be instanced, these cells are all alike. They measure thirteen feet by seven and nine feet in height, affording not excessive but sufficient room, light and air.

The furniture is of the most detailed description. A plain deal table and an equally plain deal stool are almost all to be seen beside that horrible invention, as prisoners think, their dread and woe, the plank bed, upon which every prisoner must, if he can, sleep for at least a month. Prisoners have confessed that he could not forget or forgive the plank bed.

A shelf, or double shelf, in the corner serves as a rest for the prisoner's food tin and perhaps one or two other harmless articles. Since every prisoner who can read is given a bible and prayer book of his denomination, according to the prison rules, such sacred books are generally found in most cells.

The window is barred, and the walls and floor are all of stone or brick. A table of the prison rules hangs up in the cell for the prisoner's information. For every infraction of these rules by which he is a sufferer, he has his remedy assigned, and he can be in no doubt about the manner of claiming it. There is also a bell pulley in each cell for summoning a warder in case of need. The door has a peephole through which officers may watch the inmate.

On the outside of the door is a card with the prisoner's number, his name, age denomination, crime, sentence, time served, work done, and present employment. Most of these cards are plain white. Those assigned to Roman Catholics are tinted orange. Like the prison rules and the diet, they are issued by H.M. Prisons Commissioners in London uniformly for all goals. In some cells, there is the evil-reputed 'crank', the most usual means of punishment where hard labour is prescribed.

There is no treadmill at Lewes. The crank is just what it says - a crank handle to be turned, at a considerable expenditure of physical effort, with no further object than to tire the prisoner. Besides picking half a pound of oakum, the daily task is twelve thousand turns. The number of turns completed is shown on a self-marking indicator so that there is no shirking of the task. A prisoner who does not complete his twelve thousand is reported to the governor for punishment.

One form of punishment which may be resorted to for offences cognisable under the prison rules is confinement in light punishment cells. These cells will be found at the end of the corridor on the left of the entrance. They do not differ materially from the other cells except that everything in them is made of iron, even the bed.

Moreover, everything that might be put to dangerous use, either for the destruction of prison property or else for bodily injury to the prisoner himself or others is carefully removed. Seeing the cell with its solid stone walls and floor bricks closely locked together, there would be no scope for mischief here.

However, there is plain evidence that, despite all precautions, mischief has been made. It remains a mystery how he could have managed, but not long ago, a convict detained here actually succeeded in raising, without tools, a brick out of the cement-joined floor, scooping out some of the mould underneath, which he removed. It is unknown how, but in this hollow, he concealed an improvised knife manufactured out of the rim of his food tin. The damaged place has since been made secure with cement, but the mark remains to show what human hands can do.

Near the light punishment cells are the dark cells, which are only rarely used but ought as a corrective, held in reverse, to exercise a deterrent effect, for they are far from inviting. Every ray of light is literally shut out, and the result is the blackest darkness. From the passage, all access to light or sound is barred by double doors from the outside by a thick wall.

Other modes of punishment applicable under restrictions are irons and the lash. Over both, the Home Office exercises stringent supervision; even the shape of the punitive instrument is minutely prescribed. Offenders under 18 years may be whipped with a birch rod only. Offenders over that age receive either the cat or the rod. For the administration of severe correction, there is a triangle in the basement in which prisoners are placed. Their arms are secured above their body against a post.

Fortunately, there is little occasion for resorting to this punishment. Altogether, Sussex prisoners give less trouble, we believe, than criminals in other counties. They seem less prone to mischief and more manageable. To attribute this wholly to humane treatment might imply an invidious suggestion against prison officers elsewhere, for which there is no ground.

A happy mixture of the kindness and humanity prescribed in the prison rules with the firmness required by correctional discipline has, however, unquestionably a great deal to do with the orderly behaviour generally observed where such virtues flourish. The prisoners' reception room is in the same part of the building as the punishment cells, where they may see their friends with the governor's permission. It is, of course, under difficulty, a double row of strong bars, separated by an interval across which no two arms in creation could join, keeping the interlocutors apart.

In the space between the two gratings sits or stands the watchful warder. Under such circumstances, prisoners must be highly skilled spiritualists if they are to make any mischief. Nothing distinguishes the higher cells from the lower, but a machine employed to distribute food on the upper floors deserves notice. It consists of iron rails upon which a trolley runs backwards and forward, reaching across to both galleries. The food is hoisted from the kitchen by a lift and is distributed from cell to cell on this trolley.

This arrangement is so perfect that the entire serving of food takes no more than five minutes. On the first floor of the east wing, at the back, facing the yard is the infirmary, a cell holding four beds in which prisoners enjoy more comforts. Even here, the inmates are under constant supervision. At the back of the building, the main portion of which is constructed in the form of a T, including the entrance corridor in the shape of a cross is the chapel. Here the two sexes meet, but without seeing each other.

The gallery is reserved for the females, but an ingeniously contrived grating is so fixed that they can neither see nor be seen by the males below. The chapel fittings are plain. The prisoners sit in rows facing the altar, and at either end, there are raised seats for the wardens. Two raised seats, specially marked, are reserved for the Governor and the Chief Warder. At the far end of the chapel is a font which is not infrequently put in requisition for the baptism of children born in gaol.

The regulations with regard to females newly confined are very indulgent. In the chapel, the prisoners attend every morning at nine for Morning Prayer, besides meeting for the Sunday services. The holy sacrament is administered once a month, but the discretion allowed to ministers is very properly exercised so as to refuse manifestly unworthy communicants, and we are told that, as a rule, only a few are admitted or claim admission.

In accordance with the prison rules issued by the Home Office, ample provision is made for religious instructions and pastoral supervision. Prisoners professing the Roman Catholic faith are visited by a priest of their own church. By a rather extraordinary arrangement, the prison chapel is, at certain hours, placed at the disposal of the Roman Catholic priest and his imprisoned flock, a modus vivendi with the State Church, probably unique in this kingdom.

The liberty of conscience of other denominations is equally protected. No prisoner who is not a member of the established church is compelled to attend chapel. The Chaplain is not permitted to hold communication with any prisoners, not of his own persuasion. Moreover, no Jew is obligated to work on the Sabbath. Under the new government rules, the system of secular instruction is not equally satisfactory.

The old taught classes have been discontinued, and the schoolmaster is required, if we are correctly informed, to instruct each prisoner separately in his cell. To do much good in this way, not only does an exceptionally strong head but an almost ubiquitous presence seem indispensable.

The prison establishment is, so far as personal labour is concerned, internally self-supporting, supplying its own hands for laundry, kitchen and other uses. There are strict rules in force regulating the prison diet, and the food is prepared accordingly, wholesale, of course, but the scrupulous regard to weight and other conditions.

The female prisoners are kept in a separate building, under female supervision, and the debtors again in another by themselves. These two buildings are corresponding detached wings, the former on the left of the main prison and the latter on the right.

The female prison has an outside length of 218 feet and a depth of 30 feet; it contains a corridor of 160 feet long by 10 feet wide, the cells being arranged on the front side only. The cells are of the same dimensions as those assigned to males, namely 13 feet by 7 and 9 feet high, except for two double cells at the end of the corridor, measuring 17 feet by 13.

The matrons' rooms are at the entrance end of the corridor, joining onto the debtors' wing and the female infirmary. In the basement of this wing is the officer's mess room, and there are punishment cells for females, baths, reception cells and store rooms. The debtor's wing is less in length, namely 139 feet outside, with 28 feet in depth.

The corridor measures only 90 feet by 10, with a day room for first-class debtors at one end and not for second-class debtors at the other, each measuring 22 ½ feet by 16 feet. The sleeping rooms are 11 feet by 6 ½ feet, the height being the same throughout, viz., and 9 feet.

A third-class day room with sleeping cells of the same size attached is situated on the first floor. Thus there is a separation between the sexes and also between debtors and criminal prisoners. The prison is surrounded by yards and gardens, the latter indeed partly for the growth of vegetables, partly, along with yards, for exercise.

There are four places set apart for such exercise, with circles marked off, where the prisoners keep marching in single file at the rate of about three miles an hour. A warder's box close by enables officers to watch them. The various classes of prisoners are kept separate and do not even come within sight of one another while walking. One yard is provided with two walks, an inner and an outer circle and takes more prisoners at a time accordingly. One circular walk, in the yard in the northeast corner, passes uncomfortably, and perhaps suggestively, close to the gallows pit where, among other persons, Lefroy breathed his last.

The gardens have recently been enlarged by the purchase of four acres of land, around which a wall, strong and high, is being erected. This, as well as all other work inside the prison walls or fence at present, is done by prisoners. The building proceeds only slowly. Chapter, exercise and time allowed for food rather than interfere with expedition and dispatch.

However, it is ordered that it shall be done by the prisoners. There are two scales with seven subdivisions each. Under the first scale, prisoners received at first 1 ½ pounds of bread, two pints of gruel daily and half a pint of soup daily.'

The Prison Commissioners, who dictated prison regimes, published a set of rules and regulations in the late nineteenth century that dictated criminal convicts' treatment. This document allows us to understand the harsh conditions that young George Henry Wood would have encountered.

Immediately after entering the gaol, he would have undergone a compulsory strip-searching by the head gaoler. Any prohibited or valuable items would be noted in the gaoler's journal and confiscated. During the searches, wardens were particularly vigilant for things that could be dangerous or that could facilitate escape. Once these searches were complete, the gaoler recorded the prisoner's name, age, height, weight, and distinguishing features in the nominal record. Towards the latter part of the nineteenth century, convict photos would also be taken and recorded; however, very few have survived at Lewes.

At this point, George Henry Wood was subjected to a complete examination by the prison's medical officer to determine the prisoner's health and to allow suitable work duties to be allocated. Any prisoner harbouring acute illness was excused from completing labour. Prisoners who were awaiting trial could wear their own clothes if they wished. However, parasitic infestations such as lice, mites and ticks were highly prevalent at the time and were known to spread disease. Therefore, the prison staff purified all clothing before it was allowed.

Convicted male prisoners were not afforded this option and wore a prison-issue dress, which consisted of a jacket, waistcoat, trousers, neckerchief, shirts, socks or stockings, shoes and a cap. The prison authorities provided female prisoners with a dress or jacket, petticoat, stockings, skirt, neckerchief, hat, shoes and underwear. All prison-issued clothing was covered in broad arrows to indicate that they were government property.

Most unconvicted prisoners slept in a hammock or bedstead and were provided with a mattress, pillows and blankets. Convicted prisoners were not so fortunate and were forced to sleep on a wooden plank bed without a mattress for the first three months of their sentence. This punishment was infamously uncomfortable and added to the harshness of prison sentences, as shown in the following article published in the *Islington Gazette* on the 5th of June 1899. By this time, the period was reduced to 14 days, but it was still considered too long. The article is as follows:

'The Plank Bed Torture
It must be remembered that the solitude of the cell is a real mental torture for many prisoners and, in many cases, quite unhinges the mind. All prisoners sentenced to three years and over must pass the first six months in this condition of unnatural isolation. A prisoner used to be

kept for nine months in cellular isolation. On the other hand, the plank bed is still to be retained. The first 14 days of prison life must be spent on the plank bed.

It is easy for the experienced eye to pick out the prisoner being subjected to the torture of the plank bed. He has a haggard look, a wearied eye, a worn face, listlessness, and the sheer physical debility arising from a want of sleep which stamps plank-bed prisoners.

On a recent visit to a Continental prison, I was struck by the comparatively bright look of the prisoners. 'Yes', said the governor, 'we imprison men here, but we do not torture them. Your plank bed is not a punishment but an instrument of torture.' But our official wiseacres think otherwise. Therefore, the plank bed remains.'

Each cell contained a copper sink attached to freshwater pipes for washing. Fearful of parasites and disease, the prison wardens conducted daily inspections to ensure that prisoners were clean and decent. Any dirty or unkempt prisoners would face severe punishment. Female prisoners were not forced to cut their hair unless the medical officer found parasites or extreme dirt. Similarly, male prisoners' hair was not cut any shorter than what the officials deemed necessary.

In line with the solitary regimes enforced at prisons at the time, prisoners were kept in single occupancy cells, which meant complete isolation from the other convicts. The prison authorities believed this would stop criminal friendships from developing. Wardens also enforced complete silence to promote reflection and penance.

In exceptional circumstances such as overcrowding, prisoners would share their cells with up to two other male prisoners. Similarly, prisoners suffering from conditions such as epilepsy which required nightly supervision were placed with no less than two other male prisoners. The authorities thought housing at least three or more people in shared cells would limit the possibility of '*inappropriate collusion or other unwanted behaviour*'.

Per the penal servitude act 1867, prisons ensured convicts filled their time with cleaning, hard labour and exercise. Work duties would take place in the convict cells to ensure complete isolation. Privileged prisoners would be allowed to complete work in other areas of the prison, such as the laundry or gardens if required. However, prisons that were found to be communicating would receive harsh punishments.

As stated in the previous article, some cells contained a crank machine, a penal labour device used in many English prisons in the 19th century. The contraption consisted of a hand-turned crank which forced four large cups or ladles through sand inside a drum. At Lewes, prisoners were forced to make 12,000 revolutions of the crank each day whilst facing the rear stone wall of their cell. Those who did not reach their quota received further punishment. To make matters worse, wardens would frequently tighten the cranks mechanism, which made the work even harder and led to wardens being called *'Screws'*.

Following George Henry Wood's first conviction, the short length of his sentence meant that George Henry Wood would have been allocated the crank. However, other tasks were given for longer sentences. Lewes operated the *'Marks and Class System'* like many other prisons. Marks acted as the prison currency and dictated the treatment and privileges given to prisoners.

Marks were awarded for good behaviour and completion of the allocated daily work quota. Idleness or poor conduct resulted in the deduction of marks from a convict's total. New prisoners were automatically denoted as class 1 and would have to earn enough marks to move to the next class. The types of work available to the different categories of prisoners are shown in the table below:

Regulations for the labour of convicted prisoners, pursuant to sentence:

Hard Labour for the 1st Class of Prisoner			
1.	Crank	2.	Weaving with heavy looms
3.	Pumping	4.	Making coir mats with heavy beaters
5.	Stone breaking	6.	Digging
7.	Grinding corn	8.	Sawing and cleaving wood
9.	Rope or oakum beating		
Hard Labour for the 2nd Class of Prisoner			
1.	Modified labour on the looms	2.	Shoemaking
3.	Mat-making	4.	Tailoring
5.	Picking Oakum or coir	6.	Painting
7.	Picking hair or wool	8.	Bricklaying
9.	Brush making	10.	Gardening
11.	Basket making	12.	Preparing firewood
13.	Carpentry and turning	14.	Printing and binding

As with the crank, convicted prisoners were ordered to complete a set quantity of work daily. If the work was unmeasurable, prisoners earned marks if the supervising warden deemed that the prisoner had worked diligently throughout the day. If a prisoner completed his tasks appropriately for eight hours, excluding chapel attendance and other breaks, they would receive eight pitiful marks.

However, if they completed more work than expected, they could receive slightly more. When a prisoner's mark total reached certain levels, they were rewarded with privileges as detailed in the table below:

Mark Scale. The following schedule is and shall be deemed to be the mark scale which is mentioned or referred to in and by any of the rules and regulations:

Marks to be earned	Privilege to be obtained	Time in which numbers ought to be reached
50	Bed if 1st conviction.	One week
100	Diet- second class if sentence exceeds six weeks.	Two weeks
150	One airing daily if working in a closed cell. Bed if 2nd conviction.	Three weeks
200	Bed if third conviction.	One month
250	Write a letter and receive reply.	Five weeks
350	Diet - third class.	Seven weeks
500	Privileged letter and reply (only allowed to prisoners possessing 50 extra marks).	Ten weeks
700	Diet- fourth class if sentence exceeds 3 months or Receive a visit from friends (or letter and reply in lieu or One airing daily if not already allowed.	Three months
900	Write a letter and receive reply.	Eighteen weeks
1100	Privileged letter and reply (only allowed to prisoners who possess 100 extra marks).	Twenty-three weeks
1300	Diet - fifth class if sentence exceeds 6 months or Two airings daily	Six months

	or Receive a visit from friends (or letter and reply in lieu).	
1500	Write a letter and receive a reply.	Seven months
1700	Privileged letter and reply (only allowed to prisoners who possess 150 extra marks.	Eight months
2000	Diet: sixth class if sentence exceeds 9 months or Visit from friends (or letter and reply in lieu).	Nine months
2200	Write a letter and receive a reply.	Seventeen months
2400	Privileged letter and reply (only allowed to prisoners who possess 200 extra marks.	Eighteen months
2600	Diet. Seventh class if sentence exceeds six months or Receive a visit from friends (or letter and reply in lieu).	Twelve months
2800	Write a letter and receive a reply	Thirteen months
3000	Privileged letter and reply (only allowed to prisoners who possess 250 extra marks	Fourteen months
3300	Receive a visit from friends (or letter and reply in lieu)	Fifteen months
3500	Write a letter and receive a reply	Sixteen months
3700	Privileged letter and reply (only allowed to prisoners who possess 300 extra marks	Seventeen months
3900	Receive a visit from friends (or letter and reply in lieu)	Eighteen months
4100	Write a letter and receive a reply	Nineteen months
4300	Privileged letter and reply (only allowed to prisoners who possess 350 extra marks	Twenty months
4600	Receive a visit from friends (or letter and reply in lieu)	Twenty-one months

4800	Write a letter and receive a reply	Twenty-two months
5000	Privileged letter and reply (only allowed to prisoners who possess 400 extra marks	Twenty-three months
5200	Receive a visit from friends (or letter and reply in lieu)	Two years

Enjoyable activities of any type were banned entirely, even once the prisoners had completed their daily work allocation. No gaming of any form was permitted, and any items, such as dice and cards, were seized and destroyed.

Although not compulsory, convicts were encouraged to attend the chapel each morning and evening; and did so in high numbers, no doubt, to escape the dreary and monotonous regime. All prisoners were issued with a bible, hymn and service book to fully participate in religious services, which were said to be lively and enjoyable at Lewes. Whilst these services provided a short distraction, Lewes' prisoners could not escape the heavily enforced separate system. In the chapel, prisoners were seated a yard apart, and armed wardens sat on raised chairs so that they were able to prevent any communication.

The different types of convicts held by the gaol varied greatly, and the organisation of the chapel reflected this. Debtors were seated at the rear of the chapel, away from the criminal convicts. The prison rules stipulated that prisoners awaiting trial were also segregated from convicted prisoners. This class of prisoners sat in an area separate from sentenced prisoners.

All convicts were locked in their cells from 7.30 pm until 6.30 am. The cells were approximately 12 feet long and 6 feet wide and furnished with only a wooden bed frame, a mattress and a pillow stuffed with straw if they had earned enough marks. Blankets and sheets were provided but would have offered little warmth in the frigid winter months when conditions became even more unbearable. The Governor monitored the temperature with thermometers located throughout the prison. However, when winter came, the stone walls and primitive heating system meant there was little the prison staff could do to make conditions more humane.

No alcoholic beverages or tobacco products were allowed in the jail unless ordered by the prison surgeon. The only exception was the imprisoned debtors, who were allowed to receive food, wine, malt liquor, clothing, bedding or other necessities. The sale of food or beverages to convicted prisoners was strictly prohibited. If a debtor or prisoner awaiting trial broke this rule, they would lose the privilege and receive a punishment.

Prison life was strict and unrelenting. Wardens constantly monitored the prisoner's conduct and ensured prisoners followed the rules hung in each cell. Several offences would result in harsher punishment than the loss of marks. These included the following:

- Disobedience or disregard for the prison rules and regulations.
- Common assaults by one prisoner on another.
- Profane, cursing and swearing by any prisoner.
- Irreverent behaviour at the chapel by any prisoner.
- Insulting or threatening language by any prisoner to any officer or prisoner.
- Absence from chapel without leave by any criminal prisoner.
- Idleness or negligence at work by any convicted prisoner.
- Wilful mismanagement of work by any convicted prisoner.

If the head gaoler determined that a prisoner was guilty of the offence, he would place them into solitary confinement for three days and reduce their diet to bread and water. If the prisoner repeated the violation, they would make a report to the visiting justices, who would order a greater punishment. This could include confinement in the light or dark punishment cells, leg irons and whipping. In the case of serious offences, prisoners were flogged with the Cat-o'-nine-tails.

Prison food was basic and had limited nutritious value, adding to the severity of sentences. The Dietary Scale afforded to prisoners is shown below:

Dietary Scale 1 Class I of Prisoners
For all prisoners on admission and until they have gained 100 marks will receive 1 ½ pound of bread and 2 pints of gruel daily. Prisoners will receive 3 pints of soup weekly.
Class II of Prisoners
Prisoners who have gained 100 marks until they reach 350 marks will receive 1 ½ bread, 2 pints of gruel and 1 pint of soup daily.
Class III of Prisoners

Prisoners who have gained 350 marks until they have reached 700 marks will receive 1 ½ pound of bread, 2 pints of gruel, 1 pint of soup and ½ pound of potatoes daily.
Class IV of Prisoners
Prisoners who have gained 700 marks will receive 1 ½ pounds of bread, 2 pints of gruel, 1 pint of soup and 1 pound of potatoes.
Class V of Prisoners
Prisoners who have gained 1300 marks until they have reached 2000 marks will receive 1 ½ pounds of bread, 2 pints of gruel, 1 pint of soup and 1 pound of potatoes daily. On Sundays, they will receive 1 ½ pounds of bread, 2 pints of gruel, and six ounces of cooked meat and 1 pound of potatoes.
Class VI of Prisoners
Prisoners who have gained 2000 marks until they have reached 2600 marks will receive 1 ½ pound of bread, 2 pints of gruel, 1 pint of soup and 1 pound of potatoes. On Sundays and Thursdays, prisoners will receive 1 ½ pounds of bread, 2 pints of gruel, and six ounces of cooked meat and 1 pound of potatoes.

At the end of their sentences, prisoners were given a gratuity of 1 penny for every 16 marks earned and an extra penny for every eight marks acquired above their quota. In the case of repeat offenders, this was reduced or withheld entirely. No surviving records show whether George Henry Wood received any payment as he left Lewes Prison.

Nonetheless, by June 1880, George Henry Wood found himself back in Brighton with his parents. With limited options available to him, George Henry Wood decided to enlist in the Army. On the 5th of January, 1881, he joined the 48th Brigade of the Guildford Regiment and agreed to serve his county for ten years. He was initially stationed at Stoughton Barracks, Aldershot and appeared to settle into military life.

However, on the 29th of September, after only 239 days, he was again discharged. It appears that George Henry Wood suffered from varicose veins in the legs and found himself back in Brighton; unemployed and without money or opportunity, much to his parent's dismay.

Chapter 6: *'Torn to Pieces.'*

After being charged with murder, George Henry Wood had resigned to the fact that he would remain incarcerated until Monday, the 13th of December. Aside from short periods for questioning, he remained locked in his cell and entirely oblivious to the immense public anger about Edith's gruesome murder. Despite this, he must have dreaded his upcoming court appearance, where he would be seen in public for the first time since his arrest. He had also received word that his father would also be present.

Over the course of the weekend, George Henry Wood was utterly isolated and not permitted visits by his family during this time. The only human contact he was afforded was with police constables tasked with guarding him. Although they were fully aware of the viciousness of Edith's murder, these constables showed George Henry Wood kindness and appear to have been sympathetic to his position.

During the afternoon of the 12th of December, Mr Ayres, the defending solicitor, visited the town hall to interview his client. The custody cells afforded no privacy for such a meeting, and after Mr Ayres raised objections about the conditions, Chief Constable Terry offered his office as a meeting room. At their meeting, Mr Ayres repeatedly asked George Henry Wood about his movements on the night of the murder. However, to Mr Ayres' frustration, George Henry Wood indignantly professed that he could not remember a thing. Notably, he again did not deny that he was responsible for Edith Jeal's murder.

Elsewhere, scandalous newspaper reports continued to saturate the local and national tabloids. These reports provoked further unrest in the shocked and angered Kemp Town community who by this time were baying for blood. Even though he had yet appeared before the courts, during the afternoon of the 12th, various newspapers published George Henry Wood's name, age and address, much to his family's horror.

After the meeting, Mr Ayres addressed the waiting journalists who were waiting at the station's doors. Since his client's arrest, Mr Ayres had been carefully monitoring the coverage of the murder. He had been increasingly concerned by the content being put into the public domain. Keen to protect his client's interests, he warned that such details could influence any jury hearing George Henry Wood's case. Nonetheless, reports continued to be published in most newspapers.

By the morning of the 13th of December, propelled by continuous reporting and gossip, the public's anger reached fever pitch. From an early hour, a restless, enraged mob assembled outside the town hall. Some were present to voice their disgust and anger, whilst others simply wanted to view the accused.

Inside the police station, George Henry Wood was blissfully unaware of the growing unrest outside. He awoke early and washed his face in the cell's small metal bowl after eating a small breakfast. Afterwards, he carefully dressed in his best Sunday clothes, which his father had sent on the previous day. After, he nervously paced up and down in his cell while waiting for his escort to arrive.

The Brighton Police Court where the trial was due to take place was described as a *'tolerably roomy one'* but was arranged similarly to others across the country. On each side and the back were elevated wooden galleries to allow public spectators to watch the proceedings. At the room's rear was a large and comfortable raised enclosure containing a row of extravagant magisterial chairs to seat the Magistrates. Directly beneath this bench was a small table where the court clerk would sit, usually surrounded by books and papers. Around the Clerk's table were more seats for any solicitors acting for the defence and prosecution.

Dead opposite was the Chief Constable's table, which was carefully positioned so he could monitor prisoners' behaviour in the court. Behind this was a further seating area containing two rows of seating for the press, who regularly reported on trials heard at the court. Behind the press bench were seats for the various parties involved in the day's proceedings, such as complainants, witnesses, and defendants. The wooden dock to house the accused stood directly in front of these benches.

At 9.45 am, the Stipendiary Magistrate, Mr C. G. Heathcote, entered the court to oversee George Henry Wood's sensational trial. After speaking to other officials in the court, he took his seat at the Justice's bench. Shortly after, Mr Pope, representing the Crown, also entered and began organising papers at the solicitor's table. Lastly, Mr Ayres arrived and sat beside Mr Pope.

At precisely 10.00 am, George Henry Wood was collected from his cell by several police constables and was forcefully led up to the ground floor. He walked across the grand hall and into the doors of the police court. As he came into view, a hushed silence fell over the previously bustling and noisy courtroom. Those present observed a slightly built young man of medium height with wavy fair hair, a light moustache and bright darkish eyes. As he walked across the courtroom, journalists reported that all eyes focused on the prisoner's long and thin face, which was said to be due to a *'disproportionately deep and protruding chin.'*

If George Henry Wood was concerned or worried about his position, he did very well to conceal it. Various accounts suggest that he appeared completely calm and unfazed by his situation. After being placed in the dock, he gazed about the courtroom and arrogantly stood with his arms folded. As the proceedings began, George Henry Wood noticed the public's gaze still fixed upon his person. He purposefully avoided eye contact with anyone and, instead, fixed his eyes on the dock floor or the ceiling.

Initially, he showed no emotion and maintained a neutral expression. But as the Magistrate read the charges, George Henry Wood's face changed and assumed a *'gloomy countenance'*. However, at no stage did he betray the slightest agitation or shame. It is hard to speculate whether George's relaxed demeanour was due to a lack of remorse or simply did not appreciate the severity of his situation.

The first witness to be called was Edward Villiers, the gardener who discovered Edith's brutalised body on the morning of the 11th of December. When asked by Mr Day why he had decided to look inside the barn, he explained that he had noticed that the door was wide open. He described finding Edith's body and the disarrangement of her clothing. He informed the court that Edith looked like she had been *'torn to pieces!'* which caused immense excitement in the public galleries.

He explained that he said that he had rushed back to Rock Street to find his workmate, William Stamford, and informed him that *'murder had been done.'* After, he explained, he and William Stamford returned to the field and, after a brief discussion, that he had gone to find help. He said William Stamford had spotted Doctor Humphrey in Chesham Place in his absence. Edward Villiers recalled that a short time later, the body was removed to the Freshfield Road Police Station.

William Stamford was the next witness to appear before the court. He described Edith's appearance when he entered the barn and recalled that her clothing was hitched up and blood saturated her lower body. He informed the court that whilst Edward Villiers went to get help, he had spotted Doctor Humphrey's carriage in Chichester Place. He recalled calling the doctor and asking him to accompany him to the field. In an emotional state, he explained how he had led Doctor Humphrey to the body. He described noticing several marks on Edith's neck that he had spotted as she was carried to the ambulance. Mr Ayres cross-examined William Stamford about the condition of the field's gate. He replied that the gate was locked but had forced it open to allow the ambulance access.

P.C. Herbert Pelling, who had been on duty in Sussex Square when the body was discovered, was the next witness to give evidence. He explained that at 12.50 pm, Edward Villiers came running up the road in a state of panic and informed him that a child had been murdered. He said he had accompanied Edward Villiers back to the field and, after a brief discussion with Doctor Humphrey, that he had entered the barn.

He informed the court that the body's appearance led him to believe that the cause of death was strangulation. He also stated that the disarrangement of Edith's clothes led him to conclude that an outrage had been committed. He said that after Doctor Humphrey had completed his examination, he helped carry the body to the ambulance. Afterwards, he said he had entered the barn to collect the underwear, cloth cap and chestnuts as evidence. At this point, William Stamford was recalled by Judge Heathcote, who asked whether there was usually a lock on the barn door. To the best of his knowledge, William Stamford said there was not.

The next witness to be called was Edward Jeal, who was understandably traumatised and distraught. He informed the court that on the evening of the 10th of December, he had sent his son and daughter to make a few purchases. He explained that the shop was only a few doors from their home and that his two children had made similar trips. Edward Jeal recalled that shortly after the two had left, Bertram returned home without his sister. He said in consequence of a conversation with his son, he had gone out to look for Edith and did so for almost half an hour. After he told the court, he attended the Freshfield Road Police Station and reported his daughter missing.

Edward Jeal explained that he and a police constable had searched the surrounding hills for most of the night without success. In a quiet tone, he said that he received news of Edith's murder at 1.40 pm on Friday, the 11th of December. He informed the court that, in consequence, he returned to the Freshfield Road Police Station, where he positively identified the body as that of his daughter. In response to the Magistrate, Edward Jeal approximated that the field was around a twelve-minute walk from his house.

Mr Pope, acting for the prosecution, asked Edward Jeal why Bertram had left Edith outside the shop. Edward explained that when the children reached the first grocer, they found the firewood dampened and decided to continue to the next shop.

Mr Pope asked Edward Jeal if he recognised or knew the accused. Edward Jeal replied that he knew the prisoner by sight but had not seen him on the night Edith disappeared. Finally, Mr Pope asked Edward Jeal whether George Henry Wood belonged to the same Temperance Society he attended. Edward Jeal said that he did not.

The next witness to be called was Inspector Samuel Jupp. As he entered the witness box, he generated significant interest from the public galleries, and those seated within these areas immediately started whispering. Many people in the court had noticed a pile of blood-stained clothing tucked under his arm. He informed the court that on the 11th of December, 1891, Chief Constable Terry asked if he would attend Brighton Station's goods yard at approximately 8 pm.

Inspector Jupp explained that he arrived at the Trafalgar Street entrances gate hut a short time later. He said that after a brief conversation with the supervisor, he had located George Henry Wood at work in the yard. He recalled that he had questioned George Henry Wood about his movements on the previous evening, to which George Henry Wood had replied that he was at the North Street Circus all night. Inspector Jupp explained that P.C. Tuppen had stated that he had seen a drunken man near the murder scene and had identified the individual as George Henry Wood.

Inspector Jupp explained that he had asked George Henry Wood if he could name anyone who might have seen him at the circus. He said that George Henry Wood could not provide names but half-heartedly suggested that the doorman might remember seeing him. Inspector Jupp informed the court that he had been keen to locate George Henry Wood's clothing and asked for the leggings he had worn on the night in question. He said that George Henry Wood informed him that the clothes were back at Rock Street.

Inspector Jupp said that he had, escorted George Henry Wood to the town hall. Mr Pope asked Inspector Jupp to confirm that George Henry Wood had subsequently been charged, to which Inspector Judd said he was. Mr Pope asked how George Henry Wood had responded, to which Inspector Jupp said that George Henry Wood had made several further denials. He explained that after the charges were read, George Henry Wood was taken to the lock-up cells, and that his clothing was examined.

He stated that there were no visible marks on the prisoner's body but explained there were many damp blood stains on his clothes, which appeared to have recently been washed. Inspector Jupp then detailed the suspicious stains which littered George Henry Wood's clothing. Mr Pope asked about George Henry Wood's demeanour at the point of arrest. Inspector Jupp said that he appeared dazed. Keen that the Magistrate did not doubt George Henry Wood's sanity, Inspector Jupp added that he had asked whether he understood the charges. He said that George Henry Wood had quietly responded, *'Yes, but I don't remember one particle about it.'*

Due to the time of the day, the Magistrate deferred Inspector Jupp's cross-examination. But before he formally concluded the day's proceedings, the Magistrate asked whether George Henry Wood had made any comments on the way down to the town hall. Inspector Jupp replied that he had not said a word and appeared quiet and sullen.

At this point, the Magistrate informed the court that he would take no further evidence that day. Mr Pope, acting for the prosecution, asked for a remand. He told the Magistrate that he needed time to report to the Treasury and prepare other aspects of the case. He explained that he was also due to appear at the Sussex Winter Assizes, which would take place the following week. He said this meant he would be unavailable for any other matters. He asked for a first adjournment until Tuesday, the 15th of December, and a second adjournment for a further week.

In an incredulous tone, Mr Ayres arose from his seat and fiercely objected to this proposal. He argued that the adjournment was far too long, given that the prosecution had nowhere near established guilt. He proclaimed that a lengthy remand would be unfair and would negatively prejudice his client to the public. Mr Pope calmly responded by pointing out the brutality of the crime and the perceived risk to the public.

After briefly considering the opposing arguments, Judge Heathcote ruled in favour of the Crown and ordered an adjournment. He also ruled that George would remain at the town hall cells until the case resumed on the 15th. The Magistrate then formally closed the court. George Henry Wood was flanked by six police constables who removed him from the dock and escorted him back to the basement cells.

Meanwhile, the poor Jeal family struggled to accept Edith's death at Kemp Town. The entire family withdrew and entered a period of mourning. They received frequent visits from friends and other acquaintances who wanted to convey compassion and sympathy. However, many within their community appeared oblivious to their suffering and continued to bask in the sensationalism of the murder. Around the Jeal's home, small crowds frequently gathered to gossip, hoping they would see the grieving family members.

When interviewed by the numerous journalists still present in the area, these individuals openly threatened to harm George Henry Wood if given the opportunity. However, others were unaware of George Henry Wood's arrest and stated that the murderer would never be caught due to the several hours between the crime and the body's discovery.

A short stone's throw away from Bedford Buildings, Arlington School's playing field became filled with Brighton residents who wanted to view the murder scene. Such were their numbers; Chief Constable Terry was forced to send more officers to clear the area and guard the field's entrances. However, by the time evening arrived, the temperature considerably dropped, and the site cleared, much to the police's relief.

Chapter 7: The Opening of the Inquest

Alongside the criminal proceedings relating to Edith's murder were the investigations of the Coroner, whose role dates back to 1194 and who originally carried out any action deemed to be beneficial to the Crown's revenue. Along with probing unexplained or violent deaths, *Crowners,* as they were initially named, also investigated shipwrecks, fires and the discovery of buried treasure.

The Coroner's Act of 1887 revoked much of the earlier legislation relating to fiscal matters, which allowed Coroners to focus on suspicious deaths for the benefit of the community in which they operated. Every county in England and Wales was allocated a Coroner, supported by several deputies, who serve across the county's various boroughs.

Shortly after the discovery of her body, Alfred Freeman-Gell, the Deputy Coroner of Brighton, was tasked with investigating the cause and circumstances of Edith's death. He was a prominent local figure renowned for his professionalism and knowledge. It was no coincidence that Alfred Freeman-Gell had found himself in such a prominent role. His father, Mr Alfred Gell Senior, was a qualified solicitor and worked as a justice clerk for many years. In addition, his maternal Grandfather, Mr Thomas Freeman, was also legally trained and had held the post of Brighton Commissioner for several years before he retired.

After receiving early education at St Nicholas' College in Shoreham, Alfred Freeman-Gell attended Lewes Grammar School. In 1861 he decided to follow in his father's footsteps and gained employment as a legal trainee at the legal offices of his uncle, Mr James Albert Gell. In 1868 he qualified as a solicitor and enrolled at London University 1st division, where he studied for a law degree. After completing his studies, he secured employment at offices of the Brighton Corporation, initially as the Town Clerk before being promoted to Deputy Coroner.

After being notified of Edith Jeal's death, Alfred Freeman-Gell arranged for her inquest to open on Saturday, the 12th of December, at 4 pm. The inquest was held at the Freshfield Road police station, where Edith Jeal's body lay. The late start was agreed to allow the interested parties sufficient travelling time after the police court proceedings.

On the 11th of December, the Coroner legally summoned twelve *'lawful'* men who would make up the jury. Thomas Pennicard was appointed jury foreman and would speak on behalf of the other jurors. At 3.45 pm, Mr Pope, who had appeared at the initial police court proceedings, arrived at Freshfield Road Police Station. Shortly after, Mr Ayres also came. After being welcomed by Chief Constable Terry, the pair was led into a room immediately behind the front office and was seated on a long wooden bench.

George Henry Wood was not present at the inquest. However, whether his attendance was through choice or refusal is unclear. Since his arrest, he had repeatedly denied knowledge about the crime; therefore, the authorities may have thought that his attendance was unnecessary.

At 4 pm, the Coroner welcomed the jury and watched as they took the oath of affirmation before the clerk. Immediately after, the Coroner escorted the jurors into the mortuary at the rear of the building. The jury silently entered the dimly lit room and huddled around the large stone slab positioned in the room's centre. Once the jury was in position, a police constable closed the mortuary door to prevent any disturbance to the proceedings.

After her remains arrived at the Freshfield Road Police Station, P.C. Tuppen placed a blanket over Edith's damaged body, exposing only her head. However, as soon as the doors closed, Alfred Freeman-Gell pulled back the blanket in one swift motion. The jurors were stunned and horrified at Edith's brutalised and blood-soaked body. Despite their reaction, the Coroner instructed the jury to carefully study Edith's pitiful remains.

As they did so, they would have noticed the right side of Edith's face, which bore areas of significant bruising. The marks extended from the forehead to the mouth, and told of the horror Edith had suffered at her death. They would have seen that her long brown hair lay carelessly across her head, face and neck, which bore marks of extreme violence. Even at this early stage of the inquest, having not heard a word of evidence, the jurors must have been satisfied that Edith's death was unlawful.

Once this grim task was complete, the jurors were directed back into the police station's main office by the Coroner, ready for the proceedings to begin. Edith's father, Edward Jeal, was the first witness to be called, who repeated the evidence he had provided to the police court earlier that day. The Coroner then asked Mr Ayres, defending George Henry Wood, if he wished to ask the father any questions.

Mr Ayres responded, '*I shall recall him on a future occasion.*'

The Coroner responded, '*Just as you please.*'

The Coroner turned to Edward Jeal and explained that he could leave the court. However, his words were abruptly interrupted by Mr Ayres, who had changed his mind.

Addressing Edward Jeal, he said, '*There is one point I want to make. You sent your child out to make a purchase, I think?*'

Edward Jeal: '*Yes, for a bundle of wood.*'

Mr Ayres: '*And a further purchase of some chestnuts?*'

Edward Jeal: '*Yes.*'

Mr Ayres: '*And you later ascertained that she made that purchase?*'

Edward Jeal: '*Yes.*'

Mr Ayres: '*To your knowledge, you have no idea who committed the foul crime?*'

Edward Jeal: '*Oh dear, no!*'

Mr Ayres: '*And no suspicion?*'

Edward Jeal: '*No suspicion at all.*'

Mr Ayres informed the Coroner that he had no further questions for Edward Jeal.

The Coroner turned to the jury and said, '*I don't know whether you would like to ask Mr Jeal any questions. I must say the evidence is only to be formal, and I shall take adjournment. Any questions you don't ask today may be put on a future occasion.*'

After a short discussion, the Foreman replied that they had no questions, and Edward Jeal was discharged by the Coroner. However, keen to hear the complete details about his daughter's demise, he bravely elected to remain in the room. The next witness to be called was Edward Villiers, gardener for the Brighton Corporation. He repeated the evidence he had provided to the Magistrate earlier that day about visiting the field and finding Edith's body.

The Coroner asked, '*Did you have any doubt in your mind that the child was dead?*'

Edward Villiers: '*By the appearance, I thought she was.*'

The questioning then passed to Mr Ayres, who was keen to create suspicion about Edward Villiers' motive for entering the shed on the 11th of December. He recognised that Edward Villiers had found himself at a critical location and tried to suggest that he had knowledge about the crime.

Mr Ayres: '*You were working on the road for the Corporation?*'

Edward Villiers: '*In Chesham Road and Rock Street.*'

Mr Ayres: '*Have you been in the habit of going into this field?*'

Edward Villiers: '*Yes, because there is no urinal nearer than there.*'

Mr Ayres: '*You have to go very often?*'

Edward Villiers: '*Not very often.*'

Mr Ayres: '*You have been there on several occasions?*'

Edward Villiers: '*I have been over there several times, but not on that day.*'

Mr Ayres: '*Did you think the gardener left the gate open?*'

Edward Villiers: '*The school boys go in and sometimes leave the gate open.*'

Mr Ayres: '*As a matter of fact, you found the gate was locked?*'

Edward Villiers: '*It was, so I jumped over the gate.*'

Mr Ayres: '*And you returned to your mate, and he jumped over the wall too?*'

Edward Villiers: '*Both of us.*'

Mr Ayres: '*Well now, what were the impressions on your mind when you saw this half-open door and the murdered body of the child? Did it occur to you that a murder had been committed?*'

Edward Villiers: '*I think so, and you would have thought the same!*'

Mr Ayres: '*You were asked for your impression! Some part of the child's dress was removed from the body, was it not?*'

Edward Villiers: '*I don't know anything about that. I did not stop to see any of that.*'

At this point, Mr Ayres' line of questioning began to frustrate Edward Villiers, who had become involved in the tragedy simply by being in the wrong place at the wrong time, and the disdain he felt at Mr Ayres' questions and insinuations punctured his subsequent responses.

Mr Ayres: '*Did you see any wounds on the body?*'

Edward Villiers: '*I saw that she had been violated.*'

Mr Ayres: '*I am coming to that.*'

Edward Villiers: '*You asked me the question, and I have given you the answer.*'

Mr Ayres then asked several questions about the cricket cap, chestnuts, firewood and underwear that had been found scattered around the body. Edward Villiers detailed the location and appearance of these items to the jury. This concluded Edward Villiers' evidence, and with no questions from the jury, he was thanked and dismissed by the Coroner.

P.C. Herbert Pelling was the next witness to be called and repeated the evidence he had given at the Brighton Police Court. Mr Ayres then questioned him to ascertain his thoughts on the murder.

Mr Ayres: *'In all cases, whether by accident or crime, it is part of your duty to report to your officer, is it not so?'*

P.C. Pelling: *'Yes, Sir, the first one you see.'*

Mr Ayres: *'Or when you return to the jury?'*

P.C. Pelling: *'Yes, Sir.'*

Mr Ayres: *'Have you got that report with you?'*

P.C. Pelling: *'I have not, Sir, but I believe the reports were sent to the town hall.'*

Mr Ayres: *'You have not got them, but you probably recollect what they contained?'*

P.C. Pelling: *'Yes, Sir, most of it.'*

Mr Ayres: *'Did you make a minute examination of the shed in question?'*

P.C. Pelling: *'I had very little time to make much inquiry into that, Sir, before many people were running to look in.'*

Mr Ayres: *'You made some investigation on which to find your report?'*

P.C. Pelling: *'Yes, Sir.'*

Mr Ayres: *'Did you in your report suggest any person as being guilty of this crime?'*

Mr Pope, who had been listening carefully to the evidence, interrupted the proceedings for the first time.

Mr Pope: *'I submit that the witness cannot be asked what was in the report.'*

The Coroner: *'No, strictly he cannot, but you know many things are allowed at a Coroner's inquest, which is not strictly evidence. Of course, the report can be produced on the next occasion.'*

Before Mr Pope could reply, Mr Ayres obnoxiously quipped, *'I should like it to be produced now!'*

The Coroner responded, *'This is only a preliminary hearing?'*

Mr Ayres replied, *'It may ease reflections on an innocent person.'*

The Chief Constable, Mr Terry, who was present, interrupted and said, *'I expect we can get it in a minute.'*

Mr Ayres, apparently happy with the response, said, *'The Chief Constable has given me his word very firmly.'*

The Coroner returned to P.C. Pelling. He said, *'Was the report made here or at the town hall?'*

P.C. Pelling: *'At the town hall, Sir.'*

The Coroner: *'Who made out the report?'*

P.C. Pelling: *'The sergeant on duty, I suppose, or the man in charge of the station.'*

Mr Ayres: *'Did you sign the report?'*

P.C. Pelling: *'No, Sir.'*

At this stage, Chief Superintendent Carter, who had been listening to the proceedings, quietly arose from his chair and exited the room. After a brief time, he returned and informed the Coroner that he had managed to locate the report. He passed the pile of papers to the Coroner, who, after studying the pages, read the entire document to the jury. The contents of the police report are missing from the records, and therefore, its contents are unknown.

After asking if the jury had any questions about the report's contents, which they did not, the Coroner continued with the proceedings. Doctor Douglas M. Ross of 9 Pavilion Parade was the next witness to be called. He explained that he was employed as a police surgeon for the Brighton Borough Police.

The Coroner immediately asked, *'Have you examined the body?'*

Doctor Ross: *'Yes, at Freshfield Road Police Station at 4.45 pm on the 11th of December. It is that of a well-nourished female child. It was fully dressed, except for the straw hat and drawers. These items lay on the table beside the body. The child wore lace-up boots, stockings extending above the knee, and the usual clothing I will describe later. The face and neck were smeared with blood, and the child looked almost like a Red Indian. The eyes were closed. The pinafore, two petticoats and the frock were saturated with blood on the front and lower parts. The drawers were also saturated. There was a blood clot close to the nose's left side. The child had fair hair, which was very long and matted with blood. There was no haemorrhage from the ears and no bleeding from the nose. The nose was flattened. The hands were very black and dirty and clenched. There was blood on the buttocks, particularly the left one. The left leg lay on the table, abducted and flexed. From the appearance of the lower part of the abdomen, it looked as if the blood had been wiped away. It looked so clean. There were marks of fingers on the top of the right forearm. These are distinct marks. There are two round bruises, as if made by the tips of the fingers in the same position, close to the scratches. There was an abrasion on the top of the right wrist and two scratches, and two abrasions on the back of the left hand. On washing off the blood from the face and neck, I found four marks in two pairs on the throat and four in two pairs almost opposite the chin and directly opposite the left cheek. There was extensive bruising and grazing on the right side of the neck immediately opposite those on the left. Those on the left were evidently done with the right hand. There were abrasions on the face, one at a point to the right of the middle line.*

At this point, the Coroner halted the proceedings. He noticed that his clerk struggled to keep up with Doctor Ross' lengthy statement.

Addressing Doctor Ross, he said, 'I don'*t want to stop anything, but I don't want to burden the depositions with more than is necessary.'*

Undeterred by the Coroner's comment, Doctor Ross continued with his evidence. He said, *'There are numerous abrasions and bruises on the left side. The whole of the left cheek was skinless and raw. The skin seemed to be taken off the whole of the left cheek. I did the post-mortem at 9 am today, as Mr Burchell, Coroner, requested. There were bruises extending through the scalp, and those inside corresponded with that outside. There was no fracture to the bones of the skull. The brain membranes were congested, and the veins were distended with dark fluid blood. The surface of the brain substance was very much congested, but otherwise was normal. The heart was empty of blood. There was a firmly contracted left ventricle and a flaccid right ventricle. The lungs were dark in colour and intensely congested all over with black blood. The windpipe was congested, but there was no fracture.'*

The Doctor then described the injuries relating to the egregious sexual assault that Edith had been subjected to, which caused upset in the room. The press did not report the details of these injuries and, to protect their readers, only made vague references to the rest of Doctor Ross' evidence. Disturbingly, the Doctor concluded that most of these injuries had occurred before death, which meant Edith would have likely been aware of the horrific attack she had suffered.

Doctor Ross informed the jury that Edith's lower abdomen was discoloured. He explained that this was due to an internal injury caused by a blunt instrument. Doctor Ross concluded that this trauma was caused after death as there was no blood loss. He then explained to the jurors that he believed that the cause of death was asphyxia, primarily from pressure on the throat. He added that Edith's clothes, which the assailant had thrown over Edith's head, also contributed to her death. Mr Ayres then cross-examined Doctor Ross, mainly focusing on the abdominal injury.

Mr Ayres: *'I take it from your post-mortem you did not find any trace of a knife or other sharp instrument on the body?'*

Doctor Ross: *'No.'*

Mr Ayres: *'You simply attribute death to the stoppage of the heart's action by asphyxia?'*

Doctor Ross: '*From the lungs and the injuries received. The injury to the abdomen was sufficient to cause death in time but not immediately. The injuries would set up peritonitis, but it was too early for this to set in at the time of death.*'

The next round of questions suggested that Edith was neglected, which must have been extremely painful for Edward Jeal to hear.

Mr Ayres: '*You say the child was generally dirty. Would that be of some standing?*'

Doctor Ross: '*I think it was dirty and had not been washed.*'

Mr Ayres went further, '*Neglected?*'

Doctor Ross explained, '*No, simply a child running about all day.*'

Mr Pope, who had stayed silent during the proceedings, also had questions about Edith's injuries.

Addressing Doctor Ross, he said, '*You say there was no blood from the nose but a clot on the side of the nose. Was it on the outside?*'

Doctor Ross: '*Yes, on the outside.*'

Mr Pope: '*Can you say where it came from?*'

Doctor Ross: '*It may have come from the nose?*'

Mr Pope: '*And you say there were marks of fingers on the back of the right forearm. What kind of marks were they?*'

Doctor Ross: '*From the nails and pressure of the fingertips.*'

Doctor Ross: '*Then you say the marks on the right side of the neck, immediately opposite those on the left, were done with the right hand?*'

Doctor Ross: '*Yes.*'

Mr Pope: '*Not the child's?*'

Doctor Ross: '*No.*'

Mr Pope: '*Considerable pressure must have been exercised?*'

Doctor Ross: '*Yes.*'

Mr Pope: '*Would the amount of pressure used be enough to close the throat and to cause asphyxia?*'

Doctor Ross: '*Quite. They are just in the right position. There were distinct marks as if the nails had been dug in.*'

This marked the end of Doctor Ross' evidence. The Coroner thanked him and dismissed him from the court. By now, the time was getting late. The Coroner turned to the Foreman and said,

'I don't propose to carry this further today. I understand it will suit you and other gentlemen if this inquiry is adjourned until this week. Will that suit you, Mr Pennicard? I suggest that the adjourned inquiries be at the town hall. If anyone is charged and wishes to make a statement to you, he will be at the town hall. He will be on the premises, and there is more accommodation.'

Mr Pennicard, the Foreman, asked, '*Will Doctor Humphrey be in attendance next time?*'

The Coroner replied, '*Certainly, if you wish him to be.*'

Mr Pennicard asked, '*Could the adjourned inquiry occur on Friday as Saturday was inconvenient to many jurors?*'

The Coroner: '*Unfortunately, the Winter Assizes will be sitting on the following Friday at Lewes. Both Mr Pope and I are expected at these proceedings therefore not be available that day. On Saturday, the 19th of December, the Assizes court will rise early; giving sufficient time for the inquest to resume after the Assizes closes. I propose to resume the inquest on Saturday, the 18th of December. What time would be convenient for you all?*'

The Foreman discussed the matter with his fellow jurors and informed the Coroner that 5 pm would be OK. The Coroner agreed and formally adjourned the inquest.

Chapter 8: *'The Black Maria.'*

When the police court opened on Tuesday, the 15th of December morning, in addition to the Magistrate Mr Heathcote, several other Brighton officials arrived to witness the high-profile proceedings. These included Major Alderman Ewart, Colonel Alexander, Colonel Silverthorne, and Mr W. D. Savage. As was becoming customary in the case, George Henry Wood's prior appearance was extensively covered in both local and national newspapers. These reports continued to evoke interest and excitement in the Brighton community.

Such was the intrigue in Edith's murder; large crowds had gathered at the town hall and tried to gain access to the police court. The numbers were so great the police became concerned that there would be public disorder. They also feared that the crowd would surge if the situation was not carefully managed. Chief Constable Terry instructed numerous police constables to guard the main entrances, who only permitted those with legitimate business to enter the building.

Despite this, as the unruly crowd continued to swell as the morning drew on, and the police struggled to close the doors. Inside the court, the public galleries quickly filled. As the proceedings began, the police informed the colossal crowd outside that they would not be admitted and asked them to return home, although few listened. At 10.25 am, George Henry Wood was brought up from the cells and placed in the dock. Journalists in the court noted that his beard had grown, which appeared to change his features. Nonetheless, George Henry Wood seemed relaxed and outwardly showed little concern for his dire situation.

At precisely 10.30 am, Judge Heathcote formally opened the proceedings. Mr Pope appeared again for the prosecution and Mr Ayres for the defence.

Mr Pope arose to his feet and said, *'You will remember that on the last occasion, I mentioned that this matter would have to be submitted to the Treasury. This has been done, and the Director of Public Prosecutions has agreed to take up the case. He has instructed me to continue as his agent. You will remember that I intimated on the last occasion that this would only be a formal remand. I would ask for a further remand until next Monday, the 22nd or Tuesday next, so the evidence can be brought before you in a connected form. I see no reason to depart from that course owing to the extreme gravity of the case, and then - if I may say it - the diabolical nature of the child's injuries, there is no reason for hurrying forward with the case. The prisoner could not possibly be sent for trial at the present Assizes. I understand that the legal advisor for the prisoner raises no objections to my present application for a remand.'*

Mr Ayres, who had previously argued for his client's release, stated that he had no objections on this occasion. He knew the wealth of evidence the police had linked George Henry Wood to Edith Jeal's murder. He had resigned to the fact that his client did not have an alibi and had not denied his guilt. He knew it would be pointless to argue George Henry Wood's innocence as he had no evidence to substantiate these claims. He was also aware that if he focused on the unfairness of the imprisonment, the Magistrate could order that George Henry Wood's case be heard at the Winter Assizes, which were due to open in a mere two days.

Instead, he chose to wait and formulate an alternative defence, which would take considerable time. Consequently, Mr Ayres informed the Magistrate that he would not contest the remand and was happy to wait for the Spring Assizes the following year. Upon hearing Mr Ayres' agreement, Mr Pope continued applying for a remand.

He said, *'In that case, I would merely ask you to remand the prisoner for another week. By this time, I hope to be able to place before you a connected sentiment of the case against the prisoner and complete the evidence of the child's injuries and the proof of the finding of the child. I may say that I am not sure that the matter can then be completed owing to the gravity of the case. It has been felt that the stains on the prisoner's clothing should be examined by the highest expert possible in the country, and they have been sent to Doctor Stevenson, Public Analyst. However, he is engaged at the Old Bailey and will be at Lewes. It is not certain that he will be able to complete his investigation until Monday or Tuesday next.'*

The Magistrate: *'Then you do not think there is any reason for fixing two days, for giving up practically two days for it, Monday and Tuesday?'*

Mr Pope: *'I think not.'*

The Magistrate: *'If there is a remand until this day week, will that be all that is required?'*

Mr Pope: *'I am afraid not. It would be necessary to have a further remand for Doctor Stevenson's report.'*

The Magistrate: *'If there were any possibility of finishing the case on Monday and Tuesday, I would like to arrange for that.'*

Mr Pope: *'I am afraid that there is no possibility. I do not think there is any reason to inconvenience others. The case cannot be completed before Christmas.'*

The Magistrate: *'Will you take a remand to Tuesday?'*

Mr Pope: *'If you please, Sir.'*

The Magistrate: *'And after that, there will be no object for asking a remand for less than ten days.'*

Mr Pope: *'That will depend on Doctor Stevenson. I think most probably I should have to ask for a remand for another ten days over Christmas.'*

The Magistrate conferred with his clerk for a few minutes and said, *'There is no need for fixing that today. That can be arranged at a later stage. At present, there will be a remand until next Tuesday, the 23rd of December.'*

Magistrate Heathcote then formally closed the proceedings, which had only lasted a quarter of an hour. George Henry Wood was surrounded by several police constables, removed from the dock and returned to the basement cells. However, on this occasion, his incarceration at the town hall police station was to be short-lived. Due to the remand's length, the Magistrate ordered that he be removed to Lewes Gaol and House of Correction.

This decision created a logistical nightmare for the Brighton Police. The Judge's decision spread through Brighton like wildfire, and once again, people began gathering at the town hall, believing the prisoner would emerge at some point that day. Keen to demonstrate their anger and disgust, those who had left the town hall earlier returned to the doors of the police court. As the day drew on, the streets outside became filled entirely with members of the public who were becoming increasingly agitated. To avoid any public disorder, the police delayed George Henry Wood's exit until later in the day.

Chief Constable Terry went onto the street and informed the crowd of their decision, but the unruly and hostile crowd continued to wait instead of dispersing. After watching the ever-worsening situation, the police became increasingly worried about George Henry Wood's safety and feared he would be publicly lynched. Consequently, they again postponed his transfer until the early evening.

As dusk descended on Brighton, the prison horse-drawn police car, known as the 'Black Maria', was quietly moved into East Street, which bordered one side of the town hall. It was parked dead opposite John Beale's and Son's stationary shop at 53-55 East Street. The name 'Black Maria' originated from an African American woman, Maria Lee, who lived in Boston during the Colonial era. She had kept a sailors' boarding house and would frequently support the police with any hostile prisoners. A small article in the Bognor Regis Observer on the 5th of August 1896 gives further insight into how this name came about. The article reads as follows:

'Everybody knows what the 'Black Maria' is, but probably few are aware of how its name originated. During the old colonial days, Maria Lee, a Negress kept a sailors' boarding house in Boston. She was a woman of gigantic size and prodigious strength. She greatly assisted the authorities in keeping the peace as the entire lawless element of that locality stood in awe of her.

Whenever an unusually troublesome person was to be taken to the station-house, the services of Black Maria, as she was called, were likely to be required. It is said that she took at one time, and without assistance, three riotous sailors to the lock-up. So frequently was her help needed that the expression 'Send for Black Maria' came to mean 'Take the disorderly person to Gaol.' It is easy to see how the name became fixed to the prison van which goes along the street with its complement of criminals.'

With the van in position, the anxious police waited for the right time to move. At about 6pm, Chief Constable Terry, who was monitoring the mob's behaviour closely, decided that the time was right for George Henry Wood to be escorted to his waiting transport. To protect his safety and minimise the opportunity for escape, George Henry Wood was escorted by two police constables, Chief Constable Terry, Fire Superintendent Lacroix, Inspector Parker and several other officers.

However, the disorderly crowd quickly realised what was about to occur and surged towards the police station's doors. In an attempt to mislead the masses, George Henry Wood and his guards ran up the steps to the Sanitary Office, which was situated on the eastern side of the town hall. However, some crowd members, carefully watching, noticed the movement and alerted others.

Consequently, the agitated crowd ran down the western side of the town hall in what was described as a *'perfect avalanche'* and congregated on East Street, which was already busy due to the time of day. The pavements were crammed with pedestrians, and the road was blocked by horse-drawn vehicles. The police struggled to move through the chaos, and as they stalled, members of the baying mob began encircling the prisoner and his guards. At this point,

George Henry Wood's lackadaisical and carefree demeanour changed to sheer fright. He appeared terrified and later said he believed he would be killed.

Members of the crowd initially began to boo and hiss. Curses such as *'You villain!'* and *'You hound'* were screamed by the mob, and *'let's get at you'* calls echoed around the cobbled street. The police created a human barrier around George Henry Wood, who appeared utterly stunned by the public's response to his appearance. As the group turned the corner of Bartholomew Square, George Henry Wood broke free and began to run towards the *Black Maria*.

A few seconds later, he reached the van and mounted the steps without assistance. However, this did not reduce the determination of the crowd, who quickly surrounded the vehicle and began hammering on the sides of the car, and many continued to scream angry abuse. As a result of the commotion, the horse became frightened. The large and powerful animal became increasingly unsettled and eventually began to buck. This generated further excitement amongst the crowd, who started shouting, *'Over with it!'* and *'Turn it over!'*

The police eventually managed to get to the horse and applied the whip, which caused the animal to move through the narrow street. Even though the van was moving, the crowd still did not calm and continued to shout abuse at George Henry Wood, who crouched and cowering on the floor by this time. After the vehicle had safely left the area, Chief Constable James Terry returned to his basement office.

Shortly after, Inspector Jupp entered the room and handed over George Henry Wood's clothing. James Terry carefully folded the garments and wrapped them in brown paper, ready to be posted to Guy's Hospital for analysis. The parcel's recipient, Doctor Stevenson, Home Office Analyst, had been sent a telegram requesting that he analyse the clothing urgently.

Elsewhere, as a large family living on a meagre income, the Jeals were worrying about the cost of Edith's funeral. However, due to the case's publicity, they need not have worried. The family began receiving sympathy letters and donations. Mr William Savage, a pharmaceutical chemist operating at premises at St James Street, donated a significant sum to the family. It is unclear whether he was directly connected to the family or simply offered support out of kindness.

As a result of their community's charity, Edward Jeal had employed the services of Mr F. J. Reading, High Street, Brighton, to direct Edith's funeral. By the 15th of December, the funeral arrangements were finalised, and it was reported that the funeral would take place on Wednesday, the 16th of December. Reverend M.T. McCormick agreed to conduct the service. He performed ministerial duties at St Matthew's Church, which was also known as the tin Chapel, at the corner of Sutherland Road and College Terrace. St Matthew's was renowned for encouraging and welcoming worshippers from the lower classes and the Jeal family attended regularly. Reverend McCormick was o intimate terms with the Jeals and had been offering support to the family since he heard of Edith's death. On the 15th of December, the Reverend wrote to *the Brighton Argus*. His letter is as follows:

'This sympathy has greatly supported the parents in their trial, and they feel that. He who is smitten can also heal. The husband and wife are quiet and respectable and have long resided in my parish. On their behalf, I beg to thank the many kind sympathisers that have come forward to help by word and act. I would like to especially mention Mr W. W. Savage of 109 St James Street as one who has taken a great interest in attending to the needs of the family.'

Chapter 9: *'Suffer little children to come unto me'*

Wednesday the 16th was a bright but bitterly cold day. As the soothing winter sun bore down on the town of Brighton, the sorrowful Jeal family were preparing to lay Edith to rest. The burial was set to occur at the Extra Mural Cemetery on Bear Road to the North of Brighton.

Following a report from the General Board of Health in 1849, the Brighton Corporation decided to increase its capacity for burials. Until that point, Brighton buried its dead at Hanover Church, near Brighton Station. However, the large number of interments since it had opened had caused the ground to increase by many feet above the surrounding land. To solve the issues of sanitation and overcrowding, the Brighton Extra Mural Company was formed in July 1850. Immediately after, a Board of Directors was elected, who purchased eight acres of land behind Lewes Road extending eastwards.

Unfortunately, the Directors had not paid attention to the waterworks which operated out of the adjacent land. After hearing of the proposed new cemetery, the Brighton Water Company sent a formal letter threatening to apply to the Court of Chancery for an injunction. The Marquis of Bristol, who owned land in the area and supported the new cemetery, kindly offered to exchange nine acres of his land with the Extra Mural Company. This exchange created a barrier between the cemetery and the ground used by the water company, thus preventing any contamination. Furthermore, the new land had the added benefit of a carriage road, which provided an entrance road to the cemetery.

The Directors accepted the offer, and in late 1851, work commenced. Mr Amon Henry designed the cemetery's church and chapel. Mr Wilds, who had designed the fountain and gardens at the Old Steine, created the landscaping plans for the grounds. In 1851, the

Bishop of Chichester consecrated a section of the cemetery, and the first internment occurred in November of the same year.

In 1891, the Extra Mural Cemetery was described as a *'Sheltered, wooded and gently sloping area of downland, which forms a charming retreat from the bustle and cares of life and, affording in their quiet seclusion peace to the sorrowing heart not to be found in the noisy and confined grave-yard.'* It was in this cemetery on the 16th of December that Edith was interred.

Like every aspect of the case, Edith's funeral was highly publicised and attracted significant public interest. On the morning of the 16th, thousands of Brighton residents lined the funeral route to glimpse the painful procession. At 11.30 am, the funeral procession comprising four single-horse mourning coaches and an open-top car, assembled on the eastern side of Upper Bedford Street, close to the Stag Inn. The entire road was filled with working-class residents from the Kemp Town area, who attended either through morbid curiosity or to offer support to the grieving family.

Despite the large numbers, the crowd was respectful, orderly and sympathetic to the bereaved family. Just after noon, a tiny polished elm coffin, covered in floral tributes, emerged from Bedford Buildings. The small casket, carried by four pallbearers, was tentatively placed into the first car along with several floral offerings. Around ten minutes later, more wreaths and crosses emerged from the house and were placed around the coffin. These sympathy tributes came from across the country from strangers, so moved by Edith's cruel demise that they felt compelled to send offerings to the family.

One of the inscriptions read, *'From a lady deeply sympathising with the mother.'* The family received other bouquets from Edith's friends and teachers at All Souls School. Another arrived from St Matthew's Sunday school, that little Edith had also attended. This bouquet bore the message *'From your little playmate.'* After the remaining flowers were placed in the car, the Jeal family entered the street. The crowd became highly emotional when Edith's mother appeared grief-stricken. Such was her distress; she had to be supported by her husband and two eldest children.

Behind the immediate family, fifteen other mourners followed. After pausing to look at the coffin for a few minutes, the sorrowful crowd took their places in the funeral cars, and the sad cortege set off on its long journey to the cemetery. The procession travelled down St James Street, turned into Pavilion Parade, and continued to Grand Parade. After passing St Peter's Church and the Level, the cortege slowly turned into Lewes Road. Most of the route was thickly lined with members of the public keen to see Edith's coffin. When the hearses reached the northern section of Lewes Road, they turned into Bear Road and continued until they reached the cemetery's wrought iron gates.

The police had anticipated that large crowds would attend and were stationed at the cemetery. Chief Constable James Terry, Superintendent Lacroix, Inspectors Parker and Duly roped off a large area in the northern region of the cemetery where Edith's grave was situated. Whilst this prevented the vast crowds from surging on the grave, it did not stop them from entering the cemetery, and by the time the service started, nearly a thousand people were in attendance.

The vast crowds became silent as the cars moved down the narrow cemetery lane. Many women began to cry at the tragic sight of the tiny coffin. Men bowed their heads in reverence, whilst the many children who were present clung to their parents' clothing or huddled together. As soon as the procession entered the cemetery, the chapel's bell began to toll and echo around the serene landscape. Reverend McCormick and his Curate who were already in attendance, made their way to the chapel's doors, ready to welcome the mourners.

Only relatives and friends were permitted to enter the chapel, and the police stood guard to prevent any strangers from entering. During the liturgy, Charlotte Jeal's loud and anguished sobs were heard by the crowd outside. After the service, the mourners walked solemnly to Edith's grave, close to the cemetery's northern entrance. The grave had been dug directly in front of Edith's Grandparents' graves, James and Ann Jeal, who had passed away several years before. It was also the same grave where Edith's new-born sister Ellen had been buried in 1885.

The pallbearers placed the numerous wreaths next to the grave, ready to be moved onto the mound after filling it. The crowd again began to surge as the final service took place, and the police had difficulty keeping the area secure. Reverend McCormick explained that he would like to say a few words but could not do so in the circumstances.

He said, *'We have met a great body of mourners, mourning the loss of one God had taken for himself. Suffer little children to come unto me and forbid them not, for such is the Kingdom of Heaven. I recommend that you, the family, do what the Apostles did when they lost their dear companion, go to Jesus Christ in your distress.'*

Afterwards, Reverend McCormick read the final burial verses, which appeared to cause distress to the numerous onlookers. His words were repeatedly interrupted by the gut-wrenching sobbing of Charlotte Jeal and her two younger children, looking at the grave with streaming eyes. By the final stages of the funeral, Charlotte Jeal became consumed by her grief and fell to the ground.

When the service concluded, the distraught family spent a few minutes looking at the flower-covered coffin for the last time. After, they returned to the funeral cars and began the sad journey home. Most of the crowd lingered behind after the mourners had left to look into the grave. When the cemetery finally emptied a considerable time later, the gravedigger arrived and began his melancholy task.

Public preoccupation with the murder continued to persist. Such was the interest. A *'Bodleian broadside ballad'* was written and published. These ballads would contain song lyrics, tunes and, in some instances, woodcut illustrations (as shown below). These poems would bear news, prophecies, histories, moral advice, religious warnings, political arguments, satire, comedy and bawdy tales printed cheaply on a single sheet of paper.

Ballads were sold in vast numbers on street corners, in town squares and at fairs, by travelling ballad singers. They were also pinned on the walls of alehouses and other public places. They were sung, read and viewed with pleasure by a broad audience. Edith's ballad was written and published in December 1891 by C.F. Brown and printed in Brighton. It reads as follows:

'Some Painful Lines in the Diabolical Murder of Little Edith Jeal, Aged 5 Years, In a Field. At Kemp Town, Brighton, on Thursday the 10th of December 1891.

Come listen to my painful story,
And unto you, I will unfold.
Of a little girl, who, in her glory?
Now I am lying stiff and cold.
She left her home with her brother,
On an errand, they were sent,
To get something in for their dear mother,
Hearts full of glee, these two, they went.

Chorus.

Now she's gone - she knows no sorrow -
From this sinful world of ours;
But she'll wake again tomorrow,
Up in Heaven's sunny bowers.

To a certain shop, these dear beloved ones
Made their way, some things to buy;
The boy went in to make the purchase,
And left the little girl outside.
When he came out, he could not find her,
He then soon made his way home,
But without his darling little sister
Whose missing form became soon known?

She was soon missed, and many people
Searched all night the child to find -
Father, mother, sisters and brothers -
Filled with grief and stricken minds.
Some wretched villain had betrayed her,
And took her in his arms away;
And nothing more was heard of Edie,
Until the morning of the next day.

Dear Edith Jeal, she is the victim
Of the most cruel and horrid deed;
And by a vile and wretched villain
There's not the slightest doubt to be.
In cold blood, this most disgusting monster,
Heaven bless the little child.
Although so loving and so innocent,
Cruelly murdered and defiled

This wretch had taken his little victim
To a shed that dreary night;
And when they found her little body,
It was in a most distressing plight;
Maltreated and with strangulation,
Soaked with blood were all her clothes;
Stiff and cold, her little form lay
What she went through, God only knows.

Let us hope they've found the right and guilty,
She is far too good for him,
To serve him as he served his victim,
Who never knew the thought of sin?
We know her soul has gone to Heaven,
Where there is no grief or pain;
Let's hope her dear beloved parents
Their child will one day meet again.

Chapter 10: A Letter from the Prisoner

On Friday, the 19th of December, George Henry Wood was transported from Lewes back to Brighton, ready for the reopening of the inquest on the following day. Due to security concerns, the Coroner had changed the venue from Freshfield Road to the town hall. Local newspapers continued to be saturated with stories about the case. However, on this day, these articles contained less condemnation and more compassion for George Henry Wood's family.

Members of the Wood family had spoken to the Brighton Gazette, commending Chief Constable Terry for the care and sensitivity he had shown George Henry Wood since his arrest. Whether these comments actually came from the Wood family or, instead, were, a public relations exercise by the police is unclear.

In either case, George Henry Wood did appear to trust Chief Constable Terry. On the 19th of December, 1891, He asked James Terry to deliver a letter to his parents at Rock Street, which he dutifully did. However, he also duplicated the letter and sent the copy to the Treasury. Consequently, a copy of the letter was added to the case file, which gives us an insight into George Henry Wood's thoughts, feelings and self-centred personality. The letter reads as follows:

'From your loving, loving son George. My dear Father and Loving Mother and my dear darling Lizzie. It is with deep sympathy and the love of God which I feel deep depths of my heart this morning. This is all through breaking the pledge you all thought I was keeping. I was working on the vans on Thursday as one of the men was laid up. I was appointed in his place. Brown was my mate. He drove the first two loads, and it started to rain. I drove the last three loads. We were carrying malt from the Station to Longhurst Brewery on Preston Road. I had

never broken the pledge until last Thursday since joining it. I drove the horses all right on Thursday without any accidents whatsoever. I remember going in the station gates alright Thursday night, but I do not remember anything more after I got inside the gates. I can't remember anything after, through the beastly drink. I must have been helplessly drunk. I am very sorry, very sorry to have to say such a thing. It has fairly broken me up. I prayed to the lord Jesus this morning, which has given me the courage to write to you. This crime has been brought to my feet, but as God is my keeper and helper, I honestly say that I do not remember or can't bring myself to remember anything whatsoever about it, or can I bring myself to believe it was done by your son George. I don't know, I am sure what my Dear Love Lizzie will think of me after two long years of courtship, and to think that we were going to be married at Easter and dear Nelly and all of you, what must you all think. I don't know. I am sure what this will all come to, but we must leave it to God's hand. He will see that everything is put right. If anything should happen to me, I, with all my heart, pray God will have you in his keeping and my poor Lizzie. I don't know what will become of her if anything should happen to me. Tell her to cease writing to you, for I am sure this will drive her to her sisters in Canada. But if I am not to see her anymore, tell her she must come to see me. I am sure Mr Terry will allow her to see me for a short time, but we shall see how matters stand in the course of another week. God Grant that everything may turn out to our liking. It would not be so bad if I knew what I had done, but I have not the slightest recollection of anything occurring after sed (sic.) time on Thursday has nearly driven me out of my mind. Last night I thought it was my last because I saw the golden city and the gates open wide, and there were the four little ones standing there waiting to meet me, and Grandfather and Grandmother were sheltering the little ones and looking as if they were waiting for me. God grant that I may see them someday in the beauty of holiness. I needed your advice scores of times, but I never heeded it. God grant that this may make us all love the lord Jesus Christ more and more than we have ever done before. But if I live, nothing shall ever stop me from believing in him, for he has said those that have gathered together in my name there I shall be in their midst and to bless them, for he is a very pleasant help in times of need. I needed him last week, but I need him more this morning. I found a true friend in him. He has taken it upon himself to do what is best. Please kindly ask Mr Smith to come and see me. I want to see him very particularly tomorrow if he can come. Tell Father to cheer up and also you and dear Mother and thank God that all the others are growing up in fear of God. My paper is getting very short now. Look after Lizzie. Don't go back on her. Keep her from going abroad if possible. I would like to see her very much indeed. It would cheer me up greatly if I could, and now I must say goodbye and God bless you and may his face shine upon you and may he always be near you when help is needed. Give my kind love to all and kiss them all for me, especially Dear Lizzie. Give my kind love to her and kiss her. Let God grant that she may always walk the path of righteousness for his name's sake. Amen, and ask her to pray for me. I remain your ever-dear son George.

X X X X X X X X X X X X X X X X X X X X X X X X X X X X X X X X X X X X X X X X X'

As the letter was opened and read by George and Margery Wood, they must have been devastated by their son's position. They must have recoiled at the publicity surrounding the case and wondered how they could have ended up in such a dire and humiliating position. Both were honest and hard-working individuals who had never put a foot out of place. Close acquaintances of the family described the couple as a *'Christian pair who led simple and reprehensible lives.'* Other sources described them as *'having the highest respectability and impeccable character.'*

An anonymous family member disclosed to a reporter from the *Brighton Argus* that people within the Wood's local community had quietly offered support and sympathy to the humiliated and devastated pair. The same person was critical of the gratuitous coverage by the press and felt that the public had already condemned George Henry Wood.

Meanwhile, at the town hall, George Henry Wood requested a visit from Mr William Smith, Pastor of the Belgrave Street Chapel. George Henry Wood possibly believed that the Pastor, renowned for his caring and kind manner, would give him a sympathetic ear. The Pastor had known George Henry Wood since childhood and had a close relationship with his parents. Having been ordained as an Elder, George Wood Senior worked alongside William Smith at the Belgrave Street Chapel and had done so for thirty years.

William Smith agreed, so at 9 am, he arrived at the town hall. After the short meeting, William Smith addressed the reporters, who were still assembled at the police station's doors. He described George Wood Senior as one of the best fathers and most truly Christian and self-sacrificing men he had ever known. He explained that George Wood Senior had saved £1 10s for the Sussex Home Missionary Society for over twenty years and regularly contributed to other Brighton-based religious and philanthropic agencies.

He also spoke kindly of Margery Wood, George Henry Wood's mother. The Pastor described her as a good religious woman who was highly spoken of by those who knew her. Despite suffering from ill health, he explained that Margery had taken an active role in the chapel affairs and was always willing to help.

The reporters questioned William Smith about the prisoner. Mr Smith said that he had attended his church on the Sunday before the murder and was a popular character. He explained that George Henry Wood's relatives and friends were utterly astounded by the charges laid by the police. He said that the many people who knew George Henry Wood would describe him as straightforward, compassionate, and an excellent character.

Later that day, George Henry Wood's father, sisters and brother visited the town hall. Despite the wealth of evidence against him, at this stage, his family refused to accept his guilt, which added to the painfulness of the occasion. The visit was described as harrowing and highly emotional for the father and son, as you would expect. As he entered the Chief Constable's office, George Henry Wood asked his father, *'Have you got it?'* He was expecting a letter from his fiancée. The young girl, Lizzie, whose surname is not in any records, had been engaged to George Henry Wood for nearly a year.

The wedding had been due to take place in the middle of December, but after the arrest, the nuptials were postponed until the following April. The fact that Lizzie had not cancelled the wedding suggests that she also believed in George Henry Wood's innocence at this stage. George Wood Senior responded to the request for the letter with a simple *'No.'* Immediately after, George Henry Wood was said to have suffered from a fit of some type.

The gossip continued to propagate through the Kemp Town community. On this day, talk about the case related to George Henry Wood's mother. The press reported that Mrs Wood, known to be suffering from ill health, had suddenly died. This was wholly false and likely added to the Wood family's strain. Other strange and sensational rumours were also circulating. Potential bias arising from the newspaper reports was finally acknowledged in the Brighton Argus on the 19th of December, despite the fact they themselves had published many unsubstantiated stories. The article reads as follows:

'There is nothing to wonder at the indignation and horror which have been aroused, but no one need have an intimate acquaintance with legal procedure with the working of the machinery of the law in this country, to understand that a prisoner is seriously handicapped who goes to his trial under what appears to be the prior condemnation of a least a very large section of the community. Every subject of the Queen whatever his record, whatever may be the charge against him never, is entitled to justice; the proper place to secure justice for a man accused of murder is not the Street. The proper placement is a court of justice. This is not, and it is perhaps needless to point out, written as a plea for or against the man Wood. But no man should be condemned on suspicion only.'

Ironically, alongside this plea for restraint, the Brighton Argus published sensational editorials saturated with daily speculation for many weeks.

Chapter 11: A Verdict of Wilful Murder and Outrage

Edith's inquest resumed at 5 pm on Saturday, the 19th of December at Brighton's town hall. The Deputy Coroner, Mr Albert Freeman-Gell, presided over the proceedings. The galleries again jam-packed with members of the public. However, there was far less interest and, much to the relief of the police, less anger. At 6 pm, the jury entered the police court and took the oath of affirmation.

Afterwards, they were seated at the solicitor's table. Mr Ayres was again in attendance to represent the interests of George Henry Wood and Mr Pope for the prosecution. Also within the court were the Chief Constable, Chief Superintendent Carter, and Detective Inspector Jupp, to represent the police. On the witness benches, Edward and Bertram Jeal were seated opposite to represent the deceased's family.

Doctor Frederick Abel Humphrey was the first witness to appear before the court. He recalled visiting a patient in Chesham Road on Friday, the 11th of December. He said that a man he did not know called out to him as he left the property. Doctor Humphrey said he walked over and the man informed him that a murder had been committed. Doctor Humphrey recalled that he and the man had entered the barn, where he said he saw the brutalised body of a female child.

Doctor Humphrey recalled that the girl's head was close to the eastern wall, and her feet were positioned at an oblique angle towards the southwest. He explained that Edith lay with her left leg drawn up and her right leg extended and that, aside from shoes and stockings, the body was completely naked, which generated loud gasps from the public galleries.

Having completed his evidence, Frederick Humphrey was cross-examined by Mr Ayres. He said, *'Did you make any examination?'*

Frederick Humphrey: '*No more than was necessary under those circumstances.*'

Mr Ayres: '*No minute medical examination?*'

Frederick Humphrey: '*No. The child was blue in the face and appeared to have been strangled.*'

Mr Ayres: '*Do you say her violation would cause death?*'

Frederick Humphrey: '*Not immediate death.*'

Mr Ayres: '*You weren't present at the post-mortem examination?*'

Frederick Humphrey: '*I did not see the post-mortem. My impression was that the child died from asphyxia. I examined the body to see any ligature, but I found none. I simply found that the child had been brutally injured. The appearance was sufficient to lead one to suppose the child had died from asphyxia. Rigour Mortis had set in both legs and arms.*'

Having completed his evidence, the Coroner released Frederick Humphrey from the court.

The next witness to be called was P.C. Herbert Pelling. As soon as he entered the witness box, he produced Edith's underwear which caused great excitement in the public galleries. At this point, the Magistrate asked the jury if they wished to view Edith's other clothes. After a short discussion, the Foreman of the jury replied that they did not.

The Coroner: '*Did you also find the brother's cap in the barn.*'

P.C. Pelling: '*Yes, I did, along with some chestnuts scattered on the floor.*'

At this point, P.C. Pelling produced Bertram's cap and displayed it to the jury.

Mr Ayres said, '*He had read that the father had sent the child to buy chestnuts. He has not ascertained that the nuts the child purchased were the same nuts the police constable found.*'

Poor little Bertram Jeal was the next witness to be called, who repeated the evidence about Edith's disappearance that he had given at the police court earlier in the day. He was then cross-examined by Mr Ayres, who was keen to determine if Edith had been in contact with anyone before her disappearance.

Mr Ayres began, '*After you went into the shop, you never saw her again.*'

Bertram Jeal: '*Not alive, no Sir.*'

Mr Ayres: '*You never saw her again alive after you came out of the shop?*'

Bertram Jeal: '*No.*'

Mr Ayres then tried to undermine the reliability of the young witness.

Mr Ayres: *'Members of the jury, it was raining that night, but not very hard. The witness said in his statement that he remembered it was raining. However, it did not rain until after he had removed his hat. It rained after his sister was lost. He was at home then. He is mistaken. Master Jeal, you never saw her talking to any person?'*

Bertram Jeal: *'No, Sir.'*

Mr Ayres: *'You have never been asked to identify any person?'*

Bertram Jeal: *'No, Sir.'*

This marked the end of Bertram's evidence. The small boy was asked to leave the witness stand and sit back with his father, which he did.

P.C. James Tuppen was the next witness to give evidence. He informed the court that he had been on duty in Kemp Town at around 8 pm on the 10th of December. He told the court that he had noticed George Henry Wood walking towards him as he walked along Lavender Street.

He explained that he had exchanged a few words with the prisoner and then continued walking in the opposite direction. P.C. Tuppen said that as he glanced back, he had observed George Henry Wood walk to the bottom of the street and turn left into Upper St James Street.

Mr Pope then questioned P.C. Tuppen on behalf of the prosecution.

He said, *'Did you know him?'*

P.C. Tuppen: *'Yes, Sir. I said goodnight to him, and he replied, 'Goodnight'.'*

Mr Pope: *'How was he dressed?'*

P.C. Tuppen: *'He wore a long mackintosh, leggings and an oil cloth coat just below his hips. He was also wearing a cap. I noticed that he was drunk.'*

Mr Pope: *'How long have you known him?'*

P.C. Tuppen: *'About ten years.'*

Mr Ayres then attempted to minimise the relevance of P.C. Tuppen's sighting.

He said, *'Members of the jury, he had been on duty about an hour when he saw Mr Wood. It was not busy in that part of the town that evening, as it was very windy. He also saw Brady, a postman, that night who was dressed as an ordinary postman.'*

Mr Ayres: *'Mr Tuppen, in the course of your duty, who else did you meet that night?'*

P.C. Tuppen: *'I cannot tell you any other persons in particular.'*

Mr Ayres: *'But you remember seeing the prisoner?'*

P.C. Tuppen: *'Yes.'*

Mr Ayres: *'You first met the prisoner about ten years ago and had seen him about once a week during the first ten years. You then did not meet so often.'*

P.C. Tuppen: *'Yes, Sir.'*

Mr Pope: *'Why did you notice what he was wearing this particular night?'*

P.C. Tuppen: *'I saw he was dressed as a railwayman.'*

Mr Ayres: *'You said that he was the worst for drinking. Why did you say so?'*

P.C. Tuppen: *'He staggered as he passed me.'*

Mr Ayres then began his cross-examination and used the opportunity to infer bias on the part of the police.

Addressing the jury, he said, *'Members of the jury, he had never noticed the man's dress on any other occasion during the ten years. He heard the charge that had been made against Wood and saw him at the police station on Friday night. He was on night duty on Thursday and first heard of the hue and cry of the murder at around eleven o'clock the next morning. P.C. Heath told him when he arrived for work. He did not think it necessary to tell Heath or anyone else that he had seen Wood that night. He did not see a man accompanied by a child, but others told him that a man was seen near the area of the murder wearing a long coat and leggings. It was not extraordinary for a man to wear leggings on a night like that; others may have dressed the same. Since he had known Wood, he had never seen him worse for a drink.'*

Mr Ayres's insinuation had little impact on the Coroner, who used the opportunity to point out the closeness of P.C. Tuppen's' sighting and the abduction scene to the jury. The distance between Bedford Street and Lavender Street is a mere 200 yards, placing George Henry Wood near Edith's location when she disappeared. After this, the Coroner discharged P.C. Tuppen from the court.

The next witness was Rose Leggatt, who resided at 20 Hereford Street, Kemp Town. She informed the court that she was walking to her mother's house on the evening of the 10th of December. As she reached the corner of Montague Street at about quarter past eight, the witness said she had seen a drunken man. As the man passed, Rose Leggatt said he pushed her up against a set of railings. She explained that she was unsure whether this was intentional or, instead, due to his drunken state. Rose Leggatt explained that the man had walked up the road after their encounter.

She explained that she had gone into her mother's house briefly and, after leaving, had walked towards Upper Bedford Street. She said she saw the same man leaning on a dead wall at the corner of Manchester Row. Close by was a little girl holding a bundle of firewood.

Rose Leggatt said she saw the man reach out his hand to the minor child, who matched Edith's description.

Rose Leggatt's evidence was damning and, if believed by the jury, suggested George Henry Wood had direct contact with Edith. Keen to seize on her damning evidence, Mr Pope questioned Rose Leggatt further.

He asked, '*What happened then?*'

Rose Leggatt: '*He went away, and the child went with him.*'

Mr Pope: '*Which way did they go?*'

Rose Leggatt: '*Straight up the street.*'

Mr Pope: '*Did you notice how the child was dressed?*'

Rose Leggatt: '*In a grey dress with a pinafore.*'

Mr Pope: '*Have the police sent for you since?*'

Rose Leggatt: '*I was sent on Friday night to go to the town hall.*'

Mr Pope: '*What were you brought to the town hall for?*'

Rose Leggatt: '*To pick a man out.*'

Mr Pope: '*You identified the man at the town hall?*'

Rose Leggatt: '*Yes, to the best of my ability.*'

Mr Pope: '*How was he dressed?*'

Rose Leggatt: '*In railway clothes.*'

Mr Pope: '*And when you saw him on Thursday night?*'

Rose Leggatt: '*Yes, he wore railway clothes when I saw the man and the child on Thursday night. I initially thought it was the child's father, but I was unsure. I spoke to a boy in the street, worried that the man was enticing the child away.*'

Mr Ayres, who had been listening carefully, attempted to convince the jury that the extensive newspaper coverage had influenced Rose Leggatt's testimony and could not be relied on.

He said, '*Members of the jury, the witness thought the man was enticing the child away. When she noticed that the man was worse for a drink, she concluded that he was enticing the child away. She did not say anything to the man when he pushed her. She only knew him again from his moustache, but he had his hat over his eyes. After leaving her mother's, she saw a man but did not know whether it was the same. No police officer has questioned her beyond this. Detective Jupp did not call her to the Freshfield Road police Station until Saturday night. Superintendent Carter fetched her. The man she saw in Bedford Street was dressed as a railwayman. He had on a sort of green cord trousers. She could not see them very well because he had on leggings. She says she had not read the man's description in the newspapers but saw* the man at the police station. The man she saw at the police station did not have a coat with brass buttons which she had said earlier, but he wore green cord trousers and a uniform waistcoat. She had never seen the man before. She recognised him by nothing else than his uniform trousers and waistcoat. She could not recognise him by his face because his hat was over his face.'

Mr Ayres's comments about Rose Leggatt's evidence appear to have resonated with the Foreman of the jury on this occasion.

He turned to his fellow jurymen and said, 'S*he did not know whether the man pushed her accidentally or purposely. She saw him again at the corner where Mr Trengrove's shop was. The girl followed the man away. She did not see him speak to the little girl.'*

He then turned back to Rose Leggatt and said, *'Witness, is the man you saw at the town hall the same man you saw with the little girl?'*

Rose Leggatt: *'I think so, but I could not swear it was the same man.'*

The next witness to be called was Henry Spicer of 189 Queen's Park Road, who said he was in Chesham Street at 9 pm on the 10th of December and recalled seeing a very drunk man carrying a child. Tellingly, he recalled that the child had a bundle of firewood in her hands. Henry Spicer told the court that the child was about six or seven years old and that the man's boots and trousers were filthy.

He explained that he had not seen the man's face. Henry Spicer said he attended the Freshfield Road Police Station on Friday, the 11th of December. He recalled that he had relayed his account to the duty officer and, consequently, was asked to attend the town hall. When Henry Spicer arrived, Chief Constable Terry asked him to examine the men to see if he recognised anyone. At this point, Mr Ayres interrupted the proceedings to again highlight the weaknesses in the prosecution's evidence.

He said, *'Members of the jury, he did not report his concerns. Mr Spicer was summoned to the town hall by telephone. He had previously seen a police sergeant on Friday afternoon, who asked him what he knew about the case. He responded by saying, 'What case!' He did not think it was extraordinary for a man to carry a child on such a night.'*

The Coroner: *'Mr Spicer, did you recognise the man at the town hall?'*

Henry Spicer: *'When I saw the man at the town hall, something in my breast told me that George Henry Wood was the man I had seen with the child.'*

Mr Ayres: *'But you will not swear that Wood is the same man?'*

Henry Spicer: *'No.'*

The Foreman: *'Fellow jurors, he could not swear that the man he picked out was carrying the child, but to the best of his belief, it was. He did notice that the child had a bundle of Wood.'*

Detective Inspector Jupp was the next witness to be called, who repeated the evidence he had given at the police court about George Henry Wood's arrest. He explained that Chief Constable Terry had sent the prisoner's clothing to St Guy's Hospital, London, and therefore were unavailable for the jurors.

Mr Ayres then began Inspector Jupp's cross-examination.

He said, *'Members of the jury, he had enquired about other persons besides Wood but had no suspicions of anyone in particular. Inspector Jupp, do you think George Henry Wood had time to change his clothes since the previous night?'*

Inspector Jupp: *'I do not know.'*

Mr Pope rose to his feet and addressed the jury, keen for them to know the condition of George Henry Wood's clothing on the night of the murder.

He said, *'Members of the jury, Doctor Ross examined the clothing twice. There were numerous marks of blood on Wood's clothes. The Doctor described in detail the stains on each article of clothing.'*

Mr Ayres: *'Inspector Jupp, had the trousers been soaked?*

Inspector Jupp: *'Yes, Doctor Ross said the stains were blood, but this has yet to be confirmed.'*

By this point, the Coroner felt the jury had heard sufficient evidence to make a verdict.

Addressing the Foreman, he said, *'I do not know if you would like to take the opinion of your fellow juryman as to whether you are so far satisfied and would like me to sum up and conclude the enquiry today, or whether you would like to adjourn for further evidence. It is a case in which no pains or troubles will be spared. I do not put the question of adjournment to you as a question of convenience to yourselves, but the sooner this inquest can be disposed of, the better, as there is another inquiry going on side by side.'*

The court was then cleared for a few moments to allow the jury to deliberate privately. Once the jury was ready, the Coroner, representatives of the press and the public re-entered the court. The Foreman approached the bench and conferred with the Coroner before returning to the solicitor's table and taking his seat.

Addressing the Foreman, the Coroner said, *'You wish that the case be summed up and disposed of. I have adopted the course, which is usual, but I thought I should allow you to consider* whether we have sufficient evidence. This is a case of importance to the town, and we are dealing with a crime of which we happily have few in the neighbourhood of Brighton. I sympathise most deeply with the unfortunate mother and father of the child in what must be to them a most terrible affliction. Concerning the case itself, although the circumstances are of a very horrible nature, the facts are in a tiny compass. A small child at her father's house goes out with her brother to make purchases. He left her outside a shop and did not see her again until she was found dead in the field. You have evidence that the father gave information to the police and was up all night. He searched with the police all night but obtained no clue. You have the evidence of Villiers, who found the body, the evidence of the police constable, and Doctor Ross, who defines the injuries and says death was caused by strangulation. This child had been violated and strangled by somebody. The question, of course, arises whether you fix anybody in connection with the crime. I am bound to say the evidence connecting this man who is already before the Magistrates with this crime is weak. It would be of a weak character if he were being tried before the jury for his life, but you must remember this is only a Court of Inquiry, and you must inquire into the cause of death. If you think the evidence is circumstantial enough to connect him with it, you can find a verdict of wilful murder. This means you find a prima facie case against him, and he goes to be tried before a tribunal. It is a case of identity because nobody saw the occurrence. You have the evidence of the constable, who says that at eight o'clock in the evening, he was on duty in Lavender Street and that Wood was drunk and knew him well. As far as his evidence goes, there can be no doubt that he knew the man well enough to say it was Wood he saw in the neighbourhood of Lavender Street at eight o'clock. Then you have the evidence of Mrs Leggatt, who had not seen him before, and it was hard for her to be pressed for identification. She gave her evidence as fairly as she could and tried to speak the truth about it. She says she saw a man, she supposed to be Wood, outside the shop, and he was holding his hand towards the child. She noticed that the child had a bundle of Wood, and the child went with him. They went up the street and around Somerset Street. Then you have evidence that P.C. Tuppen had seen Wood, which carries the case further. Spicer had not seen the man before, and asking him to identify him was rather hard. He sees a man carrying a child toward the field where the child was found. He says he was tipsy. The policeman who saw Wood and Spicer both say the man they saw was tipsy. Spicer says his face was covered. You must remember that when Wood was brought in as a railway servant, he was identified as a railway servant. He was not placed with other railway servants, but it is hardly fair to suppose that half a dozen men would come down with the chance that they might be identified by mistake. I do not think the police are to be blamed. They have done their best. Then comes the evidence of Detective Inspector Jupp concerning the blood stains on *the trousers and the shirts, and Doctor Ross corroborates this. I am, of course, bound to point out that beyond the evidence of the policeman and Doctor Ross, there is not much to connect Wood with the crime, but as you are only inquiring into the cause of death and as you have their evidence followed up by other witnesses, take them for what they are worth, and the Doctor's evidence as to the appearance of the clothing. If you think there is a prima facie case, I must ask you to return a verdict of wilful murder. In doing so, you are only sending the man Wood to another tribunal.'*

The Coroner again cleared the court to allow the jury's deliberations. However, a verdict was reached after only a few minutes, and the proceedings resumed.

Addressing the jury, the Coroner said, *'Gentleman, have you decided upon your verdict?'*

The Foreman: *'Yes, the jury is of the unanimous opinion that the girl Edith Jeal met her death by foul means at the hands of George Henry Wood, and our verdict is, therefore, one of wilful murder against George Henry Wood.'*

After thanking the jury for their time, the Coroner formally closed the proceedings. A message was sent to the town hall cells, and George Henry Wood was said to be in shock at the verdict. Mr Ayres was also concerned about the judgment and understood that it would be seen as significant at any future criminal trial.

The guilty verdict was featured heavily in both the local and national press. The Brighton Argus did provide coverage of the inquest to their readers. However, on the 21st of December, they also published a lengthy article under *'Topics of the Day.'* The report is critical of the abrupt way the inquest concluded and questions the Coroner's decision to allow a verdict without hearing all the evidence. The article reads as follows:

'On Saturday evening, the Coroner's jury at Brighton reached a verdict of wilful murder by George Henry Wood. We have no intention or desire to express any opinion as to the justice or otherwise of this verdict. It may or may not be borne out by the facts that will be adduced. At present, however, we cannot help thinking that all of the facts that might even be at a Coroner's inquest have not been elicited. Under these circumstances, we must confess that the Coroner's jury arrived at a decision with a promptness that does not seem to commend itself altogether. There is no question about the child being violated and murdered, but it should require the strongest evidence to substantiate that Wood was the murderer. With this man, it resolves itself into a case of life or death. If he is guilty, there is no question that hanging will be too good for him. But is he guilty? If the inquiry, which terminated Saturday evening, had

been a final expression of opinion on the matter, would public opinion have been satisfied with the verdict upon the evidence? We are not losing sight for one moment of the horrible character of the murder. It may be, too, that the evidence as it stands does cast a grave suspicion upon the accused man. Still, we would urge that these circumstances only strengthen the contention that before a Coroner's jury return such a verdict as that of wilful murder, they should endeavour to have brought before them every little of evidence that can be obtained bearing upon the case. Has this been done? We cannot but think that this is open to doubt. Police Constable Tuppen was the only witness on Saturday evening that could speak positively to the prisoner, Wood; being in the neighbourhood at the time the child was missing. Mrs Leggatt and Mr Spicer saw a man, but neither was certain that it was Wood, although both picked him out of the twelve men who were placed into a line. To the best of their belief, they thought he was the man, but on that occasion, Wood was the only man in the line attired in railway uniform. There was another fact which no doubt had great weight with the jury regarding the state of Wood's clothes and stains upon them. Doctor Ross and Detective Inspector Jupp both expressed the opinion that the stains were blood stains and that an attempt had been made to get rid of them. But as it was a known fact that the clothes were with Doctor Stevenson for analysis, would it not have been better to have awaited the opinion of this celebrated expert upon a point which is undoubtedly one of the most vital importance in this case? We urge this because we think the case is so severe that no suspicion of undue haste to the detriment of an accused person should be allowed to creep in. No one would wish that a man guilty of such a foul crime as that perpetrated upon the little child Jeal should escape the full consequences of his guilt, but on the other hand, it would be the last wish of anyone that an innocent person should be found guilty of another's crime. No mistake should be made either way that we would claim the fullness and most complete investigation, whether in the police court or at the Coroner's inquiry and in view of all the facts, we think the Coroner's jury on Saturday arrived at a somewhat premature decision that we have ventured to make these observations. Let it be clearly understood, however, that our remarks are not intended to serve in any way as a defence for Wood or to question the accuracy or otherwise of the verdict. Still, they are made with the sole object of contending that when a verdict of wilful murder is arrived at, it should only be after every possible bit of evidence has been submitted.'

Due to his reappearance at the police court the following Monday, George Henry Wood remained at the police station cells for the weekend. This, the police felt, would reduce the potential for the same public disorder that had occurred previously. To prevent any acts of self-harm, P.C. George Harris was tasked with monitoring George Henry Wood throughout the night. He sat on a small wooden chair directly outside the cell's door, enabling him to view the entire cell.

Early on Sunday evening, the 20th of December, George Henry Wood started fitting violently. In a panicked state, P.C. Harris called out for assistance and ran into the cell. A few seconds after, he was joined by P.C.'s William Jeal and James Rampton. After a brief discussion, the constables moved George Henry Wood from his cell into the corridor, where there was more room and less chance of him injuring himself. A message was sent to Chief Constable Terry, who had left for his home a few hours previously.

He immediately returned to the police station and sent for Doctor Rogers, the police surgeon, who, due to the late hour, had also returned home. After receiving word of George Henry Wood's condition, Doctor Rogers rushed back to the town hall. He tended to the prisoner for about 10 minutes. However, by this time, George Henry Wood reportedly had fully recovered.

This was the second reported *'fit'* George Henry Wood had suffered since his arrest. Doctor Ross had not witnessed either of the attacks but, after speaking to the police constables who were present at the time, concluded that the fits were epileptic in nature. This information made its way to the legal offices of Prince and Ayres, who quickly decided to use it as the basis of their defence.

Chapter 12: *'It may be true, but I hope it is not'*

On the morning of the 23rd of December, George Henry Wood's police court hearing was due to resume. On this occasion, the bench consisted of Mr G. C. Heathcote, the Mayor Alderman Doctor Ewart, Colonel Alexander, Alderman Sendall, Mr W. D. Savage and Mr G. W. Willett. As was the case previously, Mr Pope appeared for the prosecution and Mr Ayres for the defence.

Continued interest and excitement about the trial persisted, resulting in many people assembling outside the court from an early hour. As the court opened, the crowd eager to witness the proceedings immediately piled in. The public galleries quickly filled, and the police were forced to turn people away again.

At 09.50 am, George Henry Wood was led up to the cells and was seated in the dock. At precisely 10 am, the trial, the Magistrate, Mr Heathcote, formally opened the proceedings. Mr Pope arose to his feet and delivered an extended address to the court for the prosecution.

He said, *'On the first occasion that the prisoner was charged here, the only evidence given to you was the evidence of three or four persons about the finding of the body and the evidence of the constable, who brought the prisoner to the town hall. I now propose to complete the evidence of the body's finding by calling Mr Humphrey, the medical man who was called in from an adjoining street and made a cursory examination of the body while lying in the shed. I shall also be able to complete the evidence of the loss of the child by calling the child's brother Bertram Jeal, who had been sent out with the deceased child on the night in question, to buy some small articles, a bundle of wood, an egg and some chestnuts. He will depose to the fact that the child made some of these purchases, namely wood and the chestnuts with him, that he went into a grocers shop known as Trengrove's to make the remaining purchase of the egg, leaving his sister standing just outside the door, with the wood in her hand, and the chestnuts in his cap. As your Worships will remember, this cap with the chestnuts in it, or with the chestnuts scattered around, was found in the shed, and the bundle of wood was also in the shed. Therefore, it appears that the child carried the hat and the bundle of wood the whole way from where she was left, right up to the shed, and that will be important, at least regarding one witness who saw her on her way.'*

The Magistrate, who was unclear about the location Mr Pope was referring to, said, *'Where is the shop?'*
Mr Pope: *'Upper Bedford Street. It is one continuous road from Marine Parade to Eastern Road. The lower portion from Marine Parade to St James Street is called Bedford Street. The upper portion from St James Street to Eastern Road is known as Upper Bedford Street. The shop is on the right-hand side near the top corner of Manchester Row, on the south side of Manchester Street, and on the eastern side of Upper Bedford Street.'*

Still unclear about the location, the Magistrate asked, *'Is it above St James Street?'*
Mr Pope: *'Some considerable distance. More than halfway up as you go towards Eastern Road. The shop is situated at the corner of Manchester Row. The next turning on the right-hand side above is Bedford Buildings, where the murdered child resided, and the next one above is Somerset Street which will also be referred to. This plan will be put in evidence by one of the clerks from the Borough Surveyors Office, and I shall also put in a plan of the field in question. The shed is perhaps more than a shed and might be described as a barn as it is built of brick tiles with a substantial roof.'*

At this point, Mr Pope displayed a set of plans for Kemp Town to the court. He pointed out the key locations and also the closeness of the Wood family home to the crime scene. He explained that Rock Street was a continuation of Chesham Road, which bordered Arlington School's playing field, where Edith's body was found.
Continuing, he said, *'That will complete the evidence of the finding of the body and the loss of the child. And then, I propose to call the various witnesses who will speak about the prisoner's movement on the night in question and his conduct the next. I shall be able to bring witnesses who will talk of having seen the prisoner before you. First is one of his mates in the goods yard, proving that he left the goods shed in Trafalgar Street. Next is the witness who saw him in Sydney Street shortly afterwards. The time he left work was about 6.20 pm. He was next seen in Sydney Street, turning out of Trafalgar Street into Gloucester Road in a south direction at*

about 6.45 pm. He was next seen in Edward Street, at the bottom of Grosvenor Street, a little after seven and again very shortly afterwards in Edward Street at the bottom of Mount Pleasant, and this witness will speak more or less positively as to him being the same man they saw on this occasion. These witnesses had not seen the prisoner before and did not know him. I would point out that these places are in the line the prisoner would naturally take on going to the field or to his home, which is close to the barn, all in the direct line. At Mount Pleasant, he appears to have deviated from the natural course and turned down Lavender Street which runs into St James Street. This was the first instance in which he appears to have deviated from the usual route, but the important thing is that in Lavender Street, he was seen by a constable who had known him for many years. There can be no question about identity in the cross-examination identity there. That constable saw him enter Upper St James Street, still walking eastwards. The next we hear of him is from a witness who saw him at the corner of Montague Street in Upper Bedford Street. He was coming up Upper Bedford Street and was seen by a woman standing at the intersection of Montague Street.'

Mr Ayres, keen to ensure that there was no conditioning of the witnesses, said, *'Mr Pope, I must ask that these witnesses be out of the court if you are going to tell them what he was doing!'*

The Magistrate agreed and abruptly ordered all witnesses, except for Mr Humphrey, to be cleared from the court. With Mr Ayres satisfied Mr Pope again continued with his address.

He said, *'The witness to whom I have referred is Rose Leggatt, who lives in Hereford Street, which you will see turns out of Upper Bedford Street. She was going from Hereford Street to her mother's in Montague Street, and when she saw the prisoner, she was waiting at the corner of Montague Street for her mother to come down. She saw him approaching her on the east side of Upper Bedford Street. She noticed he was drunk, and as he passed, he fell against her. She went off to her mother's and returned home. She came from Montague Street into Upper Bedford Street and walked down the east side of Upper Bedford Street. The corner of Manchester Row is also where Trengrove's shop is situated. She saw a little girl standing outside the shop with something in her hand - a cap and a bundle of wood. She also saw the prisoner standing against what was described as a dead wall on the north side of Manchester Row. His back was against the wall, and he was seen talking to the child and holding his hand towards her. Before the witness reached them, the man turned up Upper Bedford Street and walked up the pavement with the child slightly in his rear. When they came to the corner of Somerset Street, which you will observe is opposite Hereford Street, where she lives, he was* still followed by the child, who took hold of its hand, and they walked down Somerset Street. The witness had left a baby of about four months old at home, and she ran home to it. She left them going down Somerset Street. I shall then be able to call before you a witness who saw them in Somerset Street a little further down. This witness lives on Somerset Street, and she saw the man carrying a child in his arms and heard screams. Those screams were instantly hushed, and they walked down Somerset Street into Montague Street and, after, into Eastern Road. The next witness will be one who saw the man carrying a child on Eastern Road close to the field. He works at a shop on the other side of Eastern Road, close to Sussex Square, a little east of St Marks Street. Coming along Eastern Road a little before 9 pm, he passed the field, bounded west by Chichester Place, and came to Chesham Street, which leads up Chesham Road into Eastern Road. As he was crossing over the top, he met a man coming across the middle of the road. He noticed that he had a child with him and also noticed that he was staggering. He turned around to see if he should trip up. That is the evidence of the last witness who saw him going in the direction of the field. That brings us up to 9 pm on the evening of the murder. Then the next witness speaks about the prisoner's conduct on Friday. It appears he went to work early, about 6.20 am. He went to breakfast between 8 and 9.15 am, and then at 1 pm, he borrowed 2d from one of the rail workers, saying he wanted a bath. Then there is the evidence of one of the corporation employees in North Road who has known the man for some time and saw him coming from the direction of the North Street baths. Then there is the evidence of another railway goods man who saw him return at around 2.30 pm to the Cheapside entrance to the goods yard. At about 3 pm, he spoke to one of the goods men of the murder under circumstances I will leave for the present. Then, at about 6.30 pm, he talked to another of the goods men about the murder. At 8 pm, he was arrested by the police. He was seen by Detective Inspector Jupp, who brought him to the station where he was charged. Those are one or two circumstances of this case, and the evidence is circumstantial. No one usually sees what occurs in these horrible cases and circumstances leading to murder. Doctor Ross will have to be called to detail the child's injuries, and on this, I should prefer not to dwell on any details as they are of a shocking and horrible nature and will cause pain to all who hear them. I desire not to refer to them in any way but to leave them to come out in the evidence. I presume it will be convenient for the evidence of Doctor Ross and Doctor Stevenson to be taken at a future date. I have a letter from Doctor Stevenson saying he cannot complete his analysis of the clothes by today but that he may be able to complete his study within a week. I wish to highlight two or three points on the evidence I have referred. The first is the position of the prisoner's house on Rock Street and the position of the railway station where he works. It will be seen from the map that his daily probability takes him past this field where this barn is situated. The field is within a hundred yards of his house. The evidence of the night in question continuously brings him from the railway station toward the field. On his way home, P.C. Tuppen speaks about having seen the prisoner in Lavender Street, and he had known him for many years. The constable cannot be mistaken for the prisoner's identity. He is next seen by a witness named Rose Leggatt in Upper Bedford Street, talking to the child carrying a bundle of wood. The child dressed in a manner the witness describes and in clothes which she subsequently identified at the police station as the clothes of the murdered child. He is next seen in Somerset Street with the child in his arms, still proceeding towards the field. The next point is the blood found on the prisoner's clothes. There were stains of blood on the inside of the trousers, on two shirts and the pockets of his trousers inside, stains which, to the present moment, the prisoner has given no explanation whatsoever. Then there is the bath the prisoner takes on Friday afternoon - a curious time I need only say for a railway employee in hard work to take a bath during his dinner hour on Friday. If he is an innocent man, why is he so anxious to have a bath and so worried that he cannot wait for his wages on Friday night? Instead, he borrows money in the middle of the day to bathe. When taken into custody, his trousers were wet, and his shirts seemed to be washed. Is there any reasonable explanation for the stains being there? Are they recent, or are they not? If they are not current, what is the necessity to remove them? If they are recent, it is an extraordinary coincidence that they should be found on the prisoner's clothing in the position they were on the day following the murder of the child. The next question is the curious coincidence that he should be speaking to his mates about this murder. It may be susceptible to explanation, and I do not desire to dwell on it too much at present, but the times are somewhat curious. The prisoner speaks to a witness at the railway station, Scarce, at 3 pm about the murder. The prisoner had not been with the witness much that day. The prisoner returned to work at 2.35 pm and spoke to Scarce about the murder. He had been with a witness named Harriott the whole day but did not mention the murder until about 6.30 pm. When asked about these comments, the prisoner said that at 3 pm, the newspaper boys were howling outside the goods yard that a child was murdered in a field at Kemp Town. He might have heard from someone coming in and out of the goods yard of the murder, and it will be for the defence to this or some other place to bring forward that evidence. At present, there is no explanation for it. I shall call witnesses to speak of when the boys called the papers. They were not issued until between 3 and 4 pm, and I put this down as a curious incident. Then again, we have the prisoner's statement when he was charged. I do not desire to press this statement too firmly. The prisoner was placed in a painful and awkward position from the charges of a serious crime like this, but some stress must be laid upon it. He said in his letter, 'I do not remember a particle about it', and there is no indignant denial *whatsoever. He asked for a pen, ink and paper to write the letter. He was told before he wrote it that it would be read, but the letter was nevertheless written and will be here today. I have the original, which will be put in. I do not know if it is necessary to read the whole letter, but if the prisoner's counsel desires, I will read it. It is addressed to his father and mother, and he uses this expression. 'This is all through breaking the pledge you thought I was keeping.' He then refers to his work on Thursday and says, 'I remember driving in the station gates alright Thursday night, but I do not remember anything more after I got inside the gates. I can't remember anything that happened after the beastly drink. I must have been helplessly drunk. This crime has been brought to my feet as good as my keeper and helper. I honestly do not remember or can't bring myself to remember anything about it. It may be true, but I hope it is not.'*

At this point, Mr Pope's words were abruptly interrupted by a wail. George Henry Wood, who had been entirely silent before, suddenly burst into tears and covered his face with his handkerchief. Whether this emotional outburst was through self-pity or as a result of the clearly defined timeline that placed him at the centre of the crime is unclear. Mr Pope paused for a few seconds to allow George Henry Wood to compose himself and then continued with his address.

He said, '*When questioned on his movements before any question of murder, he was asked if he had been in Lavender Street the night before, and he said no. He also said that he had not seen Police Constable Tuppen, who had known him for years. Then he volunteered that he had been to the circus and had been there the whole evening. This is the evidence that will be laid before you today. On its completion by Doctor Stevenson's evidence, I shall ask you to commit the prisoner to the Assizes for trial for the wilful murder of the girl Edith Jeal.*'

Mr Pope announced that his first witness of the day was Doctor Humphrey, who was summoned to the dock. He informed the court that he was a fellow of the Royal College of Surgeons and lived at 25 Marine Parade, Brighton. He repeated the evidence he had given at the Coroner's inquest about being called to the field by William Stamford on Friday, the 11th of December.

Doctor Humphrey informed the court that after he entered the shed, he had found a child lying dead on the floor. He explained that he had completed a brief examination of the body and then transported the body to Freshfield Road.

Mr Pope: '*What was the child's appearance?*'

Doctor Humphrey: *'The body was lying with the feet towards the southwest, the left leg was drawn up, and the right leg extended. The child was on its back. The lower part of the body was bare, with the clothes thrown up on the chest. I noticed the hair was matted with blood, and the face was swollen, livid, bruised, and scratched. I looked at the neck because the child looked like someone had strangled it. I looked for a ligature around the neck but found none. The lower part was very much injured, bruised and lacerated. I turned the body over and found the left thigh was bruised and scratched. A quantity of blood was underneath the body on the ground where the child lay. Blood smothered the child's clothes. The child's drawers were lying about a yard in front of the body and on the left-hand side between the body and the door. They were also saturated with blood. The child's straw hat was lying very near the head. The building floor was covered with mould and some loose dry earth. I believe that the child died from asphyxia. The child had been dead between twelve and eighteen hours when I saw it. Rigour Mortis had set in both the legs and arms. The shed was so dark I could not make a minute examination.'*

Next to be called was little eight-year-old Bertram Jeal, who repeated the same evidence he had provided at the inquest. He was then once again cross-examined.

Mr Ayres: *'What items did she have in her hands?'*

Bertram Jeal: *'She was carrying both the wood and the chestnut-filled cap.'*

Mr Ayres: *'Did you or your sister speak to anyone on the night in question?'*

Bertram Jeal: *'No, Sir.'*

Mr Ayres: *'Have you ever seen the prisoner before?'*

Bertram Jeal: *'No, Sir.'*

The next witness to be called was Mrs Eliza Dunk, who lived at 23 St Martins Place and had not attended the inquest. She informed the court that on Thursday, the 10th of December, she had been walking along Sydney Street at around 6.30 pm. She said she had observed a man speaking to a little girl. Eliza Dunk explained the man had picked the girl up in his arms, and the child had screamed loudly as he did so. She recalled that the man had walked with the child in his arms for a few steps but had fallen over.

Eliza Dunk went on to describe the man's appearance. She said he wore a railway uniform, blue or dark cord trousers and leggings and remembered that the man's waistcoat had shiny buttons. She said she had rescued the little girl and, to ensure her safety had accompanied the child to her home on New England Street. She explained that she had left the man in Sydney Street. After handing the child to her mother, she walked back home.

Eliza Dunk told the court that she had reported the encounter to the police after hearing of Edith Jeal's murder. She explained that after she made her statement, the police had asked her to attend the police court during George Henry Wood's first appearance. She recalled that the police had told her their prime suspect would be present. She explained that when she arrived at the police court, she was asked if the prisoner was the same man she had seen on the 10th of December.

Mr Ayres then cross-examined the witness. Having read through the evidence, he knew that Eliza Dunk had not attended the town hall line-up. He was unhappy that her identification had happened at the police court hearing. On this occasion, George Henry Wood had been seated in the dock, thus indicating to everyone present that he was the accused. Mr Ayres was concerned that this would have influenced anyone asked to identify him and was keen for the Magistrate to adopt a similar view.

He said, *'In what part of the building did you see the prisoner on Saturday?'*
Eliza Dunk: *'I saw him in the dock.'*
Mr Ayres: *'Did he still have his railway clothes on?'*
Eliza Dunk: *'Yes.'*
Mr Ayres: *'What were they?'*
Eliza Dunk: *'I do not know whether he had leggings in court. He had leggings when I saw him.'*
Mr Ayres: *'And a waterproof coat on?'*
Eliza Dunk: *'No, Sir.'*
Mr Ayres: *'You were told the man was in the dock?'*
Eliza Dunk: *'No, Sir.'*
Mr Ayres: *'Were you told where to look for him?'*
Eliza Dunk: *'No.'*
Mr Ayres: *'Did you know where to look for him.'*
Eliza Dunk: *'No.'*
Mr Ayres: *'Are you saying you didn't know where to look for the prisoner?'*
Eliza Dunk: *'No.'*
Mr Ayres: *'You would not look for him at the back of the court?'*
Eliza Dunk: *'No.'*
Mr Ayres: *'And as a matter of fact, you did look at the dock?'*
Eliza Dunk: *'Yes.'*

Having highlighted his concerns with Eliza Dunk's identification, Mr Ayres turned his attention to other aspects of her evidence.

Mr Ayres: *'Was the child injured?'*

Eliza Dunk: *'She hurt her knee when they fell.'*

Mr Ayres: *'Did you see any policeman that night.'*

Eliza Dunk: *'No, I did not.'*

Mr Ayres: *'The man was drunk, you say?'*

Eliza Dunk: *'Yes, Sir.'*

Mr Ayres: *'Where was he going when you saw him?'*

Eliza Dunk: *'He was going through Sydney Street near Gloucester Road.'*

Mr Ayres: *'Towards the station?'*

Eliza Dunk: *'No, Sir.'*

Mr Ayres: *'The other way?'*

Eliza Dunk: *'Yes.'*

Mr Ayres: *'Have you seen the man before about the town?'*

Eliza Dunk: *'No, Sir.'*

Mr Pope, who had carefully listened to the questioning, was keen to clarify to the court that no witness interference had occurred.

Mr Pope: *'Before you saw the prisoner in the dock, had you been spoken to by the police about the prisoner's appearance?'*

Eliza Dunk: *'No, Sir.'*

The next witness to be called was 11-year-old Fanny Pimm of 47 Meeting House Lane, Brighton. She informed the court that on Thursday, the 11th of December, in the evening, she had been in Edward Street, near the bottom of Grosvenor Street. As she walked, she described seeing the prisoner, who Fanny Pimm said she did not know but was wearing a railway uniform.

She recalled that the man who she did not know had whistled at her, which caused her to turn around. She explained that as she did so, George Henry Wood asked her where she lived, and she responded that she lived at Brighton Lanes. She said George Henry Wood had asked her to go home with him.

The Magistrate interrupted the young girl and said, *'Mr Pope, I don't think what he says is evidence against him.'*

Mr Pope: *'Whatever she says is evidence against him, so far as it is evidence.'*

The Magistrate: *'It is evidence of what was in his mind, but not what was carried out. Witness, you can continue.'*

Fanny Pimm: *'Some further conversation passed between us, and then I returned to Grosvenor Street, leaving the man in Edward Street.'*

Mr Ayres then cross-examined the young witness.

Mr Ayres: *'Tell us how the man you saw on Thursday night was dressed?'*

Fanny Pimm: *'He had railway clothes on.'*

Mr Ayres: *'What are railway clothes?'*

Fanny Pimm: *'He had brass buttons at the side.'*

Mr Ayres: *'What was the colour of the trousers?'*

Fanny Pimm: *'Green corduroy trousers.'*

Mr Ayres: *'You could see that pretty plainly.'*

Fanny Pimm: *'Yes.'*

Mr Ayres: *'Were you under a lamp or outside a shop?'*

Fanny Pimm: *'Outside a shop.'*

Mr Ayres: *'Do you know the difference between a railway and a policeman's uniform?'*

Fanny Pimm: *'Yes, Sir.'*

Mr Ayres: *'What is the difference?'*

Fanny Pimm: *'They have blue coats, blue trousers, and brass buttons.'*

Mr Ayres: *'It was only by the buttons that you recognised the man.'*

Fanny Pimm: *'Yes, Sir.'*

Mr Ayres: *'What sort of face did he have?'*

Fanny Pimm: *'He had black from hair all over his face.'*

Mr Ayres: *'What do you mean?'*

Fanny Pimm: *'Little tiny spots of hair all over his cheek.'*

The Magistrate, still confused about Fanny Pimm's description, said, *'Do you mean black hair or as if he had not been shaved?'*

Fanny Pimm: *'Yes, as if he had not been shaved.'*

Mr Ayres: *'Did your mother bring you to the police station?'*

Fanny Pimm: *'Yes.'*

Mr Ayres: *'What did the police tell you when you came in?'*

Fanny Pimm: *'They asked me if a railwayman had stopped me.'*

Mr Ayres: *'Was one man pointed out to you, or were many men pointed out?'*

Fanny Pimm: *'A lot of people.'*

Mr Ayres: *'Did you see a man dressed as a railway man among the people?'*

Fanny Pimm: '*Yes.*'
Mr Ayres: '*More than one?*'
Fanny Pimm: '*No.*'
Mr Ayres: '*When you first came, you were asked to find a railwayman?*'
Fanny Pimm: '*Yes.*'

The Magistrate, unhappy with the line of questioning and felt that Mr Ayres was leading the young witness, wasn't willing to tolerate it.

He said, '*You put words into her mouth. I do not think that is what she means. Did any police constable say anything to you about a railwayman?*'

Fanny Pimm: '*I think he asked me if one stopped me.*'

The Magistrate: '*Was anything said about a railway man when you saw these men together in the large room?*'

Fanny Pimm: '*No, Sir.*'

Believing that the Magistrate had been satisfied, Mr Ayres continued his questioning.

Mr Ayres: '*What did they ask you to do?*'
Fanny Pimm: '*They asked me to pick out a man.*'
Mr Ayres: '*A man with buttons on his coat?*'

The Magistrate, becoming increasingly disgruntled, interrupted for a second time.

He said, '*Mr Ayres! You are putting words into her mouth again!*'

Mr Ayres did not directly acknowledge the Magistrate's concerns but rephrased his question.

He said, '*How did you know the man at the town hall was the same man you saw in the street?*'

Fanny Pimm: '*By his looks.*'
Mr Ayres: '*How did you remember him to be the same?*'
Fanny Pimm: '*Because he had some hair on his face, trousers, and jacket.*'

The next witness to be called was P.C. Tuppen. He explained that on Thursday, the 10th of December, at about 8 pm, he was on duty in Lavender Street. He recalled that he had spotted George Henry Wood near the bottom of Lavender Street and had watched him continue down the street and turn into Upper St James Street. He recalled that as the prisoner passed him; he was staggering, which led him to conclude that he was intoxicated.

    P.C. Tuppen informed the court that he had known George Henry Wood for about ten.

He remembered that George Henry Wood was wearing a pair of long Mackintosh leggings, a blue cloth coat that reached down just below his hips and a cap with a peak, which he recognised as a railway uniform. Mr Ayres then cross-examined the constable.

Mr Ayres: *'When did you next see the prisoner?'*

P.C. Tuppen: *'When Inspector Jupp brought him into the hall the following night. He was wearing seminal clothes except for the leggings.'*

Mr Ayres: *'As far as you know, they were the same clothes he had been wearing when you saw him on the last occasion?'*

P.C. Tuppen: *'Yes, Sir.'*

Mr Ayres: *'You could not see the trousers because the long leggings covered them?'*

P.C. Tuppen: *'I did not see the trousers on the same night.'*

Mr Ayres: *'The leggings came to the hips?'*

P.C. Tuppen: *'They were very long.'*

Mr Ayres: *'Was it a very dark night?'*

P.C. Tuppen: *'No, Sir.'*

Mr Ayres: *'It has been described as very dark and boisterous.'*

P.C. Tuppen: *'It was very windy?'*

Mr Ayres: *'You could not see the colour of his trousers under his leggings?'*

P.C. Tuppen: *'No, Sir.'*

Mr Ayres: *'You have known the prisoner for many years?'*

P.C. Tuppen: *'I have known the prisoner for ten years.'*

Mr Ayres: *'The way he was going was towards his home?'*

P.C. Tuppen: *'Yes, Sir.'*

Mr Ayres: *'You say he was very drunk?'*

P.C. Tuppen: *'He was very rickety on his legs.'*

Mr Ayres: *'We have been told he was seen in Edward Street at about 7 pm. Would it be possible for a man in that condition to be rolling about the streets for an hour without a policeman or someone seeing him?*

P.C. Tuppen: *'I do not know.'*

Mr Ayres: *'There is an hour to account for. Would a drunken man be noticed all that time in the public street?'*

P.C. Tuppen: *'I did not see him before 8 pm.'*

Mr Ayres: *'You have not heard it suggested by anyone in the police force that he was seen during that hour.'*

P.C. Tuppen: *'No, Sir.'*

The Magistrate wanted further information about George Henry Wood's clothing on Thursday, the 10th of December.

He said, *'How high did the leggings appear to you to go?'*

P.C. Tuppen: *'They came up from the inside to the thigh.'*

The Magistrate: *'To the coat?'*

P.C. Tuppen: *'The coat came down below the leggings.'*

The Magistrate: *'Do you think there was an interval between the leggings and the coat?'*

P.C. Tuppen: *'No, Sir, I do not think there was.'*

This marked the end of P.C. Tuppen's evidence, and he was released from the court.

Rose Leggatt was the next witness to be called. She repeated the evidence she had given at the inquest. However, on this occasion, she openly stated that she could not identify George Henry Wood definitively as the man who had pushed her into the railings at Montague Street. She told the court that she believed George Henry Wood to be the man but could not be sure. Rose Leggatt explained that as the man walked up the east side of Upper Bedford Street towards her, she noticed his clothing.

Mr Pope then asked several questions to bolster his case.

He said, *'What happened in Upper Bedford Street?'*

Rose Leggatt: *'When I left my mother's, I returned to Upper Bedford Street. As I reached Manchester Row, I spotted them again at the corner, close to Me Trengrove's grocery shop. I also saw a small child waiting outside the shop, who appeared to be carrying a bundle of wood under her arm. I remember the hat and apron that the child was wearing.'*

Mr Pope: *'Where you asked to identify the girl's clothing?'*

Rose Leggatt: *'I was asked to attend the Freshfield Road Police Station, which I did. When I was there, the police showed me a bundle of wood, a hat and an apron, which I identified as the child's.'*

Mr Pope: *'What did you see the man do to the child?'*

Rose Leggatt: *'I saw the man hold his hand towards her. The man then walked away from the area, and the little girl immediately followed him.'*

Mr Pope: *'Did you see where they went?'*

Rose Leggatt: *'They walked straight up Upper Bedford Street and turned into Somerset Street. I unintentionally followed the pair and was about three or four steps behind them. I did not see them after they passed the top of Somerset Street.'*

At this point, Mr Ayres began a robust cross-examination. As a key witness, he was aware of the relevance of Rose Leggatt's evidence and was keen to highlight its weaknesses.

He asked, '*How far from Bedford Buildings was it that you last saw the child?*'

Rose Leggatt: '*A few yards. I last saw them at the corner of Somerset Street.*'

Mr Ayres: '*That is just on the other side of the road to Bedford Buildings, the child's home?*'

Rose Leggatt: '*Yes, Sir.*'

Mr Ayres: '*You told us at the inquest the other night that you are not sure that the man who pushed against you about eight o'clock was the same man you saw afterwards with the child?*'

Mr Pope was unhappy with this question and said, '*That is a question I cannot take unless it is on the depositions!*'

Mr Ayres: '*I am asking her whether she did or did not say that she was unsure.*'

The Magistrate sided with the prosecution and said, '*Mr Ayres, you are entitled to ask what she said on a previous question, but I think it would be better if you were to ask her what she thinks now.*'

Mr Ayres listened to the Magistrate's words and said, '*Did you tell a Coroner's jury that you were not sure that the man who pushed up against you was the same man with the child? Do tell us whether you are now of the same opinion?*'

The Magistrate: '*No, no, no! I don't think that's a proper way of putting the question. Ask her what she now feels on any given subject, and then you can cross-examine her on what she states.*'

Mr Ayres: '*Is it your impression that the man you saw was the same man that pushed up against you?*'

Rose Leggatt: '*I told you the truth. I never took too much notice of the child at first.*'

Mr Ayres: '*Then you came to the police court to pick out the man.*'

Rose Leggatt: '*Yes, Sir.*'

Mr Ayres: '*How did you know him again?*'

Rose Leggatt: '*Well, Sir, all I know him to be the man is by his moustache.*'

Mr Ayres: '*Was the moustache uncommon?*'

Rose Leggatt: '*Well, he looked rough and as if he had not been washed that night.*'

The Magistrate turned and said to his clerk, '*You had better note that down.*'

Mr Ayres: '*Yes! It is important for me as the witness states he looked like he had not been washed. Others said that he had a bath. Do you mean the moustache had not been washed or the man?*'

Rose Leggatt: '*It looked like the man had not been washed.*'

Mr Ayres: '*Did he look in the same condition when you saw him at the police court?*'

Rose Leggatt: '*He was not dressed alike, Sir.*'

Mr Ayres: '*What was the difference in his dress?*'

Rose Leggatt: '*I don't think he had a big overcoat when I saw him.*'

Mr Ayres: '*Had he got a big overcoat the night you saw him?*'

Rose Leggatt: '*No, Sir.*'

Mr Ayres: '*What sort, a railway or a long coat?*'

Rose Leggatt: '*No Sir, a short coat.*'

Mr Ayres: '*What sort of trousers had he got on?*'

Rose Leggatt: '*I did not see his trousers.*'

The Court Clerk, who had been making notes about the proceedings, interrupted the evidence to clarify Rose Leggatt's statement.

He said, '*The man you saw in Upper Bedford Street had a railway coat on?*'

Rose Leggatt: '*Yes, Sir, he had.*'

The Court Clerk: '*You identified the prisoner at the town hall as the man you had seen with the child?*'

Rose Leggatt: '*Yes, Sir.*'

With the Clerk satisfied, Mr Ayres continued his cross-examination. He said, '*I think you fancied that it was the child's father, did you not?*'

Rose Leggatt: '*Yes, I did.*'

Mr Ayres: '*The child was following after the man?*'

Rose Leggatt: '*Yes, she was.*'

Mr Ayres: '*You did not hear any conversation between them?*'

Rose Leggatt: '*No, Sir.*'

Mr Ayres: '*And he didn't have hold of the child in any way?*'

Rose Leggatt: '*No, he did not.*'

Court Clerk: '*You said you were not sure that the man who pushed against you and the man you saw with the child was the same.*'

Rose Leggatt: '*No, Sir. I was not sure.*'

At this point, the Court Clerk interrupted for a second time to seek further clarity.

He said, '*You said you were not certain that the man who rushed against you and the man you saw beckon to the child was the same?*'

Rose Leggatt: *'No, I am not certain, Sir.'*

Court Clerk: *'But I may suppose you are not certain they were two different men?'*

Rose Leggatt: *'I never took much notice.'*

Court Clerk: *'You cannot say whether the man who pushed against you was the same man you saw with the child?'*

Rose Leggatt: *'No, Sir, I never took much notice of the man who pushed against me, so I cannot say.'*

The Magistrate: *'Did you notice the dress of the man who pushed against you?'*

Rose Leggatt: *'No, Sir, I did not.'*

The Magistrate: *'Did you take more notice of the man than the child.'*

Rose Leggatt: *'I did.'*

Court Clerk: *'And that was the man dressed as a railway man.'*

Rose Leggatt: *'Yes, Sir.'*

Court Clerk: *'Will you tell the bench how far you can say that this man you saw with the child was, or was not, the man who pushed against you.'*

Rose Leggatt: *'Yes, Sir, he was almost the man.'*

Court Clerk: *'The prisoner was the man with the child? Do you mean to say that you do not doubt it?'*

Rose Leggatt: *'Sir, I do not doubt it.'*

With the court clerk satisfied, Mr Ayres continued with his questions.

He said, *'At the inquest, you said the man who pushed against you was in railway clothes. Do you remember saying that?'*

Rose Leggatt: *'I did not say in railway clothes.'*

Mr Pope: *'When you saw the prisoner at the town hall on Friday, did you notice anything different from what you saw the previous night?'*

Rose Leggatt: *'He did not have his leggings on.'*

Mr Pope: *'And you mentioned that at the time?'*

Rose Leggatt: *'Yes, Sir, I did.'*

Alice Guy was the last witness of the morning to be called, who did not testify at the inquest. She said she told the court that she had visited her mother during the evening of the 10th of December. She explained that she had left her house on Somerset Street at 6.15 pm and observed a man on the opposite side who was carrying a child in his arms. Alice Guy tearfully recalled that the child screamed loudly as the man walked away from her, which caused her to shout out, '*Don't hurt that little thing.*'

She recalled that the man was under a street lamp as she called out and that she saw the man's face distinctly as he was stood under a street lamp. Alice Guy added that the prisoner walked around the corner into Montague Place and continued onto Eastern Road. After being given a few minutes to console herself, Alice Guy explained that she was worried for the child as she did not have anything on her shoulders, and it was pouring hard with rain.

After hearing of the murder, Alice Guy said that she attended the Freshfield Road Police Station and made a statement regarding her observations. Alice Guy explained that she had participated in the town hall on the 12th of December and identified the prisoner in a line-up. After, she recalled that a police constable showed her a hat, which she identified as being worn by the child.

Aware of the strength of Alice Guy's evidence, Mr Ayres opted to infer that newspaper reports of George Henry Wood's appearance had influenced her identification.

He said, '*When were you first asked to give evidence in this case?*'

Alice Guy: '*I think it was on Tuesday last week.*'

Mr Ayres: '*Did you read an account in the newspapers, on Friday, of the child's body being found?*'

Alice Guy: '*No, Sir.*'

Mr Ayres: '*Did you hear anything about it?*'

Alice Guy: '*No, Sir.*'

Mr Ayres: '*When did you first hear about it?*'

Alice Guy: '*On Saturday.*'

Mr Ayres: '*Did you read it in the Sunday papers?*'

Alice Guy: '*No, Sir.*'

Mr Ayres: '*Who told you about it?*'

Alice Guy: '*A temperance friend.*'

Mr Ayres: '*Who is your temperance friend?*'

Alice Guy: '*I cannot say, Sir.*'

Mr Ayres: '*Do you know his name?*'

Alice Guy: '*Not particularly.*'

Mr Ayres: '*Was it a man or a woman?*'

Alice Guy: '*It was several temperance friends.*'

Mr Ayres: '*When were you talking about it?*'

Alice Guy: '*On the way to bible reading.*'

Mr Ayres: *'Was it on the road?'*

Alice Guy: *'Yes, Sir.'*

Mr Ayres: *'Tell me one of those who were there.'*

Alice Guy gave no response to this question, which irritated Mr Ayres.

After pausing for a few seconds, he snapped, *'Surely you can tell me the name of one of your friends? Do you remember who told you this story of the child?'*

Alice Guy: *'I do not know them particularly.'*

Mr Ayres: *'Whom did you communicate with first?'*

Alice Guy: *'I spoke to a young friend who lives above me.'*

Mr Ayres: *'What is the young friend's name? Surely you can tell me something about it, Miss Guy?'*

The Magistrate, who was also unhappy with the ambiguity of Alice Guy's evidence, said, *'You need to answer! Who was your young friend?'*

Alice Guy replied, *'Elizabeth Mockford.'*

Mr Ayres: *'When was that?'*

Alice Guy: *'I asked her on Friday morning if she had noticed a child carried by a man.'*

Mr Ayres: *'What Friday?'*

Alice Guy: *'Friday week.'*

Mr Ayres: *'Why did you ask her about the child?'*

Alice Guy: *'I don't know, Sir.'*

Mr Ayres: *'Did you suggest that the child you had seen on the night of the murder was the child whose body had been found.'*

Alice Guy: *'No, Sir.'*

Mr Ayres: *'You did not know anything about it?'*

Alice Guy: *'No, Sir.'*

Mr Ayres: *'Until the Sunday you went to the bible class, you had not heard about the murder?'*

Alice Guy: *'Not particularly.'*

Mr Ayres: *'You mean to say, living where you do, you did not hear about this dreadful murder?'*

At this point, the court clerk, who was also increasingly annoyed with Alice Guy's responses, interrupted the proceedings to seek clarity.

He said, *'Have you heard of the child being found dead?'*

Alice Guy: *'Yes, I heard of the child being found.'*

Court Clerk: *'When did you hear about it?'*
Alice Guy: *'I do not know that. I can't tell you.'*

The questioning then returned to Mr Ayres.
He said, *'Did you not think it was important?'*
Alice Guy: *'We hear of so many crimes.'*
Mr Ayres: *'Many crimes in your neighbourhood.'*
Alice Guy: *'Yes, Sir.'*
Mr Ayres: *'Did you hear on a Saturday that a crime had been committed?'*
Alice Guy: *'Yes, Sir, I heard of the particulars in the morning.'*
Mr Ayres: *'Did you buy a paper?'*
Alice Guy: *'I am not in the habit of buying papers.'*
Mr Ayres: *'Did you have one given to you? Did you read it in the newspaper?'*
Alice Guy: *'No, Sir.'*
Mr Ayres: *'Well, who told you about the murder?'*
Alice Guy: *'I cannot remember. It was a long time ago.'*
Mr Ayres: *'It is not long ago. It is only a week. If your memory is as defective as this, not much weight can be placed on what you have told us.'*
The Magistrate: *'Mr Ayres that is her comment.'*

Mr Ayres, who was losing his patience with Alice Guy's refusal to be, evident in her the evidence she was giving.
Addressing the Magistrate, he said, *'How can it be that she cannot remember anything else?'*
The Magistrate turned to Alice Guy and said, *'You say you cannot remember who told you about the murder.'*
Alice Guy: *'No, Sir, I cannot.'*
The Magistrate: *'But it was on Saturday?'*
Alice Guy: *'Yes.'*
Mr Ayres: *'Did it occur to you that it was the same child that the man you saw that was carrying a child?'*
Alice Guy: *'No, Sir.'*
Mr Ayres: *'Did you think it was a father and child you saw?'*
Alice Guy: *'Yes, Sir, I did.'*
Mr Ayres: *'And you were interested to know where he lived, so you followed him?'*
Alice Guy: *'Yes, I thought it was a long distance for the child to be carried away.'*

Mr Ayres: *'But you considered the father was carrying her?'*

Alice Guy: *'He seemed incapable of carrying it.'*

Mr Ayres: *'Why did you notice the child, supposing its father was carrying it?'*

Alice Guy: *'So many children are lost.'*

Mr Ayres: *'Do you follow every man you see with a child in his arms?'*

Alice Guy: *'I do not.'*

Mr Ayres: *'Although it was pouring torrents, you were curious enough to know where the man lived.'*

Alice Guy: *'No, Sir.'*

Mr Ayres: *'Did you find out where he lived?'*

Alice Guy: *'No, Sir.'*

Mr Ayres: *'Then your curiosity stopped when you had gone about half a mile?'*

Alice Guy: *'I do not understand.'*

The Magistrate: *'She says she only went to the corner of Somerset Street.'*

Mr Ayres: *'You are positive about when you saw the prisoner?'*

Alice Guy: *'Yes.'*

Mr Ayres: *'Had you an umbrella with you?'*

Alice Guy: *'No, Sir, it is not far to go.'*

Mr Ayres: *'Had it been a wet evening?'*

Alice Guy: *'Yes, Sir, it came on gusty but sometimes cleared up beautifully.'*

Mr Ayres: *'But it was raining at quarter past eight?'*

Alice Guy: *'Yes.'*

Mr Ayres: *'And if the Constable said it was not raining, he was incorrect?'*

The Magistrate was unhappy with this comment as he knew that no police constable had referenced the weather during the police court proceedings.

He said, *'Mr Ayres, the Constable has not said that yet.'*

Mr Ayres changed his question, *'If the child's brother said it was not raining, is it not correct?'*

The Magistrate again interrupted and said, *'The brother did not say it either!'*

Mr Ayres replied, *'The child has said so, pardon me!'*

The Magistrate: *'He may have said it at the inquest, but he has not said it here. You do not have the right to put the question as to what was said elsewhere. The brother has not said anything about the rain!'*

Mr Ayres accepted the judge's advice and changed tact.

He said, *'You heard about the murder on Saturday night. You did not think it important to communicate with the police until Friday?'*

Alice Guy: *'I did not hear from the police until Friday.'*

Mr Ayres: *'Did they communicate with you?'*

Alice Guy: *'Yes, Sir.'*

Mr Ayres: *'Have you read the accounts in the paper from day to day.'*

Alice Guy: *'No.'*

Mr Ayres: *'Nothing at all?'*

Alice Guy: *'I did not feel interested enough in it.'*

Mr Ayres: *'When did you see the prisoner identify him?'*

Alice Guy: *'In the morning.'*

Mr Ayres: *'Is he the same in appearance today as when you saw him on Friday night?'*

Alice Guy: *'He has more whiskers now than I saw him.'*

Mr Ayres: *'In every other respect, he is the same?'*

Alice Guy: *'Yes, Sir.'*

Mr Ayres: *'The same clothes?'*

Alice Guy: *'Oh no, Sir.'*

Mr Ayres: *'And you are sure this man here is the man you saw under the lamp?'*

Alice Guy: *'I feel confident.'*

Mr Ayres: *'You swear to it. Do you swear it is the same man?'*

Alice Guy: *'I feel confident that he is the same.'*

Mr Ayres: *'Do you swear it?'*

The Magistrate again rebuked Mr Ayres for badgering the witness.

He said, *'You cannot go saying that. She says she is confident. You may ask if she's positive about it. You may ask if she makes a distinction between confident and positive.'*

Mr Ayres: *'Are you certain it is the same man?'*

Alice Guy: *'Yes, Sir.'*

Mr Ayres: *'And before you heard of the murder, you spoke to your friend about the child.'*

Alice Guy: *'Yes, Sir.'*

At this point, the Magistrate informed Alice Guy that she could leave the court. As she did so, the gravity of the situation caused her to become overwhelmed, and as she walked, she quietly sobbed into a handkerchief. After she had left, the Magistrate informed the court that the proceedings would pause for lunch. After the courtroom cleared, George Henry Wood was returned to the cells.

Chapter 13: *'What dreadful news it is?'*

Following a thirty-minute interval for lunch, George Henry Wood was brought back up to the police court, and the trial resumed. The first witness of the afternoon was Henry Spicer. He said on the 10th of December, as he walked along Eastern Road, he spotted a man carrying a child at the top of Chesham Street. He told the court that he had identified the man as the prisoner at the town hall. Henry Spicer was then cross-examined by the defence.

Mr Ayres said, 'Was it raining *when you saw the man?'*

Henry Spicer: *'No, it was not raining.'*

Mr Ayres: *'Did you see the man's face?'*

Henry Spicer: *'No, Sir.'*

Mr Ayres: *'Did you notice anything else about the man?'*

Henry Spicer: *'I noticed that his boots were filthy.'*

Court Clerk: *'What made you believe this was the same man?'*

Henry Spicer: *'I came down to the town hall on the 11th of December to see if I could identify the man, and to the best of my belief, the prisoner is the same man.'*

Traiton Harriot, a Foreman at the Brighton Station Goods Yard, was the next witness to be called. He explained that he could not remember when George Henry Wood left work on the 10th of December, but did recall that he had been delivering malt to Longhurst Brewery. He stated that George Henry Wood usually finished his work duties at about twenty minutes past six in the evening, but this was only sometimes the case.

Traiton Harriot recalled that the prisoner wore an oilskin cap, leggings and a coat. He said that on the day after the murder, George Henry Wood came to the porter's lodge at about

5.45 am to sign in and left for dinner at 1 pm. He could not remember him saying anything suspicious in nature. Traiton Harriott said he left the porters lodge at around 6.30 pm on the 11th of December and made his way down Trafalgar Street. He recalled that as he reached the entrance to the goods yard, he bumped into George Henry Wood again.

He said that on this occasion, George Henry Wood had said, '*Don't you think a man must be mad to murder a little child?*'

Traiton Harriott explained to the court that he did not understand the comment and had simply replied, '*What child?*' He remembered that George Henry Wood had answered, '*Have you not heard of the murder at Kemp Town?*' Traiton Harriott said he had not, and the two parted company. He explained that he had thought it strange that the two had been working together for most of the day, yet George Henry Wood had not mentioned the murder before this point.

Mr Ayres then cross-examined Traiton Harriott.

He said, '*When you saw him on Thursday, was he wearing his oilskins?*'

Traiton Harriott: '*Yes.*'

Mr Ayres: '*Was it raining hard?*'

Traiton Harriott: '*It was raining off and on.*'

Mr Ayres: '*He drove the horse up Trafalgar Street?*'

Traiton Harriott: '*I think his mate drove the horses.*'

Mr Ayres: '*At times, you work very late at the station?*'

Traiton Harriott: '*Yes, at times.*'

Mr Ayres: '*Is there anything unusual in a man having a warm bath in the middle of the day? What other time would he have it?*'

Traiton Harriott: '*I cannot say.*'

Mr Ayres: '*You were with him on Friday?*'

Traiton Harriott: '*Yes, most of the day.*'

Mr Ayres: '*Did he appear strange in his manner, anything unusual.*'

Traiton Harriott: '*No, I did not notice anything. We are always busy and have no time to take much notice.*'

Mr Ayres: '*He was wearing the same clothes he had the day before?*'

Traiton Harriott: '*As far as I know.*'

Mr Ayres: '*Did you see any blood marks on them?*'

Traiton Harriott: '*No.*'

Mr Ayres: '*What character has he borne?*'

Traiton Harriott: '*He was a steady man as far as I know.*'

Mr Ayres: *'He had been a teetotaller for some months?'*
Traiton Harriott: *'I always thought he was a teetotaller.'*
Mr Ayres: *'You have never seen him drunk before?'*
Traiton Harriott: *'No.'*
Mr Ayres: *'Do you recall him bursting a varicose vein in his leg some months ago?'*
Traiton Harriott: *'Yes.'*
Mr Ayres: *'He had something wrong with his leg and went to the hospital in London?'*
Traiton Harriott: *'That was before he worked for me.'*
Mr Ayres: *'How long has he been with you?'*
Traiton Harriott: *'Twelve months.'*

The following three witnesses to be called by the prosecution were intended to prove that George Henry Wood had taken a bath the day after the murder. Although their evidence is circumstantial, having a bath in the middle of the day would support the fact that George Henry Wood wanted to remove blood from his person.

The first of these witnesses was Martin Marchant, a 28-year-old goods cabman who lived at 28 London Street. He explained that on Friday, the 11th of December, George Henry Wood borrowed two pence from him. He said George Henry Wood had told him he wanted a bath. Similar evidence was given by Albert Fisher, a 28-year-old railway porter who lived at Belmont Street. He explained that on the 11th, he had also lent George Henry Wood a penny because he wanted to go for a bath.

The last of the three witnesses was John Winder, who lived at Devonshire Street, who described seeing George Henry Wood coming out of the North Street Baths at about 2.30 pm on the 11th of December. John Scrase, a railway cabman, was the next witness to be called to give evidence. He told the court that he had seen the prisoner on Friday, the 11th of December, at about 3 pm at Brighton Station. He recalled that George Henry Wood said, *'What dreadful news it is?'* John Scrase explained that he did not know what George Henry Wood was referring to and replied as such.

John Scrase said that George Henry Wood had explained that a little girl had been outraged and murdered in a field near his house. After outlining the details of the crime, George Henry Wood said, *'I would have whoever did it served the same or worse.'*

P.C. Thorpe was next to appearing before the Magistrate. He explained that on Sunday, the 13th of December, he was in charge of the prisoners at the town hall cells. At about 11 am, he said George Henry Wood asked for writing paper and a pen. P.C. Thorpe explained to the court that he had complied with George Henry Wood's request but informed him that whatever he wrote would be read. He said that he had watched the prisoner write a letter. P.C Thorpe explained that he reminded George Henry Wood several times that the letter would be read. He said George Henry Wood was still writing the letter when his shift finished.

P.C. Rampton was the next witness to be called. He explained that he had relieved P.C. Thorpe at about 1 pm on Sunday, the 13th of December and was tasked with supervising the custody cells. He said that George Henry Wood handed him a letter shortly after his shift began. He told the court that he had read the first portion of the letter but had handed it over to Inspector Jupp for further inspection. At this point, Mr Pope produced the letter and showed it to P.C. Rampton, who confirmed that it was the letter George Henry Wood, had written.

P.C. Rampton's evidence was followed by that of Detective Inspector Jupp. He stated that he received a letter from P.C. Rampton in the afternoon of the 13th of December and handed it to Chief Constable Terry. He explained to the court that George Henry Wood lived at 11 Rock Street, a continuation eastward from Chesham Road.

Mr Ayres then cross-examined Inspector Jupp.

Mr Ayres: *'You have been there lots of times?'*

Inspector Jupp: *'Not recently.'*

Mr Ayres: *'Since the murder, have you only been there once in connection with the whole affair?'*

Inspector Jupp: *'Yes.'*

Mr Ayres: *'Was it last Monday?'*

Inspector Jupp: *'A week ago.'*

Mr Ayres: *'Did you go to the house after you arrested him?'*

Inspector Jupp: *'Yes.'*

Mr Ayres: *'You thoroughly investigated and scraped up the floorboards?'*

Inspector Jupp: *'No. It was in consequence of a remark about the house's structure that I went there. I searched the basement, and that is all.'*

Mr Ayres: *'Did you go to the bedroom?'*

Inspector Jupp: *'No.'*

Mr Ayres: *'You found nothing as the result of the search?'*

Inspector Jupp: *'Nothing.'*

Mr Ayres: *'Was all assistance given?'*

Inspector Jupp: *'Yes.'*

Mr Ayres: *'I want to hear from the policemen who searched the bedroom. It might be suggested that there was blood on the sheets perhaps.'*

A confused Mr Pope interrupted the evidence and said, *'We do not suggest this at all!'*

Mr Ayres appeared to have been satisfied with Mr Pope's comment and sat back at the solicitor's table. Mr Pope then informed the court that he would read George Henry Wood's letter, detailed in a previous chapter. As Mr Pope's words reverberated around the courtroom, George Henry Wood bowed his head and again burst into tears.

Doctor Ross was the final witness of the day to be called. He repeated the evidence he had provided at the inquest regarding Edith's general injuries and appearance. He told the court that, in his opinion, Edith's injuries had been caused by someone who used extreme violence. He also said that a blunt instrument may have caused some damage. At this point, the Magistrate formally closed the proceedings for the day and ordered that George Henry Wood remain in custody until the 29th of December. The prisoner was quickly removed from the witness box and returned to the basement cells.

Outside the town hall, in St Bartholomew's Square, a large crowd, once again, gathered and besieged the area, hoping that they would catch a glimpse of the prisoner as he walked out to the Black Maria. The crowd excitedly discussed the details of the murder and debated George Henry Wood's guilt. They knew that the Magistrate had ordered his removal to Lewes Gaol and waited to see this occur.

The large numbers again unnerved the police, who believed a siege was likely. The police locked down the court and stationed officers at the police station's doors. However, the prison van did not arrive, and within an hour, the crowd dispersed. Inside the police station, a chaotic scene was unfolding. After the police court proceedings closed, George Henry Wood was reportedly seized with another fit. Within a short time, he apparently recovered but suffered a further two attacks in quick succession, which the police said left him in a weak state of health. As a result, Chief Constable James Terry postponed George Henry Wood's removal to Lewes until the following day.

By the morning of the 23rd of December, George Henry Wood was said to be in good health. A few minutes before 9 am, the Black Maria pulled into East Street. Around fifty members of the public had gathered on this occasion. George Henry Wood, who was already in handcuffs, was quickly led out of the police station by Superintendent Carter and several other officers. When the group reached the van, Superintendent Carter opened the door and pushed the prisoner into the cab.

He and Fire Superintendent Lacroix followed George Henry Wood into the compartment and quickly closed the door. A few seconds later, without any commotion, the van began its journey to Lewes, much to the relief of the police.

The Christmas holiday was extremely special to the Wood family as a deeply religious family. Usually, the family spent time together worshipping and celebrating the birth of Christ. However, this year, the latest remand meant this would not be true. Consequently, the family spent the holidays praying for their son and trying to avoid public appearances. George Henry Wood, who had been placed in a cell, tried to readjust to Lewes House of Correction's harsh conditions and regime.

Chapter 14: Committed to Trial

On the morning of the 29th of December, George Henry Wood undertook the now-familiar journey from Lewes House of Correction to Brighton Town Hall. As the van pulled up at the end of East Street, it was greeted by several police constables who quickly removed the prisoner from the van and escorted him into the police station. On the floor directly above, the Stipendiary Magistrate, Mr C.G Heathcote, The Mayor, Alderman Doctor Ewart, Colonel Alexander, Colonel Silverthorne, Alderman Brigden, Alderman Reeves, Alderman Sendall and Mr J Martin were taking their seats in the police court.

As was the case in his previous appearances, the public galleries were entirely filled, and those unable to access the proceedings congregated outside the town hall's doors. Several police constables once again guarded the entrances in case the crowd surged. Mr Pope and Mr Ayres were both again in attendance. At 10 am, George Henry Wood was led up from the cells and was seated in the dock. Mr Pope started the proceedings with a short address to outline the evidence he would be presenting that day.

He said, *'The principal witness I have to call today to complete the evidence against the prisoner is Doctor Stevenson, who has completed his examination of the prisoner's clothing and will be able to give his result. There are one or two more witnesses regarding the facts necessary to complete the other evidence. The witness on the last occasion spoke of the prisoner wearing an oilskin coat when he left the goods yard. I shall call a witness who saw him remove the coat before he left the goods yard and put it in a hut there. You will remember that some witnesses who saw him later did not mention his coat. It will be necessary to show whether the prisoner wore his oilskin coat when he was seen later.'*

The court clerk, who had been busily taking notes, paused briefly and said, '*That is not necessary, surely?*'

Mr Pope replied, '*It is essential! Another witness said he had the oilskin coat on. His identification must show he took it off before he left the yard. It seems desirable on the part of the prosecution to show this. If one saw him with the coat and the next witness without it, showing he took it off is desirable. I shall call the evidence of two gatekeepers who work at Brighton Station, one at the Cheapside gate and one at the Trafalgar Street gate. Both will say that to the best of their beliefs, the prisoner did not go out of the yard after coming from lunch and that they heard nothing of the newspaper boys calling about the murder, so there seems to be no means by which the prisoner could have known it except by evidence called on his behalf. There will also be evidence from the two evening papers, giving the correct publication time. Afterwards, Doctor Stevenson will say the majority of the stains spoken to by Detective Jupp are bloodstains. The trousers which, as your Worships will remember are not corduroy trousers but have a flap that falls down. This leaves the pockets bare against the man's leg. They were considerably stained with blood, almost saturated. There are also smears on the pocket and bloodstains on the flannel shirt, which appeared to have been washed and rubbed. Blood stains were on the woollen drawers in front, outside and inside. In addition, there are stains in the interior of the right-hand coat pocket, as if a person's hand had been covered with blood and placed into the pocket. There were stains on the edge and lining of that pocket. There were also bloodstains near the shirt's collar, as if a finger with blood on it had touched the top of the shirt. An expert can't say that blood stains are of human blood. Doctor Stevenson can go as far as any expert can. He can say that the stains agree in every character with human blood and can confirm that they are mammalian blood. He will be able to state positively from his examination of the whole of the stains that they were made between the 7th of December and the 14th of December.*'

Having completed his opening address, Mr Pope called his first witness, Sydney Gladwin. He informed the court that he was employed as a Goods Department Clerk at the Brighton Station Goods Yard. Sydney Gladwin explained that he had seen the prisoner at 7 pm on the evening of the 10th of December at the watchman's hut. He recalled to the court that the prisoner had tried to remove his coat, but he was unable to due to intoxication. Sydney Gladwin said he had helped George Henry Wood remove his coat and hung it over the hut's fire hose reel, which was mounted on the wall. Sydney Gladwin was then cross-examined by Mr Ayres.

He said, '*What was the prisoner's condition? Was he drunk?*'

Sydney Gladwin: '*Yes, but not very drunk.*'

Mr Ayres: *'But he was too drunk to take off his coat?'*
Sydney Gladwin: *'Yes.'*

The next witness to be called was Francis Simmons, also of Station Street, who worked as a gatekeeper at the Trafalgar Street entrance to the goods yard. He recalled that on Friday, the 11th of December, he had been on duty at the watch hut from 2 to 6 pm. He informed the court that he did not see George Henry Wood during this time. He explained that he was responsible for logging the names and timings of anyone leaving the yard during work hours aside from their lunch breaks.

He told the court that he would have seen George Henry Wood if he had left the goods yard and that he first heard about the murder at 5 pm but refused to swear the exact time. Mr Ayres then arose to begin his cross-examination. He knew that George Henry Wood had made several detailed comments about Edith's murder to various people. He was also aware that the prosecution alleges this was because he had committed the murder.

During George Henry Wood's interviews, he had informed the police that he had learned of the murder from the numerous paper boys standing at Brighton Station's entrances, calling out the day's headlines. However, Francis Simmons had stated that George Henry Wood had not left the good's yard during the day, which cast doubt on his reasons for knowing about the murder.

Mr Ayres wanted to cast doubt about the significance of Francis Simmons' evidence and used the cross-examination.

He said, *'Do you put down in a book all the times people come in and go out?'*
Francis Simmons: *'Yes, Sir, I do.'*
Mr Ayres: *'Have you got the book here?'*
Francis Simmons: *'No, Sir. It is a book provided at the station, about the size of a prayer book.'*
Mr Ayres: *'You mean to say no man can come in and out without you recording his time? I don't say so. There may be a rush of traffic at the time, and he may slip out by the side of a van. He might have gone out without you noticing him?'*
Francis Simmons: *'I won't swear the prisoner did not go out, but I certainly did not see him.'*
Mr Ayres: *'Then what your evidence comes to is this. As you know, he did not leave the yard between four and six?'*
Francis Simmons: *'As far as I know.'*

At this point, Mr Pope rose to his feet and objected.

He said, *'Mr Ayres! He did not say four! He said two!'*

Mr Ayres corrected his question and said, *'Okay, he did not leave the yard between two and six?'*

Francis Simmons: *'The last time I saw him that day was almost 1 pm. I did not see him again that day.'*

Mr Ayres: *'Mr Simmons, will you tell the bench what has been his general character while he has been employed by the company?'*

Francis Simmonds: *'Well, I know nothing against his character whatsoever. I have never worked with him. He has come to the hut at breakfast and dinner when I have been here.'*

Mr Ayres: *'But you have had an opportunity of seeing him every day?'*

Francis Simmonds: *'Yes, I have known him for two years, and he has always borne a good character as far as I know.'*

Court Clerk: *'You believe he has borne a good character?'*

Francis Simmonds: *'Yes, of course, but I never saw him outside the goods yard.'*

The next witness to be called was Horace Mockett, General Manager of the Evening Times, who the prosecution felt would highlight the suspicious nature of George Henry Wood's comments about the murder. He informed the court that the first issue of his publication which contained any reference to the murder, was at 3.15 pm on the 11th of December. Mr Ayres then cross-examined the witness.

He said, *'Does your paper generally get the first news?'*

Horace Mockett: *'It certainly did on that occasion.'*

Mr Ayres: *'Will you be surprised that The Brighton Argus had it an hour before that?'*

Horace Mockett: *'I should be shocked. Regarding the news, the first time we received word of the murder was soon after 2 pm.'*

Court Clerk: *'The first issue of yours with the murder was 3.15 pm?'*

Horace Mockett: *'Yes.'*

Mr Ayres: *'The first issue of any paper containing the news in the town?'*

Horace Mockett: *'Yes.'*

Mr Pope: *'How many evening papers are in the town?'*

Horace Mockett: *'Two.'*

Court Clerk: *'And you first heard of the murder about two o'clock?'*

Horace Mockett: 'Yes.'

The final witness to be called was Doctor Thomas Stevenson, Official Analyst to the Home Office, who had travelled from London earlier that day. He explained that he had received a parcel from Inspector Jupp on the 14th of December, which contained various clothing items. Doctor Stevenson informed the court that he had examined the clothing and subjected them to chemical and microscopic analysis. Mr Pope then asked Doctor Stevenson to detail his findings.

He said, *'I found stains on the outside and inside of the pocket, which appeared to be blood smears. On the front of the trousers, near the bottom, there were more minor blood smears. The inner side of the flaps of the trousers had extensive smears of blood and other stains, nearly covering the flaps inside. When I received the trousers, the flap was damp and almost wet. There were also blood stains on the outer part of the right pocket. When I examined the flannel vest, I found three distinct blood spots that originated from the inside and had soaked through the material. These stains were also wet as if someone had tried to wash them off. The third stain was near the bottom of the vest, which likely originated from the left thigh. There were further blood stains on the shirt, below the collar button, which I believe had been caused by a blood-stained finger. Finally, there were blood stains on the left of the front opening of the drawers. During my analysis, I confirmed that the blood was mammalian and similar to human blood. The blood stains appear to have been made four or five days before I received the clothing and within a week.'*

At this stage, Mr Pope produced George Henry Wood's clothing and showed them to Doctor Stevenson, who confirmed they were the clothes he had examined. The Magistrates Clerk asked whether Mr Ayres had any questions for the witness, to which he replied that he did not. After Doctor Stevenson concluded his evidence, Mr Pope informed the Stipendiary Magistrate that the prosecution's case was completed. Per the Indictable Offences Act (1848), the court clerk read the witnesses' depositions to the Magistrate in the accused's presence.

Once this was done, George Henry Wood and the Magistrates signed the testimonies to confirm their accuracy. Afterwards, the Magistrate read and explained the formal charges to the court. He then addressed the prisoner.

He said, *'George Henry Wood, do you wish to say anything in answer to the charge? You are not obliged to unless you desire to do so, but whatever you do will be written down and presented at your trial.'*

George Henry Wood: *'No, Sir. I reserve my defence.'*

The Magistrate: *'Do you have any witnesses to call?'*

George Henry Wood: *'No, Sir.'*

The Magistrate: *'Therefore, you stand committed for trial at the Spring Assizes for the County of Sussex on this charge.'*

The Magistrate then informed the witnesses that they were compelled to appear at the next Court of Assize. George Henry Wood was removed from the dock and returned to the basement cells. Reports state that while in the cells, George Henry Wood suffered from several further fits, which were similar to those he had suffered after his last court appearance. The police feared the prisoner's ill health would delay his removal to Lewes.

However, he quickly recovered and was deemed fit to be moved later that day. During the latter part of the afternoon, George Henry Wood received a visit from his father, mother, brother and sister and the family engaged in warm conversation. At 5.45 pm, the *'Black Maria'* arrived on East Street. To the police's relief, only three or four people had gathered around the Black Maria to see the prisoner's removal.

At 6 pm George Henry Wood was escorted from the police station in handcuffs and quickly placed in the van. Immediately the van pulled off and began the short journey towards the House of Correction at Lewes. As the vehicle arrived at the looming gatehouse, feelings of apprehension and dread must have overcome George Henry Wood. He had served sentences here before, but only for short sentences and must have been spurred on by the fact he would soon be free.

On this occasion, things were entirely different. Minimally, George Henry Wood knew he would not return to Brighton until at least April if his defence succeeded. However, having heard the wealth of evidence against him by this point, he was likely aware that he would never be freed again. To add to his woes, he also knew that if the jury at the Court of Assize believed in his guilt, he would be hung.

Chapter 15: *'A Neurotic Subject'*

By early January 1892, Prince and Ayres were concerned that they had still not agreed on a defence strategy. Having directly participated in the police court proceedings, Prince and Ayres must have been under no illusion that they faced an uphill battle. The prosecution's evidence against their client was continuous, compelling and credible. Mr Ayres had worked tirelessly during cross-examination to discredit the reliability of the prosecution's witnesses. He had repeatedly made suggestions of confirmation bias and police interference and urged the court to consider the negative impact of media reports on his client's case.

Yet, despite his best efforts, the Magistrate had committed George Henry Wood for trial. Adding to their problems was that their client had no alibi and had not denied that he committed Edith's despicable murder. Prince and Ayres also knew other aggravating factors would further galvanise the prosecution's case. The Assizes jurors would also hear that Edith Jeal was not the only girl George Henry Wood had approached on the 10th of December.

In addition, there was also the impact of George Henry Wood's previous convictions to consider. Honesty and truthfulness were strongly regarded characteristics in the Victorian era. As a rule, society looked dimly at anyone considered dishonest or involved in criminality, and Prince and Ayres understood that this stance would likely be mirrored by any jury.

If Prince and Ayres were to save George Henry Wood from the gallows, they knew they needed to find a credible defence for his actions beyond simple denials, which they could not substantiate. During their conversations. George Wood Senior had informed the solicitors that his son had experienced ill health during childhood and had suffered some type of seizures. He disclosed that his son had previously travelled to Manitoba and experienced similar symptoms there. They were also aware that there were statements from the police which stated that George Henry Wood had suffered from further fits since his arrest.

Consequently, by early January, with the spring Assizes fast approaching, Prince and Ayres decided to pursue several different defences. Firstly, they would argue that George Henry Wood was intoxicated, which led to the onset of a seizure. Secondly, they would argue that lust from the sexual assault on Edith Jeal further aggravated the seizure. They intended to argue that at the time of the crime, George Henry Wood's seizures led to epileptic mania. This they intended to suggest led to unconsciousness, and insanity which meant he was criminally not culpable for his actions.

Today, epilepsy is understood to be a neurological condition that causes seizures through abnormal brain activity. However, this has not always been the case. Throughout history, doctors did not understand the pathological basis of the condition. They attributed the condition's causes to various nonsensical reasons such as sexual deviancy, demonic possession and witchcraft. It was also widely believed that people with epilepsy were emotionally and intellectually disturbed. They were thought to have harmful personality traits such as irritability, violence, aggression and rage. High-profile criminals such as Jack the Ripper were frequently reported to be sufferers of epilepsy.

These societal misconceptions leaked into broader society, which led to people with epilepsy becoming ostracised. Epileptic sufferers would struggle to obtain work and experience poor living conditions and, in many instances, poverty. The shame and fear associated with epilepsy led to sufferers being away in asylums or forced into workhouses. Experts of the time also linked epilepsy to criminality, while others went further and named epilepsy the primary cause of most crimes.

Today, experts accept that people with epilepsy are no more likely to act aggressively or commit crimes than those without the condition. However, in 1891 these facts were not known, and due to these misconceptions, a defence of epileptic mania was commonly offered and must have appeared to be the perfect defence for George Henry Wood. However, the solicitors understood they would require further evidence to convince a jury that George Henry Wood was not responsible for his actions.

Consequently, Prince and Ayres decided to obtain evidence from a medical expert. As previously alluded, the Wood family was of lowly means and needed more money to employ an expert witness. As a result, Prince and Ayres wrote to the Secretary of State, The Right Honourable Henry Matthews, at Whitehall to request assistance for George Henry Wood.

The letter reads as follows:

'Sir,

Regina V George Henry Wood,

We have been consulted by relatives of the prisoner (a man for some time in the employ of The London & Brighton South Coast Railway Company), who now stands committed for trial on a charge of murder at Brighton, and who will be tried at the next Gaol delivery at the Lewes Assizes. We are informed that the Treasury has taken up the prosecution, and the accused's family now instructs us to appeal to you for professional assistance in the prisoner's defence.

To meet the justice of the case, medical evidence must be forthcoming as also legal assistance for the prisoner, and we shall be obliged if you will inform us to what extent you can assist our clients in the matter. The accused is entirely destitute of means, and unless assistance is afforded him, his case cannot be adequately put before the Judge of Assizes. We are informed that in cases of this nature, it is the custom of the Home Office to assign medical assistance and counsel for persons accused of so great a crime. Several medical men in Brighton could afford the necessary assistance if so instructed. On the question of counsel, it may assist you if you allow us to suggest the names of some members of the Bar practising on the South Eastern Circuit. The father of the accused, although very poor, is a most respectable man, and so far as we can ascertain, nothing is known against any family member.

We are, Sir,

Yours obediently, Prince and Ayres'

Mr Lubbe, Director of Public Prosecutions, was handed the letter on the 8th of January 1892. He was aware that in recent years other individuals accused of murder had been given legal assistance by the Crown. Consequently, he passed the letter to the Treasury for consideration. Prince and Ayres' request was raised at a Home Office meeting on the 8th of January 1892.

      The Secretary of State, Henry Matthews, stated that he had no funds to enable him to comply with Prince and Ayre's application. He also felt that it was unusual for the court to assign counsel to defend a prisoner who would be otherwise without legal assistance. The Under Secretary wrote back to the Director of Public Prosecutions, Edward Leigh Pemberton, on the 11th of January to that effect. The letter reads:

'Sir,

Reg V Geo Henry Wood

With reference to your letter of the 8th of January and enclosure. I think Messrs. Prince and Ayres may, if the Secretary of State sees fit, properly be informed that it is not within his power to provide professional assistance to the accused, but that, if no counsel has been retained for the defence before the Assizes, the judge who tried the case will no doubt assign counsel for the defence, and that they may further be informed as regards the medical evidence referred to in their letter, the nature of which they do not indicate, that if the suggestion is that the defence of insanity may be set up at the trial, the solicitor to the Treasury if he is so informed and is furnished with any facts concerning such defence, he will by the standing directions of the Secretary of State, take steps to have the prisoner duly examined by a medical expert, and will furnish a copy of the medical evidence to the defence. If, however, the medical assistant asked for it is not of this nature. Messrs. Prince and Ayres will let the Secretary of State know what witness or witnesses they desire to consult and call at the trial. He will communicate with the solicitor to the Treasury to give the defence such assistance on this point as may be reasonable.

I am Sir, your obedient servant.
H. Lubbe'

After receiving the affirmative response, Prince and Ayres began searching local directories for a suitable medical expert. First and foremost, the expert they chose would have to support the fact that people with epilepsy were prone to insanity. Secondly, for the jury to accept the testimony, any expert must be broadly experienced and have sufficient qualifications. After scrutinising and canvasing the different candidates, they decided to recruit Doctor Charles Edward Saunders, who met both elements of Prince and Ayres' criteria.

He had initially undertaken a general education at Cheltenham College and went on to study at St. Thomas Hospital. In 1861, he qualified with an M.D. (Hons) at Aberdeen. After graduating, he practised at Cuckfield, Sussex, until acquiring the post of Surgical Registrar at St Thomas', where he had previously studied. A few years later, Doctor Saunders became elected as Medical Officer for Health for the districts of Middlesex and Hereford. Finally, in 1888, he was elected Superintendent Medical Officer at Sussex County Lunatic Asylum at Haywards Heath.

Associates described Doctor Saunders as a man of fine presence with a manner full of tact and charm. He was said to show a *'persona grata'* with his patients and colleagues and was renowned for being upright and courteous. Alongside his education and experience, these jury-pleasing qualities may have also contributed to Prince and Ayres' selection.

In February 1891, Prince and Ayres wrote to Doctor Saunders to ask if he would be willing to examine their client, to which Doctor Saunders replied that he would. In the late 19th century, any person entering a Prison needed permission from the Secretary of State. Consequently, on the 19th of January, Prince and Ayres again wrote to the Home Office to request that he give Doctor Saunders permission to examine George Henry Wood.

It is unclear what happened to the letter, but in any case, it did not arrive at the Home Office. Prince and Ayres waited four weeks, believing the Home Secretary was considering their request. However, having not received a response by the end of February, Prince and Ayres wrote to the Home Office for a third time, urging the Home Secretary to give Doctor Thomas permission to examine their client. Their letter was received and again discussed at a Treasury meeting. The Secretary of State was aware that George Henry Wood was due to be medically examined at the request of the Director of Public Prosecutions by an expert selected by the Crown. However, Henry Matthews acknowledged that the accused also had the right to be assessed by his own expert.

Consequently, he instructed Edward Leigh Pemberton to telegram Prince and Ayres on the 25th of February, stating that their expert could visit George Henry Wood if they were willing to provide a name. With no time to lose, the solicitors responded immediately, naming Doctor Charles Saunders as the defence's medical expert.

On the 29th of February 1892, Prince and Ayres wrote to Doctor Saunders and told him that the Secretary of State had agreed to grant him access to Lewes Gaol. Doctor Saunders contacted Captain Crickett, Governor at Lewes Gaol, to inform him that he would visit George Henry Wood on the 12th and 19th of March 1892. On both days, he arrived early and spent the entire day examining his patient. Afterwards, he compiled a detailed report which he sent to Prince Ayres and the Treasury. His report reads as follows:

'Sussex County Asylum,
Haywards Heath
March 21st 1892

Reg. V: George Henry Wood - Murder
In accordance with the instructions contained in your letter of the 8th of March, I have paid two visits on the 12th and 19th of March to Geo. Henry Wood, a prisoner now awaiting his trial at Lewes Gaol charged with the wilful murder of Edith Jeal on the 10th of December 1891.

The prisoner was calm and collected and gave me an outline of the chief incidents of his life from childhood upwards, omitting, as was perhaps only natural, any allusion to his criminal career, which appears now by his own admission and corroborative evidence, not to have commenced the severe offence with which he stands at present charged. His memory for recent and remote events is good.

His fixity of attention is fair, and there is no evidence of mental derangement at the present moment. At my first interview, I purposely did not refer to the events of the 10th of December. Still, the prisoner volunteered his statement that he knew nothing of what had happened from the time he got off his van on the evening of the 10th of December until the following morning when he awoke with a bad headache, which he attributed to the drunken state in which he had been on the previous afternoon and evening. He, however, got up and went to his work at the usual time.

There is nothing to point to mental disturbance other than caused by intoxication for some considerable time (2 years at least) before the 10th of December. Still, there is abundant evidence to prove that the man, whilst in Canada, had repeated attacks of epilepsy. Granting that the man is an epileptic, his irresponsibility for his committed deed may be strongly affirmed. Epileptics are subject to mental unconsciousness and to explosions of nerve force which they are wholly unable to control.

The frightfully atrocious nature of the injuries inflicted on the prisoner's victim is more in keeping with the blind fury or passion of an epileptic than with the action of a responsible individual, however sensual or brutalised or drunken he might be. Alcohol exerts itself in the most marked of all its baneful effects on the epileptic, and whether the prisoner was drunk on the 10th of December is not disputed.

Doctor Echeverria, late Physician in Chief to the Hospital for Epileptics and Paralytics, New York, states that as a result of his experience, intemperance alone has acted as a cause of alcoholic epilepsy in 30.8% of the cases in which this latter broke out as its immediate consequence and that the most remarkable feature in traumatic patients was that their paroxysms were attended with impulsive explosions of the most dangerous character.

It is alleged that the prisoner had some head injury, but beyond a superficial scar on the vertex of the scalp, there is no evidence of this. This visible scar is attributed to a trivial accident when he was a schoolboy. The prisoner now says that he did not fall from a mast. The absence of any apparent attempt to conceal the body of the child Jeal is evidence of the murderer's disregard for consequences, his inability to control his volition, or his unconsciousness of the act done.

The fact is at variance with the belief that the perpetrator of the act was of a disposing mind. The prisoner's letter to his parents reads like the canting whine of an epileptic. The prisoner's career affords evidence of his criminality on other occasions, and it may be of some value to quote figures showing the relation of epilepsy to crime.

The statistics of the Broadmoor Criminal Lunatic Asylum, as collated by Doctor John Baker (Journal of Mental Science - July 1888), state that of the entire admissions during 23 years, 77% have been epileptics, while of the total number of patients of all classes admitted, charged with murder 11.1% were epileptics. Of the homicidal offences perpetrated by epileptics, the greater numbers have been committed by those between the ages of 25 and 30, showing that those are the periods when epileptics are most dangerous. The following table shows the nature of the crimes of epileptics patients admitted into Broadmoor Asylum during 23 years (1864-1887):

Section A Crimes of Personal Violence	Males	Females	Total
(1) Homicidal Offences			
Murder	36	15	51
Manslaughter	2	1	3
Attempt to murder	29	2	31
Total	67	18	85
(2) Non-homicidal Offences			
Assault with intent to rape	2		2
Attempted suicide	2		2
Total	4		4
Total crimes of personal violence (section A)	71	18	89
Section B - Other crimes			
Larceny	18	5	23
Burglary	6		6
Arson	4		4
Sheep Stealing	2		2

Forgery	2			2	
Placing obstruction on railway	1			1	
Vagrancy	1			1	
Total (section B)		34	5		39
Grand total of all crimes		103	23		128

Rape, it will be seen, is not a common crime among epileptics. However, still, it finds a place in these statistics. Epileptic fits have been known to occur immediately before, during and after coitus. Concerning the absence of symptoms of brain affliction other than the epileptic nervosa, I can only repeat my firm conviction that epileptics frequently act automatically and unconsciously.

No epileptic is safe from such a controllable impulse as may compel him to perform acts of such complexity, whether criminal or otherwise, agreeing with M. Delasiame, who writes (Journal De Médecine Mental'e), 'It is certain that on passing by an epileptic we elbow one might be on occasion, and that epilepsy, through the fancies, more or less delusional, that it originates, furnishes a considerable share of the crimes reported by the daily press and described as mental alienation.' And equally, do I agree with Doctor Echeveria when he says, 'Epileptics cannot be held responsible for any act of violence perpetrated during their unconscious automatism, which they have no power to control or capacity to judge.'

The evidence of the prisoner being an epileptic was so intense I had not thought it necessary to inquire closely about the family history.

I have the honour to be, Sir, your obedient servant.
C. E. Saunders M.D'

As is clear from his report, Doctor Saunders had concluded that George Henry Wood was not responsible for the murder and outrage of Edith Jeal. He quotes various statistics and references scientific sources to cement his position. He goes on to suggest that the sexual assault of the young girl may have contributed to the violent nature of the attack. However, it is shocking that he fails to recognise that 28-Year-old George Henry Wood should not have been sexually abusing such a small child in the first place.

Obviously, there is now a greater awareness and understanding of paedophilia and child sexual exploitation compared to a time when consent could be given at the young age of thirteen. However, even in the Victorian era, abuse of such a small child was considered abhorrent, immoral and unnatural, and it is surprising that Doctor Saunders' does not acknowledge that any sexual act carried out on such a small child was inexcusable.

However, he offers another aggravating factor that appears far more relevant - alcohol. Today it is accepted that alcohol can increase the risk of epileptic seizures in sufferers, and Doctor Saunders' report acknowledges this. However, withdrawal from alcohol after prolonged use can also cause seizures, even in individuals without epileptic conditions.

As previously stated, George Henry Wood had admitted to Doctor Saunders that he had been drinking alcohol for a considerable time. Therefore the fits may have been brought on by alcohol withdrawal rather than epilepsy. Whilst George Henry Wood stated that he had experienced attacks throughout his life, there was no corroborating evidence to support his claims at this stage. It may be that the fits both followed his arrest and were a direct result of alcohol withdrawal.

In any case, Prince and Ayres finally had the expert testimony they would need to defend George Henry Wood. However, they also knew that the prosecution would have George Henry Wood examined by their own experts, who, because they were working for the Crown, would likely form the opposite opinion. The first medical report which contradicted the defence's position came from Richard Turner, Medical Officer at Lewes Prison. His report is as follows:

'In Re: George Henry Wood
Charged with Murder

H. M. Civil Prison Lewes
29th of February 1891
When this prisoner was received here on the 15th of December 1891, he was alleged to have had a fit of some kind in the police Cells at Brighton. He told me that he used to have fits in Canada but had not had one before his apprehension in 1888 and that he did not know what kind of fits they were.

On the 22nd of December 1891, he went on remand to Brighton and had another fit which the police surgeon has recently told me (the 13th of February 1892) was a severe epileptic fit. At his reception on the 15th of December 1891, he was placed in a normal cell and ordered to be watched every half-hour day and night.

He was then perfectly coherent and rational and has never been otherwise here. Nothing occurred until the 3rd of February 1892 when he was found in a fit on his mattress on his face at 7 pm.

He was seen by the Deputy Medical Officer, Mr J Stack, at 7.45 pm. In his judgement, there were no signs of epilepsy, but it was more of the character of syncope with hysteria. As the regulations require, he has been under the care of outside attendants daily and night.

On the 5th of February, he had another attack at 4.20 am, which lasted 10 minutes only and was seen by Duty Warder C Haskell. On the 12th of February 1892, he had another seizure at 7.45 pm and was seen by Warder James Spinks - it again lasted only 10 minutes. On the 26th of February 1892, he had another episode at 5.45 am, which lasted only five minutes and was seen by the Chief Warder, Mr G Farr.

According to Warder G. Brown, sprinkling with cold water on each occasion brought him to. He has had no convulsions, foaming at the mouth, or tongue biting, nor has he been violent as usual in epilepsy. The prison being a mile away from my residence, so the attacks were over before the Deputy Medical Officer or I could arrive.

He has been seen daily by the Medical Officer on duty since he has been here and is always coherent and rational when spoken to. The prisoner says he had been drinking for nearly a week before his apprehension and has a sister who suffers from fits.

I have the honour to be your obedient servant.

Rich Turner
Med. Officer
H.M.C Prison, Lewes'

In addition, the Director of Public Prosecutions had recruited Doctor Edgar Sheppard, Professor of Psychological Medicine at Kings College, as an expert witness. Doctor Sheppard was much older, qualified and experienced than Doctor Saunders. He was born in 1819 in Worcestershire and received a general education locally. He joined the Medical Register of Certified Surgeons in 1846 and became a fellow of the same society in 1859.

He received his M.D. in 1855 at St Andrews, Scotland, and joined the Medical Register of Certified Professors in 1859. Before his employment at King's College, Doctor Sheppard had worked as the Medical Superintendent at Colney Hatch Lunatic Asylum. In 1892 he had been employed at Kings College Hospital, London, for over twenty years.

Alongside his extensive education and experience in psychological illnesses, Doctor Sheppard assessed and treated numerous epileptic patients throughout his career. Due to his status, he was frequently called upon by the Home Office to give his opinion on criminal cases. He was a familiar face in the criminal courts and well-versed in providing evidence. He was well-read in British and Foreign Medical Literature and wrote several notable papers. He was known for having a familiar presence and well-refined taste and manners.

After seeking permission from the Home Office, on the 4th of April, Doctor Shepherd also visited George Henry Wood at Lewes Prison and examined him. Doctor Sheppard, too, wrote a report of his findings which he sent to the Home Office. His statement reads as follows:

'Reg v Geo. Henry Wood
Report from Doctor Edgar Sheppard, M.D, F.R.C.J, M.R.C.P, late Professor of Psychological Medicine in King's College, London and formerly (For 20 years) and Medical Superintendent of Colney Hatch Asylum.

Lewes
April 4th 1892

In compliance with instructions from the Treasury, I have visited the above-named in H.M Prison (Civil) at Lewes, where he stands committed on a charge of murder, at Brighton, on the 10th of December 1891. He is a man of ordinary stature, relatively well-nourished, coherent and collected, answering questions without hesitation.

He is naturally depressed by what is behind him and the severe position immediately in front of him. The prisoner's cranial conformation is unsuitable, and he has a narrow and highly arched palate. There is a slight scar, not of recent origin, on the vertex of the scalp, which he says is occasionally tender.

I have carefully read the depositions in this case, the official reports of the Medical Superintendent of the County Asylum and the Prison Surgeon, and various documents bearing on the prisoner's antecedents in health and disease. The case is interesting in its psychology and not free from any complications.

It seems to me to be well established that the prisoner has suffered from some form of epilepsy in Canada, and his general life aggravated rather than subdued this distressing malady. Be that as it may, it appears that having returned to this country, he has of late been doing duty in the service of the Brighton Railway Company satisfactorily.

There is no evidence of a recurrence of epilepsy for more than two years or of any strangeness of conduct to attract the observation of others, and this probably is because he has abstained from drinking. Alcoholic intemperance now and again (as so often) assaults the citadel of this confessedly neurotic subject and conditions to frightful crimes.

The question presents itself to me: are these crimes due to the uncontrollable impulse of an irresponsible epileptic? Or are they the result of an undue indulgence in alcohol by those who have often experienced its power for evil and were prevented by disease from estimating and considering it?

I subscribe to the latter of these two positions. I believe that the prisoner did not know what he was doing when he committed these criminal acts - not because he was insane but because he was intoxicated. And indeed, he is not insane at the present time. It may be conceded that alcohol does act with peculiar force upon epileptics and gives their aggressive acts a savage ferocity which at once suggests insanity.

It may also be conceded that those who suffer from instability of nerve elements and, notably, epileptics are more or less handicapped in the struggle of life. But such persons are often highly intelligent, capable of active duties, and filling responsible positions.

I think I should also state that it is quite what might be expected that after a debauch and an act of lust, the prisoner should have a recurrence of epilepsy even after its long remission. Still, from what I gather at Lewes Gaol from four trained warders who are familiar with epileptic convulsions and who have severally observed the prison when down with fits, I am bound to add that these seizures were of a passive and ephemeral character and had none of the explosive characteristics which go to make up the homicidal violence of epileptics.

Edgar Sheppard'

The report shows that Doctor Sheppard agreed with Richard Turner's assessment of George Henry Wood's state of mind. Although he accepted that George Henry Wood had likely suffered from epilepsy in previous years, Doctor Sheppard concluded that this was not why he murdered Edith Jeal. Instead, he cited alcohol abuse as the cause and suggested his actions could have been avoided through temperance.

Shortly after it was written, a copy of the report was sent to Prince and Ayres at Middle Street, who must have been disheartened by its contents. They understood that the upper classes, from which the jury would be selected, looked dimly upon alcohol abuse, particularly when it related to individuals in the lower classes.

They must have recognised that these comments would further reduce the likelihood of any sympathy towards their client, who, at the Court of Assize, was to be classified as a drunken child murderer. Nonetheless, the Assizes were fast approaching, and the pair continued to work on their client's defence.

Chapter 16: A *'Painfull'* Experience.

Having received George Henry Wood's medical reports, Prince and Ayres turned their attention to other aspects of the defence's case. Since his son's arrest, George Wood Senior had repeatedly met with the solicitors and was questioned about his son's history. Having extensively studied Doctor Sheppard's report, Prince and Ayres had become aware that George Henry Wood had previously travelled to Manitoba. The medical reports also reference the Manitoba Penitentiary, which was of concern.

Consequently, Prince and Ayres questioned the weary father about the circumstances of his son's travels and troubles. George Wood Senior explained that he had reached his limit after his son's last conviction at Brighton. He explained that he had decided to no longer tolerate his son's humiliating behaviour. He explained that his son could not hold down a job and had damaged his family's reputation at this time. George Wood Senior explained that he had been at a loss for how to remedy the situation and looked for a permanent solution.

During the 1880s, the Canadian Government heavily promoted migration to its country's North West. As part of their campaign, glossy advertisements championing the scheme were placed in British post offices, train stations and official buildings. These detailed the benefits for people willing to move, including assisted passage and free land grants. Those unsuited to labouring were promised employment, good pay and a higher quality of life.

After learning of this opportunity, George Wood Senior said he had decided that his son should travel to Canada. He explained that at the time, he believed that the move would give George Henry Wood a fresh start and an opportunity to rehabilitate his character. It also meant that the family would avoid further embarrassment. Initially, George Henry Wood resisted the idea but eventually agreed.

It was not uncommon for fathers from the upper classes to send their troublesome sons abroad. These remittance men, who were usually drunken, dissolute or prone to criminality, would be sent regular payments by their wealthy families for as long as they stayed away. George Wood Senior could not provide his son with this level of support. He explained to Prince and Ayres that he did, however, agree to fund the travelling expenses; and offered a small amount of money to tide George Henry Wood over.

Consequently, George Henry Wood booked a steerage class ticket with the Allan Line. This nautical service operated a fleet of transatlantic steamships that sailed from Liverpool to Dublin, Nova Scotia and Manitoba, where George Henry Wood had decided to settle. On the 11th of April 1882, George Henry Wood went from Brighton to Liverpool by train and walked the short distance to the docks. He stayed at a lodging house while waiting for the 3983-ton Polynesian Ship to arrive.

The following morning, George Henry Wood boarded the vessel with optimism. However, he needed to prepare for the abysmal conditions he would endure for the next ten days. Whilst there is no account of George Henry Wood's journey, various high-profile national newspapers, including The Times, published reports about the awful conditions steerage passengers suffered.

The living quarters were riddled with rats, fleas and other parasitic lice. The provided diet consisted of gruel that tasted sour and watery stews made from often mouldy leftovers. The provided coffee and tea were impossible to drink, and water was extraordinarily scarce. Steerage officers harshly berated passengers if they complained or requested additional supplies.

Ventilation in the bowels of the ships was also insufficient and led to an uncomfortably warm and oppressive environment. Due to the unsanitary conditions, many migrants would develop illnesses during the journey and would often be denied medical treatment. It was not uncommon for migrants from the lower classes to perish during these journeys.

Yet despite the harsh conditions of his voyage, George Henry Wood arrived safely in the Port of Manitoba. After reaching dry land, George Henry Wood wrote to his parents to inform them that he had come to his destination. George Wood Senior recalled to Prince and Ayres that when he received his son's letter, he felt a sense of relief and optimism that his son would finally make a success of himself. However, life in Manitoba was far from what the positive advertisements had suggested.

The Government pamphlets were frequently criticised for containing *'gross misrepresentations'*. Although the Canadian Government provided immigrants with land grants as promised, the size and location of the land differed from what was promised/ Furthermore, many immigrants needed more funds to buy the necessary farming equipment, and the land would often remain unworked and uninhabited. These impoverished migrants would be forced to move to the nearest town and, to survive, would have to undertake labouring jobs which paid significantly less than similar jobs back in England.

Life for migrants was extremely tough. They were forced to reside in shanty houses scattered across the prairie land. A few of these dwellings were built from logs or wooden boards. However, most were constructed from layers of sod which made up the walls and roof. Two uncovered holes allowed for a window and door. The interiors of these primitive residences were also basic and, due to their remoteness, contained little homely comforts. Most only included a homemade table, a grid-iron bed, a stove and a few boxes or kegs for chairs.

When it rained, dirty water streamed through the sods, adding further discomfort for the occupants. The weather was also challenging. Winters saw temperatures as low as minus 38 degrees Celsius. Violent and heavy blizzards were common in winter and could lay up to ten feet of snow. Anyone forced to go out in these conditions often suffered from frostbite on their extremities.

The difficulties faced by Manitoba's migrants were detailed in the New York Herald in 1889 but were later reproduced in the Pall Mall Gazette. The article is titled *'Long Letters from Manitoba'*, criticising the Canadian Government. The report reads as follows:

'Long letters from Manitoba have appeared recently in the New York Herald, complaining in strong terms of the neglect of the Canadian Government to fulfil its promises to migrants. Instead of a well-surveyed road being found 150 miles westward from Winnipeg, the prairie was in such a condition that only 100 miles were accomplished in a fortnight due to the heavy rains. Unloading wagons and doubling teams was an everyday incident of the march.

On arriving in the district where free homesteads of 160 acres had been promised, it was found that, under one excuse or another, nearly all the workable land was already disposed of. The discovery settled the matter for a member of the party, who immediately left for Dakota or Minnesota.

The writer of one of the letters referred to resolved to try his luck further and got as far as the little Saskatchewan district. Here he found that his promised grant of 160 acres was reduced to 80. Instead, moreover, of the offer of the pre-emption of 160 acres more at a dollar an acre being adhered to, an offer was made of the pre-emption of 80 acres at 60 dollars if within five miles of the proposed Pacific railway of the same quantity at a dollar an acre at a hundred miles distance from the line.

The pleasing succession of seasons promised in the official handbook is reported to be a myth. The winter comes on in October and never relaxes its hold until May. The snow is then lying 6 to 10 feet deep, and as Manitoba is all one dead level, there is no proper drainage. The water is absorbed into the earth or remains in pools until the sun dries it up.

Red River fever, a species of violent dysentery, prevails in consequence. Another writer asserts that nothing can improve the country regarding drainage, but the deepening of the Assiniboine and Nelson River beds. Were this done, Manitoba would become a dry land with a deep black loam soil resting on lacustrine clay.'

Without sufficient resources or the required work ethic, George Henry Wood quickly concluded that prairie farming was not for him, and made his way towards Winnipeg, the nearest town.

Back at number 12 Middle Street, George Wood Senior recalled that the trip did not have the required effect on his son. When asked to elaborate, he finally disclosed that his wayward child had spent nearly four years at the Manitoba Penitentiary following a conviction for horse stealing. George Wood Senior also explained that his son had experienced epileptic seizures while incarcerated.

Knowing that the prosecution would also know these facts, Prince and Ayres knew they needed to have the full particulars of their client's conviction. Consequently, they wrote to Lewes Prison on the 13th of January 1892, asking George Henry Wood to provide a statement about his time in Canada. On the same day, he replied. His illiterate account reads as follows:

'From G. H. Wood H.M Prison, Lewes
Thursday the 14th of January 1892

Dear Sir,
I received your letter this morning (Thursday), but the work you have asked me to do will be a very painfull (Sic.) task for me, but I will try and think of everything that I did from when I left Brighton until I returned. I have had to put up with a very hard life during these eight long years I was away. It will all be for the best, perhaps. My first situation was with Captain Munroe, Winnipeg. Father has the address. I believe it was Vaughan Street, Winnipeg. I was the driver of a pair of horses all the first summer, and then I went to Portage la Prairie and was hired by Mr Rulan and Rogers to work on the Railroad on the Beautiful Plains, close to Neepawa. It was there I had the first fitt (sic). It was the month of January. It was too cold to work much that day, so all the men went on the drink, me being a teetotaller and not drink with

them. 3 or 4 being the worst for liquor, got hold of and nearly strangled me, job my head on some bricks face downwards broke to (sic) front teeth out. This is what caused the first fitt (sic). A man by the name of Madge Buckwell was a Foreman. Some of the workers that were with me were sent to Neepawa for a doctor. He called to see me and staid (sic) all night with me. The men paid the Doctor 5 dollars, which is one pound of our money because I was not able to at the time. I had three fitts (sic) following one another, and the last fitt (sic) lasted 18 hours. It was two weeks before I was able to resume my work by riting (sic) to Rulan and Rogers. You might find this Buckwell, but I don't know whether you will find him or not being out on the railroad them days we used to carry all our kitt (sic.) with us. We had no homes, only tents to call homes those days while working for the same party on porch creek haymaking for the horses (the company used to make their own hay save buying). One night there was a dreadful prairie fire about twenty miles away from where we were camped. It was travelling at the rate of 45 miles per hour, and we were close beside a creek and the bottom wase (sic) very soft. We had no other way of escape, only by crossing this creek as the fire had burnt the bridge that crossed the creek. We got across and pitched our tents, and then it came onto rain until we thought it was never going to leave off thundered and lightened. You could pick up in the grass when it lightened during the night, it lightened so bad that one of the men that were in the tent was killed with lightning the other man and I were struck that bad that we could not speak to each other or move or do anything. After this, I went to work cutting down loggs (sic) for a man named Mr McActy on the Lake of the Woods all winter and in the spring. I went to work with James Ritchie Post Office Gladstone (farmer). I could not get at the end of my time the amount of wages that was promised to me. I got engaged and almost mad caused me to steal a man's horse and bolt with it. The consequence was I was arrested and taken to Portage la Prairie there to await my trial. Here was another place I had fitts (sic). I forget the Doctor's name they called in to see me, but by riting (sic) to Mr Moss Jailer Portage la Prairie, you will find out all about me. I was sentenced to three years and ten months to serve my time at the Manitoba Penitentiary. It was here where I had fitts (sic) every now and again. The warder's name was Colonel Bedson, Deputy Mr McDonald. During my time there, my number was 15. Mr Sutherland was the Doctor, and Mr Burke was a dispensary man. When I served my time, my friends sent me enough money to come home. I had only been home about three weeks when I got to work in London at the Gas house during the strike. Whilst there, I twisted a varicose vein on the skin of my left leg, which caused me to leave the gass (sic) house. Father has got the name of the Doctor that operated on me at Kings College Hospital, and then I got work as a porter at the Brighton Goods Department. The Doctor would not pass me because of the veins in my leg and the Governor, liking my way of working and the good

character I was when I got the situation, did not want me to leave and said at the time he would like two or three such as me men what knew how to work so he sent me to London to pass the Doctor the second time and this time, through a letter from the Governor to the Doctor at King's College Hospital. Doctor Ross was on his holiday at the time, but the Doctor that took his place during his absence is the one that operated on me and ever since the operation, I have never been thoroughly right in the head ever since. Doctor Ross is the Company Doctor. I have not sent you the name of the Doctor in Neepawa because I never knew him and the names of the others and their addresses. I could not tell you because men like me had no place to call our homes, only tents or empty logg (sic) houses should happen to come across any. I can't go any further than this because the country being so wild and the towns so few and far between are very likely the men that were with me then building a railway over three thousands of miles. I think this is as correct as I can get it. I must close and remain your humble servant.
Geo. Henry Wood.'

George Henry Wood's statement is both implausible and unconvincing. It gives an insight into George Henry Wood's egotistical personality and self-pitying tendencies. Nonetheless, after receiving and reviewing the report, Mr Ayres wrote to Manitoban authorities to ask for confirmation of George Henry Wood's convictions. With George Henry Wood's ill health still in mind, they also wanted to verify that he had suffered from fits whilst imprisoned.

In February 1892, Prince and Ayres began receiving responses from Manitoba. Although some of the replies contained helpful information, some only added to the challenges of the case. This must have been the turning point if Prince and Ayres doubted George Henry Wood's dishonesty and propensity for lying. The letters stated that he had, in fact, been imprisoned on three separate occasions - a fact he had failed to mention. These convictions occurred in 1883, 1885 and 1886. The solicitors' first response was from Doctor William Sutherland, a Surgeon at Manitoba Penitentiary. His letter reads as follows:

'The 12th of February 1892

Sir,
George Henry Wood confined here as convict No: 15 during 1887, 1888 and 1889, was repeatedly under my care at the Penitentiary. He suffered from repeated attacks of epilepsy. Some are more severe than others when admitting him to the hospital would become

necessary. The total number of days spent in the hospital during his imprisonment was nine. He was convalescent and unfit for duty for 84 days.

If my case notes are correct, this is a history of injury to the skull from a fall to the deck from a ship's mast. This can, however, be easily verified by personal examination.

Yours faithfully,
Mr W. R. D Sutherland. M. D. Surgeon'

As they read Doctor Sutherland's response, Prince and Ayres must have felt some relief. The Doctor had not only confirmed that George Henry Wood had suffered epileptic fits, which were so severe they had required hospital treatment, which supported the solicitor's line of defence. On the 13th of February, they received a second response from the Manitoba Penitentiary. The letter reads as follows:

'*Manitoba Penitentiary,*
Stony Mountain
February 13th 1892

Gentleman,
Your letter addressed to Col. Bedson, late Warden of this Penitentiary, was handed to me two days ago. Col. Bedson died last July, and your letter was delivered to his widow, which accounts for the delay in these particulars reaching you. George Henry Wood, a native of Brighton, was sentenced to this Penitentiary on the 23rd of August 1886, at Portage la Prairie, Manitoba, to a term of three years and ten months for horse stealing. He was discharged on the 4th of November 1889, going directly to England. His father had assisted in his passage home. Whilst here, he was well-behaved and received all the remission of time possible for him to obtain. He was subject to fits, as testified in an enclosed letter from the Surgeon of the Penitentiary. Wood had an injury to his skull, which he stated resulted from a fall from a ship's mast. I have requested that the Revd. Mr Goulding, Protestant Chaplain, write to you. I would be extremely obliged to you for the particulars of this man's case and the trial result. Trusting that this may reach you in time to be of use.

I have the honour to be Sir, your obedient servant
Geo. P. Foster (Warder).'

The third response arrived on the 17th of February from William Moss, the chief Gaoler at the Central Judicial District Gaol at Portage la Prairie. His letter reads as follows:

'Dear Sirs,

Re: George Henry Wood,
I may say I had Wood under my charge on three different occasions. On the 29th of December, 1883, he was sentenced to one week. On the 6th of August, 1885, he was sentenced to three months, and on the 28th of August, 1886, he was sentenced to three years and ten months at Penitentiary Stony Mountain. I consider him a character not responsible for his actions and should certainly not be out of some place of keeping. He had fitted on two different occasions while here, once in the courtroom whilst receiving his trial, and the case had to be adjourned for one week before the prisoner(Wood)could appear again, and after that, he had an awful fit in the Gaol. The Doctor who attended to him died only a few weeks ago. I don't fancy I can give any information that would influence his trial or strengthen your defence.

Yours truly,
William Moss
Gaoler C.J.G.'

William Moss' and George Foster's letters also corroborated that George Henry Wood suffered from several fits whilst he was imprisoned. Both letters recall that some of these episodes were severe in nature. Furthermore, William Moss suggests that George Henry Wood lacked intelligence and character and even went as far as to suggest that he should not be held responsible for his actions.

    As they read the responses, Prince and Ayres must have felt some relief and believed they were progressing in the case. Whilst they had agreed to present insanity as a defence, they had feared that they lacked sufficient evidence to fully convince a jury of these claims. However, the letters from Canada supported their defence, which led to optimism.

    The fourth response arrived on the 17th of February from Mr Burke, Hospital Overseer and School Master at Manitoba Penitentiary. His letter reads as follows:

'Gentlemen,

I am honoured to acknowledge the receipt of your letter requesting information regarding George. H. Wood, ex-convict no 15 and especially about whether he was subject to epileptic fits while in our prison. In reply, I beg to say that I have seen a copy of a letter by our Surgeon, Doctor W.R. Sutherland, of, I think, the 12th inst. Bearing on this matter, and as I presume his letter was forwarded to you, I have nothing important to add to what the Surgeon has stated. The man, Wood, was subject to epileptic fits. There were periods in which those fits were of daily occurrence, and he found it necessary to assign employment at which no danger could arise from his falling down.

I have the honour of being your humble servant.

D.D Burke.'

The final letter received from Canada by Prince and Ayres arrived on the 17th of February. This letter's author was Mr Aneas McDonnell, Chief Keeper at Manitoba Penitentiary. His letter reads as follows:

'Gentlemen,

I received yours dated the 2nd of February inst. (re Wood) yesterday. I remember you're Client Wood, ex No 15, very well. It is quite correct that he served a term here in this Penitentiary and had several fits 'epileptic' to my knowledge, but I cannot say positively how many he had. The Doctor's address is W.R.D Sutherland, Surgeon, Manitoba Penitentiary, and Stony Mountain, Canada. At that time, he was not a resident physician but regularly visited the institution. I have just learned that you had written to the latter Warden (Mr Bedson), the letter falling into the hands of the Revd. Mr Goulding, Protestant Chaplain to the Penitentiary. I believe that he has answered it. If necessary, I can substantiate in court as to the fits.

Yours Obediently,
A. D. O McDonnell.'

As mentioned, Prince and Ayres must have felt that the letters were highly beneficial to their client. They had multiple written statements confirming that George Henry Wood had suffered from fits for an extended period. Mr McDowell had also offered to testify in person at the court of Assizes in George Henry Wood's defence. However, their optimism could not have lasted very long. After discussing their progress with George Wood Senior, their hopes were utterly dashed. It became apparent that the lowly bootmaker could not subsidise Mr McDowell's travelling expenses. The hearsay nature of the letters meant that any judge would object to them being read in court. Much to their disappointment, Prince and Ayres resigned to the fact that they would have to proceed without the Canadian witnesses.

The left image shows one of the Broadside Ballad pamphlets, many of which were printed to commemorate George Henry Wood's execution at Lewes. The record is held at the East Sussex Record Office, Brighton. (Author's own image.)

The right image shows the entrance archway to Bedford Buildings. The archway was set into the Stag Inn and led directly onto a cobbled lane, which was lined with slum tenement as shown.

The image above shows the Bedford Building tenements shortly before they were demolished as part of Brighton's slum clearances. Image supplied courtesy of the James Gray Collection.

The image above shows artist's impression frontage of the Lewes House of Correction. The image shows the main entrance and Governor's (left) and Chaplains (right) residences. The record is held at the East Sussex Record Office. (Author's own image.)

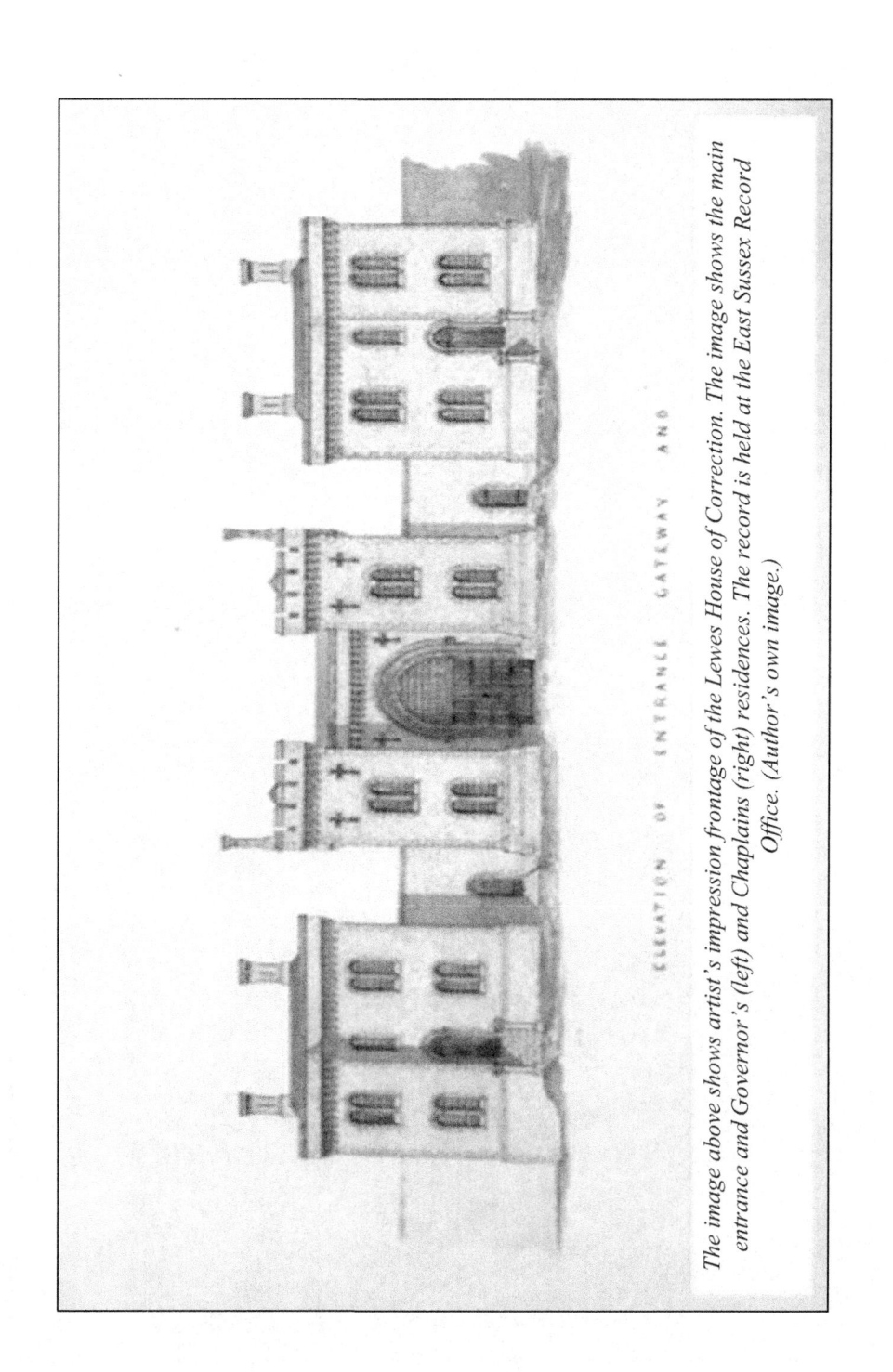

The image above shows an artist's depiction of the scene outside Brighton police court on the 19th of December 1891, as George Henry Wood made his way from the police cells to the 'Black Maria', and the police struggled to protect him from a public lynching. Image supplied courtesy of the British Library.

The image above shows artist's impression of the Manitoba Penitentiary as it appeared in 1887. Image supplied courtesy of the Manitoba Archives.

The above image shows the entrance to the original Brighton Borough Police Station at the north eastern corner of the town hall. Image supplied courtesy of the James Gray Collection.

The above image shows Rock Street, Kemp Town. The Rock Inn is clearly visible in the image. Number 11, the home of the Wood family is straight opposite the rear of the bus. Image supplied courtesy of the James Gray Collection.

The image to the above shows Manchester Row before it was demolished during the slum clearances. The dead wall that George Henry Wood was seen to be leaning against is visible on the right of the image. Image supplied courtesy of the James Gray Collection.

The left image shows an artist's impression of George Henry Wood during his appearance at the Brighton Police Court, on the 19th of December 1891. Image supplied courtesy of the British Library.

The right image shows Reverend Arthur William Goulding, Chaplain of the Manitoba Penitentiary. Image supplied courtesy of the Manitoba Archives.

The image above shows the ventilation grates and restraints within cell number 1 at the Brighton town hall police cells. This is likely the cell that George Henry Wood was placed into after his arrest. (Authors own collection.)

The image on the left shows the cells underneath Brighton's Town Hall. The complex can still be visited and is known as the Old Police Cells Museum. (Author's own collection.)

The above image shows All Souls School, where Edith and Bertram Jeal attended. The school is situated in Essex Street. The building survives today, although it has been many years since it was used for educational purposes. Image supplied courtesy of the James Gray Collection.

The image above shows the head offices of the Sussex Dairy Company at the corner of Montague Place and St Georges Road, Kemp Town. This was Edward Jeal's employer in 1891. A number of milkmen can be seen in the image, although they are not named in the record. Image supplied courtesy of the James Gray Collection.

The image above shows an image taken from the front page of the Illustrated Police News on Saturday the 19th of December 1891. Image supplied courtesy of the British Library.

The above image shows an aerial view of the Eastern quarter of Kemp Town. The central area consists of Sussex Square and Lewes Crescent. Image supplied courtesy of the James Gray Collection.

The image above shows Arlington School's playing field, where Edith lost her life. The access gate was located in the far left corner. The barn was located midway along the boundary on the left of the image. Image supplied courtesy of the James Gray Collection.

The above image shows the chapel at the Extra Mural Cemetery, Brighton, where Edith's sorrowful funeral was held. (Author's own collection.)

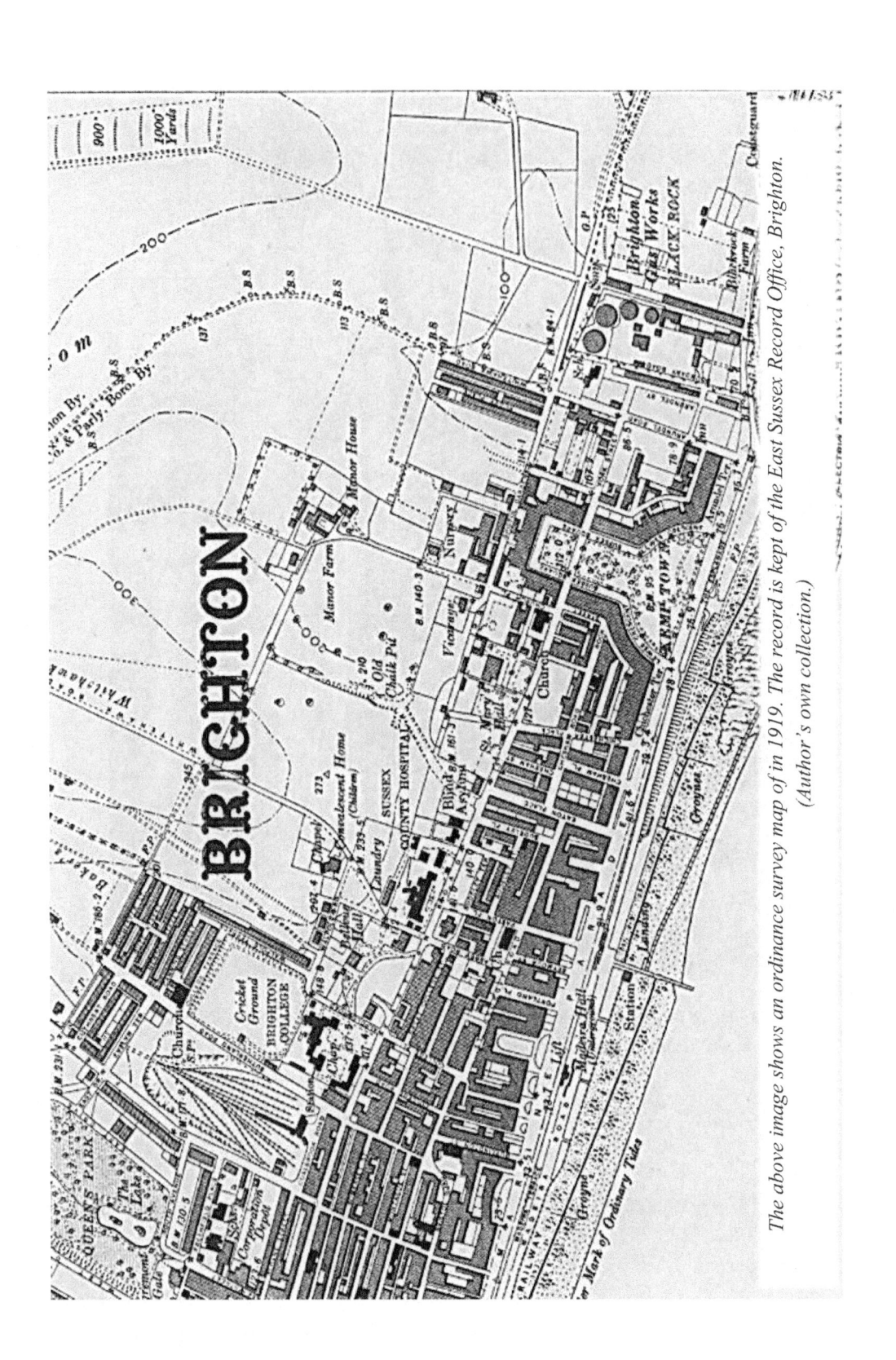

The above image shows an ordinance survey map of in 1919. The record is kept of the East Sussex Record Office, Brighton. (Author's own collection.)

The above image shows the Arlington School playing field's North West boundary wall. The upper section of Chichester {Place can be seen to the right. Image supplied courtesy of the James Gray Collection.

The above image shows St Matthews Church, Sutherland Road, Kemp Town, where the entire Jeal Family used to worship. Also known as the Tin Chapel, many residents from the slum areas of Kemp Town used to attend mass here. In 1891, the church was managed by Reverend McCormick, who was tasked with delivering Edith's Funeral. Image supplied courtesy of the James Gray Collection.

Chapter 17: *'A Half-Witted Imbecile'*

As Prince and Ayres continued to liaise with their client, they learned that he obtained employment as a horse driver very quickly after George Henry Wood arrived in Manitoba. Despite this, George Henry Wood quickly fell into criminality and appeared before the courts during his first year. The criminal case file for this conviction has not survived, and the case does not appear in local newspaper reports.

Therefore, the exact nature of the conviction remains a mystery. It is, however, apparent that George Henry Wood was only imprisoned for seven days. The light nature of the sentence suggests that George Henry Wood had committed a petty crime such as theft, letter opening or cattle stealing. The letters from Canada also confirm that he served his sentence at the ominous Vaughan Street Gaol, otherwise known as the Eastern Provincial Gaol.

The oppressive institution was built in 1881 and housed men, women and children, and its exercise yard was used for public executions. George Henry Wood was likely housed in the east wing, which contained less severe offenders at the time. After his release, it appears that George Henry Wood lived a transient lifestyle, moving around the outer districts of Winnipeg, such as Portage la Prairie, Neepawa and Gladstone.

By May of 1885, he obtained work as a farm labourer at the homestead of James Pool in Glendale, Manitoba. In addition to paying his wages, James Pool offered room and board. George Henry Wood was welcomed into the house and permitted to join the family at the dinner table. As time passed, the family appeared to have increasingly trusted the outwardly naive young labourer and paid less supervision to his activities.

Also residing at the homestead was James Pool's niece, Louisa Jane Fulton, who had turned six the previous May. Since she arrived, George Henry Wood found himself with increasing access to the vulnerable little girl. Within a few days, he started grooming her, and when the opportunity presented itself, he sexually abused her on multiple occasions. Despite the fear and shame, she must have felt, Louisa Fulton bravely told her horrified aunt, Rebecca, who immediately told her husband, James Pool.

On the twenty-seventh day of July 1885, James and Rebecca Pool visited Marmaduke Fieldhouse, a Justice of the Peace for the Province of Manitoba. They informed him of Louisa Fulton's disclosure. The Judge told the pair that they could not lay charges themselves and would need to send for Louisa's mother, Charlotte Fulton. In the intervening time, the Judge advised the pair not to alert George Henry Wood to Louisa's disclosures if he fled the area.

James Pool sent a telegram to Charlotte Fulton asking that she visit urgently. On the same day, Charlotte Fulton made the journey to Neepawa, and shortly after she arrived, she was informed about her daughter's abuse. James Pool returned to Mr Fieldhouse with Charlotte and Louisa Fulton in tow. After questioning Louisa, the Judge was satisfied that she was telling the truth and issued a warrant for George Henry Wood's arrest.

Later that day, George Henry Wood was arrested by the Canadian Mounted Police at the Pool residence. When questioned, he declared he was innocent and stated that James Pool had made the accusations because he owed him wages. Nonetheless, George Henry Wood was taken back to the Vaughan Street Gaol to await his trial scheduled for the following day. George Henry Wood retained Mr Robertson, Portage la Prairie, to defend the case.

On the 10th of August 1885, at the Central Judicial Criminal Court, George Henry Wood appeared faced with *'unlawfully and feloniously attempting to carnally know and abuse Louisa Fulton, a child under ten years old.'* The Justices of the Peace, Marmaduke Fieldhouse and James Hamilton, presided over the committal hearing to determine whether there was sufficient evidence to send the accused to the Court of the Queen's Bench.

The first witness to be called was Louisa Jane Fulton. The Magistrates asked the small child several questions to ensure she understood the difference between telling the truth and lying. Having satisfied the Judges, Louisa Fulton took the oath of affirmation. The heartbreaking statement she gave to the court is as follows:

'I am stopping with my uncle James Pool. I am six years old. I know the prisoner. He is called George Henry Wood. The prisoner came to my bed upstairs. He put his finger between my legs, unbuttoned his pants, and tried to put his tool into me. He came upstairs to my bed three times, repeated what he did first, and then offered to get me candies if I would not tell anyone what he did. When Ellen Pool was out milking at night, George Wood came to my bed. George Wood came when I was outside the stable where the hogs had been, and he did the same thing

to me there that he did before upstairs. The next place he attempted to abuse me was when I was out watching the oxen, and the prisoner brought out a dipper for me to pick berries, and he did the same to me in the berry field. He again did the same thing to me in another field. I think it was the next day. He did the same thing one day in the house. I was in the house minding the baby, and the prisoner came in with a plate of berries. He has not molested me since I told my aunt. When George Henry Wood abused me, he hurt me, but I did not cry. He did not say he would do anything to me if I told on him.'

Louisa's testimony is horrifying, heart-breaking and shows George Henry Wood's paedophilic tendencies. During the few weeks he was staying at the Pool family home, he repeatedly abused Louisa Jane Fulton in the most heinous and manipulative way. He carefully watched and waited for her to be unsupervised by her aunt and uncle so that he could meet his perverted needs. He stalked her into the surrounding fields and used simple rewards such as berries and sweets to coerce her into not telling.

These facts would have benefitted the prosecution in Edith Jeal's murder had they taken the time to obtain the case file. However, they did not request any details relating to George Henry Wood's second Canadian conviction, and therefore the details were never put before the court.

In any case, the next witness to be called was Ellen Pool. She was the younger sister of James Pool and had also been staying at the Pool residence for some time. She shared an upstairs bedroom with Louisa Jane Fulton. George Henry Wood also stored his belongings in this room, which conveniently gave him reason to enter the room as he wished. Ellen Pool's brief statement reads as follows:

'I know the prisoner George Wood. He is working at my brother's James Pool. I am living with my brother and going to school. I saw the prisoner come downstairs from where Louisa Jane Fulton slept.'

The final witness to be called was James Pool. After taking the oath, he said, *'I am James Pool of Glendale, Farmer. I know the prisoner George Wood. He came into my employ on the twenty-second day of June 1885. Louisa Jane Fulton lives with me. She is the niece of my wife. Louisa told my wife that George Wood abused her, and then she told me the same. She told me about the matter on or around the twenty-eighth day of July 1885. On the 27th or 28th, the prisoner took a dipper to a field where Louisa was. This was before Louisa told me of the* matter. The evidence Louisa gave to the court today was substantially the same as made to me when she told me of the matter. I had no suspicion of anything until Louisa told me.'

Having heard the evidence, Hamilton Marmaduke addressed George Henry Wood. He re-read the charges to the accused and then said, *'Having heard the evidence, do you wish to say anything in answer to the charge? You are not obliged to say anything unless you desire to, but whatever you say will be taken down in writing and may be given in evidence against you at your trial.'*

Unlike his response at the Brighton police court in 1891, George Henry Wood made a lengthy response to the charge. His statement reads as follows:

'The first time Louisa Jane Fulton says I was upstairs with her, I went up to my trunk to get some writing paper. There was none there (in the house), and I got asked by Jas Pool. I thought the little girl was asleep. She raised her head as I was looking in my trunk. I sat down on the side of the bed and pulled the sheet from over her head. I placed my hand on the outside of the bedclothes, not knowing that I hurt her, as she stated. That was the only time I was upstairs. The next time I was hass-sowing in the field. I left my vest out in the field the day before. At noon, James Pool told me I was to finish the Hass-sowing and go ploughing. He told me to take the oxen out to hitch onto the plough to keep the weeds under. I took the little girl up to where the berries were because I had to go that way to get my vest. I did not ill-treat nor do anything wrong to her. I went out with her the day she went out around the oxen. I told her if she went out while I had a smoke, I would bring the dipper out for her to pick berries sown where my plough was and went right on with my work leaving her picking berries. What she said was done at the stable I know nothing about. I turned twenty-three last November. I came to this Country in 1880. I had a good character written for me when I left. The character will be found at Mr Jameson, 372 Main Street, Winnipeg, and Lawyer. The lady's name was Mrs Chamberlain, 17 Lewes Crescent, Brighton, England, and Mr Wilson, who I think was once Mayor of Brighton, 11 Chichester Terrace, England. My mother and father are home in England, George Wood shoe manufacturer - 11 Rock Street, Brighton.'

George Henry Wood's statement marked the end of the short trial's evidence. After reading the court clerk's notes aloud, Mr Fieldhouse proclaimed, *'After consideration of the evidence, it has been determined to send the prisoner to stand his trial at the next court of competent jurisdiction at Portage la Prairie in the central Judicial District. A warrant of commitment will be made out.'*

As dictated by the Speedy Trials Act, Mr Hamilton asked George Henry Wood whether he would like the trial's verdict to be decided by a judge or jury. George Henry Wood was aware that he would be remanded until his trial and therefore chose the quickest option: to have his case heard by a Judge. However, the prosecution's case was not ready to proceed, so Mr Fieldhouse adjourned until the following day. The Judge issued a warrant of commitment, and immediately after, George Henry Wood was removed from the court and transported back to the Vaughan Street Gaol.

George Henry Wood's Court appearance was featured in several local newspapers. One such report appeared in the *Minnedosa Tribune*, on the 14th of August 1885, just before his second appearance at the Court of the Queen's Bench. The short article explains how spectators perceived George Henry Wood at the committal hearing. The article reads as follows:

'A half-witted ignoramus named Woods committed an indecent assault upon a little seven-year-old girl of Mrs George Fulton's on Monday last. Information was laid the day before yesterday, and the scamp was brought before M. H. Fieldhouse the day before yesterday. J. P. and, after a preliminary examination, was committed to taking his trial at the Assizes Neepawa Canadian.'

On the fourteenth day of July, George Henry Wood appeared before Judge Ryan at the Court of the Queen's Bench, Portage la Prairie. After opening the proceedings and reading the formal charges, Judge Ryan called the witnesses for the prosecution. The first witness to be called was Louisa Fulton's mother, Charlotte Jane Fulton.

She said, *'I am the mother of Louisa Jane Fulton. She was six years old last May. She was living with my brother in laws, Jas Pool, about 3 miles from Deputy P.O. I do not know the County or the number of the lot. I have been living in Portage la Prairie since the charge against the prisoner. I have previously instructed Louisa Jane Fulton on the nature of an oath or affirmation. She knows well evil and the punishment consequences of telling lies. I got a telegram from Jas Pool to go up on Monday, the twenty-seventh day of July. James Pool is married to my sister. I have not got the telegram with me. Due to the telegram, I got up to Neepawa the same day. I spoke to the child about the trouble. I did not tell her she had been naughty. The prisoner had been at Pool's house for about a month. Pool did not tell me that he* owed the prisoner wages. I did not speak to the prisoners about the matter. I thought it best to take legal action. I did not think it extraordinary that Jas Pool had done nothing. They did not know until shortly before I went up. They told me they sent me word as soon as they could. I did not blame them for allowing the prisoner to remain in the house. After the charge, my sister told me she did not allow the child out of sight. I did not think it proper that anyone should speak to the prisoners about the charge. I did think it proper to instruct the child about an oath of affirmation. Before I instructed her, she knew good from bad. Sometimes, but not often, I have known her to tell untruths, but when I questioned her closely, she always told the truth as far as I could learn. She may occasionally tell stories but, when questioned, will tell the truth. Since the twenty-fourth day of March, she has been at Jas Pool's away from me. Jas Pool told me that the little girl told her that the little girl told him that the prisoner had carnally known her, so far as he could, without killing her. These were the words that she had used. I understand from Mrs Pool that the prisoner had penetrated the child's person to some extent. Mrs Pool told me that the child had told me the prisoner went up to the little girl's bed and pulled the sheet off the little girl, put his fingers into her private parts, and put his penis into her private parts. The child told Woods that he was hurting her a little, and she complained of being sore. Mrs Pool told me that the little girl had told her that the offence had occurred seven times. I have had the child examined by a Doctor who said that if he had seen the child sooner, he could have told if carnal knowledge had taken place. So far as he could tell, the child was not injured. The child said that the prisoner hurt her on each occasion. I did not reproach the child who was afraid I would whip her. She was a little nervous and afraid I would whip her. Mrs Pool gave me no reason other than I stated why I was not notified sooner.'

Seven-year-old Louisa Jane Fulton was the next witness to be called. She bravely said, 'The first time the prisoner did anything to me, I was upstairs in bed. I was undressed. He pulled the clothes off, put his fingers into my pea, and unbuttoned his pants and pea into mine. He hurt me. The prisoner did this to me three times upstairs. He did it downstairs in the lounge and over at the stable and the berry patches. I first told my aunt Beckie. I did not tell her the first time Woods did it because I did not like to. My Ma asked me this question before. I have told what Woods did more than once. Aunt Beckie did not tell me Ma would whip me. I was afraid Ma would whip me. Aunt told me if I told a story, I would be whipped. She would whip me if I told Ma the story was a lie. I was not hurt much by Wood in the bed.'

At this point, George Henry Wood conveniently appeared to have some type of fit, possibly brought on by stress. However, it would later be suggested that George Henry Wood could fake seizures when it suited him. In any case, the court adjourned until 11 am the following day to allow George Henry Wood to recover from the episode.

When the trial resumed, Louisa Jane Fulton was again sworn in and continued with her evidence.

She said, *'I did not speak to Ma or anyone else about what happened yesterday. No one said anything last night about me being whipped. I did not tell Aunt Beckie any sooner because I did not like to. I know what Woods did to me was wrong. I remember the first time Woods came upstairs. I do not remember him unlocking his trunk to get paper. I do not remember what woke me. I was not asleep. He had a trunk upstairs. I do not think he opened his trunk. He sat down on the side of the bed. I do not remember if he spoke to me. I do not think he did. I do not remember if he spoke to me before he left. He put his arm across me. He hurt me a little. I do not know if he meant to hurt me. He did more to me than put his arms across me. It was not his arm that hurt me. Aunt Beckie first told me Woods had done what was wrong. She did not tell me why it was wrong. I know Mr Fieldhouse. I told him what Woods had done more than once before I went to Mr Fieldhouse. I told the matter a second time to Aunt Beckie. She did not tell me I would be whipped. No one told me I would be whipped. No one told me I would be whipped if I told a story. I remember Ma was at Grandma's when Woods did what he did. He came up after I saw them. When Ma arrived at Aunt Beckie's, I was afraid I would be whipped. Mama used to whip me when I told stories. What I had said about Woods was not a lie, and I was not afraid I would be whipped because it was not a lie.'*

Heartbreakingly, Mr Robertson, acting for the defence, asked for Charlotte Fulton, Louisa's mother, to be removed from the court. He then asked Louisa if she was afraid that she would be whipped because of what she had told her aunt. Poor little Louisa Jane Fulton then burst into tears and refused to answer. Mr Robertson repeated his question several times until Louisa answered in a quiet tone, *'Yes.'*

The next witness to be called was 12-year-old Margaret Ellen Pool. She said, *'I live in the Municipality of Glendale in the County of Beautiful Plains with my brother James Pool, about three miles from Deputy P.O. Charlotte Fulton is unrelated to me. Louisa Jane lived at my brother's house before the twenty-seventh day of July for a couple of months. James Pool, his wife, myself, Louisa Jane Fulton and George Wood lived there. The defendant is sometimes called George Henry Wood. Wood lived for about a month with James Pool. I recollect the* twenty-seventh day of July. Louisa Jane Fulton said that Woods had assaulted her on the twenty-eighth day of July. I slept with the little girl upstairs. No one else slept there but us. Louisa went to bed at about eight o'clock. I generally went to bed at 9 o'clock. I did not see the defendant going upstairs while Louisa was in bed. I saw him coming down from upstairs while Louisa was in bed, it was before the twenty-seventh day of July, but I could not say how long, about a week perhaps. He had nothing in his hands. I did not think his coming downstairs was strange as his box was there. It was what I would expect from him going to his chest. I have known him for about a month. So far as I knew, his conduct was good. I was astonished when I heard the charge. Louisa told me in the house. I told her nothing when she told me of it. I thought she ought to complain to someone but did not tell her so. I have known the child for a couple of months. I did not find her inclined to tell stories. I remember when the child's mother came; the mother talked to her about the matter. That I heard. She told Mrs Pool before she told me. I was there at the time. I told my mother about it. I stopped at Mrs Fulton's mother last night but did not speak of the matter to anyone. I do not know if the child was afraid of being whipped when her mother came up or if she is usually afraid of her mother. About a week has passed between the child's complaint and the taking of proceedings, and in the meantime, Woods eats at the table as usual. She did not tell me anything but that he put his hand on her private parts. She said he did that and more. She told me about the matter at different times and gave me the same account. I do not know how often she told the story. She told me three times. I did not complain to Mr Pool or object to eating with Woods.'

The final witness to be called was given by James Pool. He gave the following account:

'I know, Wood. He lived with me on and before the twenty-seventh day of July as my hired man. My sister's wife and Louisa Jane lived with me simultaneously. My wife was subpoenaed but could not come as she expected to be sick. Louisa calls my wife, Aunt Beckie. My wife told me first about the matter. I heard of it on the 27th and 28th when information was laid on the 4th or 5th of August. Mrs Charlotte Fulton told me the little girl had given her evidence very well yesterday. Mrs Fulton did not tell me what evidence the little girl had. I spoke to my sister, the last witness since yesterday. All I said was not to be bashful and tell the truth. I stopped at Mr Hall's last night. Nothing was said except how little the girl was. I did not speak to Woods about the charge and allowed him to remain in the house. The little girl was not afraid when her mother was coming up. She was glad. She knew what her mother was coming up for. I know nothing of my wife's knowledge. So far as I know, the prisoner behaved very well. The little girl told me of the matter once after her mother was sent for. I did not reproach Louisa *for not telling before. She said the matter had gone on for some time and that she had objected. I allowed Woods to remain as usual because Judge Fieldhouse advised me to send for her mother. He would leave if I had allowed the prisoner to know that we would complain. I would have had to give him a reason for not allowing him to sit at the table as usual. The child is, in my opinion, truthful.'*

Finally, the Magistrate read George Henry Wood's statement to the court. Having heard all of the evidence, Judge Ryan found George Henry Wood guilty and sentenced him to imprisonment for three months, to be served at the Vaughan Street Gaol. As he was removed from the court, George Henry Wood was said to be indignant and showed no remorse for his actions.

Chapter 18: Manitoba Penitentiary

George Henry Wood was released from the Vaughan Street Gaol in October 1886. At the time, the Canadian Pacific Railway was in the process of building the country's transcontinental railroad. By this point, the line had already connected from Vancouver to Montreal. But in 1886, the Company tried extending the line to Winnipeg to the east and west rail lines.

Due to the country's rapid expansion, there was a severe shortage of labourers, and it was not difficult for anyone willing to work long hours to obtain work. George Henry Wood's statement suggests he did work on the railway for a time. However, for reasons unknown, George Henry Wood's employment on the railway was short-lived, and by 1886 George Henry Wood had resumed working as a farm labourer.

By August 1886, he found employment with James Ritchie in Neepawa, but within a year of being released from Vaughan Street, George Henry Wood again found himself in trouble with the law. On the 14th of August 1886, he stole a horse from the town of Gladstone. On that day, Joseph McAlpine and his wife decided to visit some friends in the local community. While they were out, George Henry Woods snuck into the McAlpine's stables, stole a horse, and fled toward Winnipeg. Joseph McAlpine returned home to discover his horse missing.

He was also informed that George Henry Wood had also disappeared. Putting two and two together, he reported the matter to Edward McDonald, Justice of the Peace, who issued a warrant for George Henry Wood's arrest. The document was immediately sent to Constable Corrigal of the Canadian Mounted Police, who began searching the surrounding hills and fields. He successfully apprehended George Henry Wood on the 16th of August 1886, near Headingley.

After his arrest, George Henry Wood was formally charged and incarcerated at the Vaughan Street Gaol, Portage la Prairie, for the third occasion. Later that day, he appeared at Winnipeg's Central Judicial District Court for a committal hearing. After opening the proceedings, Judge McDonald informed George Henry Wood that he was charged with feloniously stealing one bay mare. The Judge asked George Henry Wood for his plea, to which he replied, '*Guilty.*'

The Judge then read Joseph McAlpine's statement to the court, which reads as follows:

'I am the part owner of a dark and which bay mare was in my possession and in charge on Sunday 15th instant. She was in my stable at Gladstone. I know the accused. My wife and I went to McDoors on Sunday, and the accused took the mare during my absence. I missed the mare and the accused and, from that, supposed that he had stolen her. The first clue I got after enquiries was that he had passed Woodside. Next, he passed through Westbourne and Donald Station. He also stopped at James Rutledge's farm north of Portage la Prairie. I also heard that he passed Poplar Point. I have not seen the mare since Sunday morning, and she was then in the stable. Strictly speaking, the mare is not my property, but I am responsible to her owner Neil McIves for her keep and safety. The prisoner never admitted to me that he had taken the mare. On Monday, 16th inst., I got a warrant out for the arrest of the accused. The prisoner is who I suspect of stealing the mare and is known by George Henry Wood.'

The Judge then read Constable Corrigal's statement to the court, which read as follows:

'I was given the warrant to arrest George Henry Wood for stealing a bay mare, and the prisoner is the man I arrested. I did not find the property with him. After I arrested him, he denied being the man Woods. He said his name was Fraser, and he knew nothing of the mare. I arrested him. I did not get the mare. I have no idea where she is, but George Henry Wood admitted to taking her in his given account. I found him in possession of a pony which was not the mare I was after. The pony I left in charge of a woman.'

The Judge then informed George Henry Wood that he would appear at the Court of the Queen's Bench on the 23rd of August 1886 and ordered a remand at the Vaughan Street Gaol. George Henry Wood's short trial again appeared in the local newspapers. One such report was published in the *Portage la Prairie Weekly* on the 20th of August, 1886. The report contained the shocking reason for George Henry Wood's hasty and criminal behaviour on the 26th of August 1886. The article reads as follows:

'Provincial Policeman Corrigal Captured George Woods, the horse thief, on House's Place at Pigeon Lake between here and Winnipeg. The prisoner served a sentence about a year ago for assault on a small girl at Neepawa. A few days ago, it was said that he attempted rape on a young girl near Gladstone but was nearly brained by a neck yoke in the hands of her father. Fearing prosecution, he stole a horse from Mr McAlpine, a farmer at Gladstone. He pushed past Portage La Prairie on his way to the boundary when he was promptly overhauled by the energetic Corrigal. He appeared yesterday before a magistrate and was committed for trial, taking up board with Governor Moss in the meantime.'

There is no mention of attempted rape in either witness statements or official court papers. However, it is clear from several newspaper reports that George Henry Wood had tried to rape another young girl before stealing the horse. Whilst the lack of charges means that the victim is not identifiable, it is highly likely, although not sure, that the victim was a child within or close to James Ritchie's family.

Why George Henry Wood was not charged with attempted rape on this occasion is unknown. However, it may be due to societal attitudes towards victims of sexual crime at the time. During this era, victims and their families often chose not to pursue charges relating to sexual crimes. Those who did were often shamed and disbelieved by their communities.

Additionally, those who did go to court were treated poorly and unsympathetically. Victims of sexual crimes had their reputations tarnished, and potential husbands would see their history as unacceptable. These facts led to victims declining to press charges through choice or coercion.

A further article of interest appeared in the *Brandon Mail* on the same day. The report reads as follows:

'Geo. Wood, a young man from the vicinity of Gladstone, who served a term in jail for committing a rape on a little girl in Neepawa, is again in the clutches of the law. Last Sunday, he stole a horse in charge of Mr McAlpine of Gladstone and started for the east. At once, Mr McAlpine got a warrant and placed it in the hands of Constable Corrigal of this place for execution. Corrigal, after deciding the most likely direction that the thief would take, started in pursuit and, on Tuesday, succeeded in overtaking his man between the houses and Headingly. Wood was arrested and brought back to Portage when he was jailed. Woods was making for the States, but he could not find a trail through the woods. He endeavoured to elude the pursuit by driving his horse into the river, but the native cunning of Corrigal proved equal to the occasion, as the sequel shows. The prisoner appeared before Ed McDonald J.P. on Tuesday *and was committed for trial on the evidence adduced. When Woods was sentenced for the abovementioned crime, the Judge dealt leniently with him as it was thought he was suffering from mental debility. But it now transpires that he can play the idiot to perfection.'*

George Henry Wood was of low intelligence, but he was clearly highly manipulative and cunning. On no less than two occasions, he had successfully ingratiated himself into people's homes and convinced his community that he was an honest and decent man. George Henry Wood's Canadian convictions might also provide further insight into why George Wood Senior had been adamant that his son should move and stay away. Soon after Edith's body was discovered, amongst the newspaper reports were suggestions that other young girls in the area had been '*mistreated*' in the Kemp Town area. Was George Henry Wood responsible for other crimes in England that never ended up in court?

In any case, had the prosecution been aware of these prior convictions in 1891, any suggestion of insanity, whether through epilepsy or otherwise, could have easily been disproved. Additionally, the Canadian convictions should have clarified any questions about George Henry Wood's motives. By all accounts, he appears to have been a predatory paedophile with a perverted attraction to young girls, which he could not control.

On the 23rd of August 1886, George Henry Wood appeared for the second time at the Central Judicial District Court before Judge Ryan. On this occasion, George Henry Wood pled guilty, so the Judge didn't call any witnesses. The motive for his guilty plea may have been to avoid speaking about his criminal actions towards another young girl. Alternatively, he may have realised that the Judge would never take his word over Constable Corrigan, who had observed George Henry Wood fleeing on the stolen horse before arresting him.

Nonetheless, Judge Ryan found him guilty and sentenced him to 3 years and ten months. Due to the length of the sentence and nature of the crime, Judge Ryan ordered that George Henry Wood serve his sentence at the local Penitentiary.

Manitoba Provincial Penitentiary, also known as Stony Mountain, is located around 24 km North of Winnipeg in the municipality of Rockwood. Following confederation, the Canadian Government ordered its construction to cope with the rising number of convicts and to ease the overcrowding at Kingston Penitentiary. The Canadian Government expropriated land for the project's site in the latter part of 1872, approximately 11 miles from Lower Fort Garry, where Sir Garnet Wolseley and his troops were stationed during the Red River rebellion.

In 1869, Indigenous people of the Red and Saskatchewan River colonies feared for their rights, land and survival following confederation. The Métis organised a resistance movement and elected an independent government, hoping they would negotiate better terms for their people. However, the Rebellion's elected leader, Louis Riel, was declared an outlaw by the Canadian Government. He was eventually caught, convicted of treason and hanged in 1885. Louis Riel's death did not stop the uprising and conflict between the Canadian authorities, and the indigenous people continued for many years.

Colonel Samuel Lawrence Bedson, who had fought alongside Sir Garnet Wolseley at Fort Garry during the Red River rebellion, stayed in the area after Louis Riel's execution and became the first appointed Warden of the new Penitentiary. By 1886 when George Henry Wood was incarcerated, the prison contained 106 cells and approximately 140 prisoners. Overcrowding was a significant issue, and Warden Bedson was forced to house the surplus prisoners in the attic and corridors.

The facilities at the institution were extremely basic and primitive. The Penitentiary lacked a hospital, the bathrooms were not fit for purpose, and the laundry was said to be dangerous and inconvenient. To add to his misery, the regime was draconian and bleak. The guards harshly enforced the silent system. Anyone who spoke to other prisoners or broke the rules could be sentenced to a diet of bread and water or, in some cases, deprived of food entirely. Other punishments included using a ball and chain and dark punishment cells. In the case of more severe or repeated infringements of the rules, prisoners would receive lashes.

The warders gave convicts a stick on entry to the prison, their only means of communication. The four-foot rod was painted white, with one end coloured red and the other black. If prisoners needed anything, they would pass the rod through the grate in their cell door to alert the guards. The black end was shown for any usual request, whereas the red indicated an urgent need.

As soon as they arrived at the Penitentiary, prisoners underwent an assessment by the medical officer, whose report detailed the individual's physical capabilities for work purposes. As was the case at Lewes, various types of work were available, including shoe-making, groundwork, and broom and mat manufacturing. Prisoners were expected to work every day except Sunday.

The Penitentiary was entirely self-sufficient. Consequently, some prisoners were expected to work the surrounding farmland or tend to the prison's livestock. All prisoners worked ten hours a day with only a break for lunch and were not permitted to stop until the tower bell rang to signal that the workday was over.

An article published in the Toronto Daily Mail on the 31st of August 1885 gives insight into the interior and conditions of the Penitentiary. Representatives from the publication had visited the prison to see Chief Pound Maker. The Chief was part of the red river resistance but surrendered along with several of his men after the capture of Louis Riel. After a short trial, he received a sentence of three years at Manitoba Penitentiary. The report is as follows:

'Arriving at the Penitentiary, we arrived at the front door, slightly blown but still active. Here we met Head Warder McDonald. After a quick handshake, we are conducted through the corridor, with its fine collection of stuffed animals. After a short while, we reached the business office, where Warden Bedson sat at his desk, surrounded with papers and documents, and up to his eyes in the business.

Notwithstanding this, however, we received a cordial welcome and, taking a seat, explained the object of the visit. 'Very well, gentlemen, I shall be happy to show you', said the Warden, 'and I will show you all the lions of the place, including the rebel prisoners. I have no objection to your speaking to them on general matters, but gentlemen, no rebellion, please!

You will find the establishment rather upset at present as it is undergoing alterations and enlargement, and in consequence, we are considerably cramped for room. As for the rebel, prisoners have not been set to work yet as no tasks can be assigned to them until after they have been examined by Doctor Sutherland today for that purpose.'

The Warden led the way from his office up a narrow flight of stairs to the third floor of the building. At the head of the stairs, the passage widened into a hall of considerable size, with two doors on the right and one on the left.

Directly opposite the stairs stood two small brown-coloured wooden tables and stools, and beside each table lay a neat roll of blankets and a coverlet. On each table were a small perforated tin containing salt and an inkstand. A bible also lay there, and a work of fiction was on one table.

Passing through the doorway to the left, we entered a large square room, around the walls of which were fourteen outfits for as many convicts, comprising mattress, blanket, coverlet, table stool wash-bowl, salt cellar, inkstand and Bible. Everything was spotless and neat, even to the point of pain.

Descending the stairs again, we were taken into the basement, where several convicts worked. A massive grating of iron bars was opened by an elderly convict, and turning down a short passage, we entered the tailoring establishment. 'Attention!' called the guard as Colonel Bedson entered, and every convict doffed his cap and rose to his feet. 'To work!' came the command from the Warden, and business was resumed.

The convict tailors were employed to make the chaste uniform of the institution, some cutting, others sewing, but all silent under the eye of the watchful guard. What a life for men to live! Just mere existence, taking no interest in the outside world, toiling silently for a stern taskmaster who never pays wages.

Prisoners have nothing to look forward to, no change, no variety, and the one brooding through that but for their own transgression, they would now be breathing pure air, beneath the bright sun of liberty, without the hateful garb of shame upon them and no taskmaster forever watching.

What do those silent prisoners think of as they sit at work all day? Do they think of their grey-headed old father and mother away from home, sorrowing for an erring son? Do they think of a heartbroken wife struggling daily to earn bread for little ones? No sign of such thoughts appears upon their pale, passionless faces as they bend over their tasks.
Their day of liberty must come eventually, and that is their only consoling thought, enabling them to bear up against the crushing monotony of prison life.

Next to the tailor's shop is the stocking manufactory, and seven or eight convicts were busily engaged in making woollen stockings by machinery. At the furthest table, a fair-complexioned, intelligent-looking convict is manipulating the knitting machine, whilst sitting on a stool close to him is a full-blooded Indian convict stitching up the gaps in the stocking toes. Another young Indian at the end of the table is running a second machine, and he manages it very deftly.

Passing this department, we ascended a short flight of stairs, entered the corridor where the cells were located and walked down the aisle admiring the brightness and cleanliness of everything. The steel bars of which the cell doors are made are all polished until they fairly glitter and the interior of every cell is neat and tidy. Before reaching the bottom of the aisle, we pass a convict shoemaker, busily employed at his last, and then we come to the visitor's register, where we sign our names. At the end of this ceremony, we walk up the passage on the opposite side and, passing through the basement once more, we come out into the open air.'

It was within this harsh environment that George Henry Wood completed his sentence. During his three-and-a-half-year term, George Henry Wood established a close relationship with the Penitentiary's chaplain, Reverend Arthur William Goulding. Very quickly after the two became acquainted, it was apparent that Reverend Goulding was increasingly concerned for George Henry Wood.

As a result, he decided to visit Mr and Mrs Wood in Brighton, England, to urge them to bring their son home. The Reverend did not publicly state the nature of his concerns; therefore, it is unclear whether he was worried about George Henry Wood's sexual predation or his supposed ill health. It may also be the case that the kind and caring chaplain was manipulated by his parishioner.

In any case, in 1891, Reverend Goulding travelled to England to visit George Henry Wood's parents at 11 Rock Street. Travelling so far was an extreme course of action for the Reverend to undertake and shows the extent of his concerns. The chaplain did persuade George Wood Senior to allow his son to return home, and he even funded his passage. Shortly after, Reverend Goulding returned to Canada and informed George Henry Wood of his father's decision.

In January 1892, Reverend Goulding was alerted to George Henry Wood's position back at Brighton, and on the 13th of February, he wrote directly to Prince and Ayres himself. His letter is as follows:

'Sir,
The Governor of this institution has just handed to me your letter of the thirtieth day of December last addressed to our late Governor Col. Bedson, re one George Henry Wood at one time an inmate here now indicted for murder, in which letter my name occurs as having during the summer visited his parents. This is quite correct. But before this visit, I needed to write to them about their son's illness.

During his stay here, he was for different periods confined to hospital, and I think a majority of the cause emanated from the epileptic fits spoken of. My visit to his parents was to try and urge upon them the necessity of getting him home to England where he could be carefully watched and attended by them. And in this, I was successful.

Whilst here, his conduct was good. He manifested the most significant interest in my ministries and was a communicant in the Church of England. I cannot express my deep sorrow to think he should now stand in such an awful position. I had hoped for much better things from personal contact and observation with this man for over three years.
Surely if guilty, the man must be beside himself. Kindly convey to his parents my heartfelt sympathy.

I am Sirs,
Yours respectfully, Arthur W.G. Goulding B.D.'

On the 25th of February 1892, having taken time to consider the impact of George Henry Wood's situation on his parents, Reverend Arthur Goulding also wrote a sympathetic and supportive letter to George Wood Senior. His letter reads as follows:

'Sir,

I cannot express my surprise hearing of your son's trouble and your great grief from Messrs. Prince and Ayres. Not having heard from you or him for some time, I concluded that he was doing well. I have written to your solicitors as entirely as I can regarding his having suffered from epilepsy, and the Doctor has done likewise. The latter's report is the most valuable for your son's defence as he was his attendant all the time he was here, and he can speak authoritatively on the point.

I remember on one occasion, Dr Sutherland tried to get your boy to undergo an operation for some injury received in the head whilst at sea, but he would not consent to it. I would like it very much if you would send me a copy of the paper containing an account of the trial as I am very interested in your behalf.

May God grant you grace and strength to bear this severe trial. I know how terrible it must feel to think that one of your bloods should stand convicted of such an awful charge. If you can see your boy, remember me to him and say how sorry I am for him but that he has my earnest prayer for his soul. Why did he give way to that accursed drink? May he seek mercy from God through Christ for pardon for his past life as the worst may soon be realised.

With kind regards and heartfelt sympathy to you and yours.

Believe me to be, yours faithfully,
A.W. Goulding.'

Chapter 19: The Court of Assize

On Tuesday, the 6th of April, the Honourable Sir James Charles Mathews, who had been charged with overseeing Sussex's spring Assizes, travelled from his house in Queen's Gate Gardens to London Victoria Station. From here, he boarded the early train and, a short while later, arrived at Lewes Railway Station. After disembarking, he exited the station where he was met by the High Sheriff of Sussex (Mr Wilfrid Hans Loder), his Chaplain (Reverend Canon Copper, Vicar of Cuckfield), and the Under Sheriff (Mr Walter Bartlett).

After some brief pleasantries, the Judge was escorted by the police and a troupe of trumpeters from Preston Barracks to the Judge's Apartments in School Hill, Lewes, where he would lodge for the duration of the Assizes. A few weeks before, the Treasury selected Judge Mathews to oversee the proceedings due to his professional qualities and extensive experience. He was said to have a *'strong natural aptitude for the practical side of the law, and from the outset of his career, he showed impatience with technicalities and determination to get at the real points at issue.'*

Having been appointed to the Queen's Counsel Bench in 1874, Judge Mathews had overseen many high-profile trials. Early in his career, Judge Mathews was described by commentators as 'being *too impatient with slowness and dullness.*' However, he eventually became the best *Nisi Prius* judge of his time.

As was customary, Sussex's Court of Assize was to be heard at County Hall, Lewes, which had been in operation since it was erected in 1812. In 1808, the building's exterior was constructed using limestone quarried at Portland Island, Dorset. The design involves a symmetrical main frontage of five bays which faces onto the High Street.

The central section of three bays features a recess with six Doric order columns supporting the upper floors. There are casement windows on the first floor and flanking wings projecting forwards. Above the first-floor windows are reliefs which depict *Wisdom, Justice* and *Mercy*. Later, the town's authorities extended the building by two bays eastwards in a similar style.

When the building opened in 1812, it was used primarily for dispensing criminal justice. However, following the implementation of the Local Government Act of 1888, which established councils in every county, it also became the meeting place of East Sussex County Council. However, later, it was solely used as a court of law. The structure still stands today and is now known as Lewes Crown Court, and continues to host some of Sussex's most high-profile trials.

On the morning of the 7th of April, Judge Mathews drove directly to Lewes High Street, where he attended mass at St Anne's Church as was customary. After the service, he walked the short distance to the courthouse, where he was greeted by various local dignitaries. The Mayor arrived a few minutes later, adorned in the robes of office and followed by the Mace-bearer.

The proceedings began at precisely 11 am. The jurors, which included Sir Anchitel Ashburnham - Foreman, Anthony Biddulph, Hugh Wyatt, Mr Shenstone, Mr Wisden, Mr Blencowe, Francis Barchard, Reginald, J. Graham, Baron George de Worms, Phillip Worms, Phillip Rawson and J. H. Nix. The group were welcomed, seated and instructed to take the oath of affirmation.

After formally opening the proceedings, Judge Mathews outlined the cases the jury would hear in the coming days. He informed the court that the calendar contained the names of 15 prisoners concerned in 14 cases. As was usual, he briefly touched on the ability of the prisoners to read and write. Judge Mathews explained that very few of the prisoners had previous convictions and attributed this to the vigilance and hard work of the Sussex Police Constabulary.

Eventually, he came to Edith's murder, the most high-profile case of the proceedings, Judge Mathews solemnly said, *'I regret to inform you there are two cases involving inquiry into the loss of life, one a very terrible case, a charge against a man, George Henry Wood. There can be no doubt a dreadful outrage was committed and followed by the murder of a helpless little girl who was five years old. Of course, in a case of this kind, you do not usually have evidence of any eyewitness. Still, many circumstances of great significance concur in pointing to the accused as guilty of the crime, and it will be your duty to return a true bill.'*

His comments suggest that the Judge, who had already studied the case file at length, was satisfied that George Henry Wood was guilty. This type of statement would not be allowed in a court of law today and would likely form the basis for a post-conviction appeal. Unfortunately for George Henry Wood, in 1892, judges could make such comments to the accused's detriment.

Afterwards, the proceedings began in earnest. The first case heard by the jury was Robert Piper, a gardener from Sompting, who was charged with feloniously shooting at Frank Bushby with intent to murder on the 2nd of April 1892. The prosecutor explained that the victim was the brother-in-law of the accused. Frank Bushby was called to the stand and explained that on the evening of the 1st of April, he had sat with Robert Piper for the entire night. He said that he had left the residence early the following morning and began walking towards the garden gate and as he went, he heard a scuffle which caused him to turn around.

As he did so, he saw Robert Piper standing immediately behind him with a gun in his hand. Frank Busby said he threw himself to one side, but the gun fired. Frank Bushby recalled to the court that the prisoner had said, *'Here is another one. I'll do it for him!'*
Eventually, the two men struggled until someone came to Frank Bushby's assistance and called the police, who arrested Robert Piper. The defending counsel explained that Robert Piper was under the influence of alcohol at the time of the offence and had been abusing alcohol for several months.

The defence indicated that Robert Piper had experienced epileptic fits whilst under alcohol. He was also said to be suffering from delirium and was in a nervous state. Frank Bushby pled guilty to causing grievous bodily harm and was sentenced to four months of hard labour to be served at Lewes.

Catherine Frances Pickett, a servant from Upper Beeding, was the next prisoner to appear before the court. The eighteen-year-old pleaded guilty to setting fire to the dwelling house of her employer, Mr Henry Stapley. The prosecutor informed the court that the police could not establish a motive for the act. The accused's mother was called a witness and said that Catherine Pickett acted strangely as a child. After hearing the evidence, Judge Mathews ordered the prisoner to return to her mother's care.

The third case was that of Louisa Horn, from Eastbourne. She stood charged with unlawfully trying to conceal the birth of her two children on the 30th of November, 1891. Louisa Horn confessed to hiding her new-born twins under Eastbourne Pier shortly after their birth. Before the Judge delivered his sentence, the prosecuting barrister explained that he did not want to press the case. He told the jury that Louisa Horn had found herself pregnant with twins without any means to provide for them. He informed the court that she was *a 'good girl'* who had found herself in troubled times. Judge Mathews showed compassion for Louisa Horn's situation and sentenced her to one day's imprisonment.

Francis Horton, a commission agent from Brighton, was the next prisoner to appear before the court. He was charged with theft, having been accused of stealing letters containing cheques from Hove's pillar boxes. He also faced a second charge of forging an endorsement to a cheque. Francis Horton pled guilty to two theft charges and received a sentence of three years of penal servitude. Newspaper reports about his conviction suggest that Francis Horton's younger brother, Ethelbert Horton received a sentence at the Hampshire Assizes for a similar charge. During the proceedings he said he only followed his older brother's instructions. Luckily for Francis Horton, Judge Mathews was unaware of this claim during his trial.

Frederick Scrivens and James Elliott were the following prisoners to appear before the court. The pair faced charges of feloniously breaking the Parish Church of St Peter's, Brighton, and stealing the sum of 2d. 2s. Frederick Scrivens pleaded guilty, but James Elliott denied the charges and was found not guilty.

The following case to be heard was that of Frederick Willard, a labourer who had failed to surrender to bail at the last Brighton Borough Court Sessions. He faced charges of indecently assaulting eight-year-old Emily Budd on the 6th of March. The prisoner pleaded not guilty but was convicted and received a sentence of three months of hard labour.

Annie Martin, a servant, was the next prisoner to be called. She stood charged with the wilful murder of her newly-born female child at St. Leonard's, Hastings. The defence provided evidence about Anne Martin's background and financial instability, described as complicated. Having heard these facts, Judge Mathews substituted the capital charge with one of manslaughter. The jury returned a verdict of not guilty, and Anne Martin was discharged from the court.

The following case to be heard was that of Nelson Wren, a carpenter, who stood facing charges of perjury. Nelson Wren had given evidence in a poaching case heard before the Uckfield Magistrates on the 3rd of December 1891. The prosecution suggested that he had provided a false alibi for a man named Baker, who was subsequently convicted. After hearing all of the evidence, the jury found Nelson Wren not guilty.

Hargraves Brown, a schoolmaster from Itchingfield, was the next prisoner to appear before the court. Mr Brown stood charged with attempting to procure for the commission of gross indecencies, which at the time was a term used for describing homosexuality. The Uckfield police charged him with indecent assault between December and February 1891. Hargreaves Brown received a glowing reference from the Reverend John Moses, Rector of Itchingfield, and was found not guilty afterwards.

The final case was that of Stephen Hinkley, Wadhurst, who pleaded guilty to having carnal knowledge of Fanny Smith, a girl under 16 who had been in prisoner's employment. The prosecution informed the court that the prisoner had been a local preacher in the Wesleyan community. During sentencing, the Judge told the accused that he was an *'arrogant hypocrite, as there was no doubt the girl had been entrusted to his care by her parents on the character he bore of a moral and religious man'*.

At this point, Judge Mathews adjourned the proceedings until the following day, which would solely deal with George Henry Wood's case.

Chapter 20: The Day of Reckoning

On the morning of the 8th of April, after waking early, George Henry Wood washed, dressed and ate breakfast in his cell. At 8 am, he was handcuffed and led out to the Black Maria, parked at Lewes Gaol's front. Accompanied by 2 prison warders, George Henry Wood was placed into the cab, and after only a few moments, the vehicle began the short distance to County Hall, Lewes.

The 8th of April 1892 was said to be warmer and sunnier than usual. As George Henry Wood glanced out of the barred window of the vehicle and glimpsed the glorious spring weather, he must have been overcome with dread. He was aware of the publicity and anger that Edith Jeal's murder had evoked and likely dreaded being seen publicly again. To add to his woes, he had received word that his father would attend his trial and hear the overwhelming evidence against him.

At 8.20 am, the van arrived at the courthouse and parked close to its main doors. George Henry Wood was led from the car's safety, into the court and down to custody cells below. Much to his relief, only a few people were waiting to watch his arrival, and all stood calmly as they crossed the pavement to the court.

Once in the cells, he was left with thoughts and worries about the upcoming day's events. It is apparent from the case file that George Henry Wood viewed himself as the real victim of the situation. However, I wonder if he spared two minutes during this time to consider the horrendous ordeal that his actions had placed at the feet of the Jeal family. Did he consider that his not-guilty plea would force them to endure the horrific evidence about their daughter's murder again?

Inside the small courtroom, every available area was filled with public spectators, as eager as ever to hear the crime's gruesome details. No women were said to be present at the proceedings, which reporters attributed to the shocking nature of Edith's death. Due to the seriousness of the charges, Barristers of the Queen's Counsel had been recruited to represent both the prosecution and the defence.

Prince and Ayres had instructed Charles Frederick Gill to take up the case for the defence case. The Treasury had selected Mr Day to oversee the prosecution, with the support of Mr Grantham. Both arrived early and made their way to the barrister's chamber to finish the preparation of their cases.

At 10.25 am, Mr Gill, defending counsel, entered the court, took his place at the solicitors' desk and started unloading documents from the large red bag he had been carrying. He was described as having a *'troubled countenance and grave expression'*, and who could blame him? He would have realised the serious nature of his task and the potential outcome if the defence failed. A few minutes later, Mr Day and Mr Grantham, both acting for the Treasury, also entered and took their positions beside Mr Gill.

At precisely 10.30 am trumpeters in the outer hall played the customary shrill fanfare. Everyone inside the courtroom immediately rose as the sharp melody echoed through the courtroom. As the trumpets ceased, Justice Charles Matthews, dressed in red and white robes, entered the courtroom and took his seat at the magisterial bench. He was immediately followed by his Chaplain and the High Sheriff Walter Bartlett, Lewes, and other county gentlemen who took their positions at and around the Judge's bench.

Graham Denman, the Clerk of the Arraigns, thundered, *'George Henry Wood!'* to which the prisoner, surrounded by police officers, entered the courtroom. Despite the apparent tension, George Henry Wood was said to have walked with *'an air of jauntiness and a soldier-like manner.'* Reporters, who were overly represented in the courtroom, attributed this to the fact that George Henry Wood had served in the army and navy rather than intentional bravado. I wonder if, at this point, they were aware of the short period that he had actually served in the forces.

In any case, George Henry Wood was led across the courtroom and was placed into the dock. As he did so, every spectator turned their eyes to study his form. He was described *'as being under medium height with an extraordinarily weak and characterless face, a low forehead and a flat cranium'*. Other spectators described his head as *'curiously small compared to his rather broad shoulders.'* The Brighton Herald described George Henry Wood's appearance as *'A certain physical smartness but very little intelligence.'* This latter observation mirrored the public perception following George Henry Wood's Canadian court appearances.

After the accused's entrance, Judge Mathews requested that the jury enter the courtroom. George Henry Wood watched as the twelve jurors entered the courtroom and took their seats. As they silently filed in, he carefully studied each man as they entered the jury box, possibly attempting to read their mood and character.

After listening to each jury member pledge the oath of affirmation, Judge Mathews formally opened the proceedings. As the Judge's words echoed around the packed room, George Henry Wood nervously moved his lips and chin, and his lower jaw quivered convulsively. His eyes kept wandering in different directions and were not fixed on anyone or anything for more than a few seconds.

After the opening address, the Clerk of the Arraigns rose to his feet. In a stern, sombre tone, he said, *'George Henry Wood, the charges are that you feloniously, wilfully, and with malice aforethought killed Edith Jeal at Brighton on the 10th of December, 1891. The same charges are given on the coroner's inquisition.'*

At this point the court clerk turned to George Henry Wood and asked for his plea. In a distinct but quiet voice, he replied, *'Not guilty, Sir.'* With the formalities out of the way, Mr Day took to his feet and began his opening statement for the crown, centring on a recital of the facts.

He said, *'I have to lie before you very shortly, and I hope clearly, the facts upon which the prosecution relies to bring the terrible charge against the prisoner. It is usual in a case of such a severe nature and where consequences were so awful to ask the jury to pay careful attention to the evidence laid before them. However, from my experience of juries in the county, I know full well that even when the liberty of a fellow man is in peril, jurors give the facts the most anxious attention. Therefore I feel it unnecessary to ask you for that attention when a man's life is at stake. It is also usual to ask a jury to lay aside what they may have heard or read on the subject and focus on the case's merits before you. You have sworn to give a verdict according to the evidence and to fulfil your duty. I am confident that you will put away any preconceived ideas you might have or anything you have read on the subject. In a case where the circumstances can make the feelings of humanity revolt, you should not look at the man in the dock and assume him to be the perpetrator. Until the charge is proven, I am sure you will not give way to such feelings but will consider without prejudice, only on the evidence before you whether the man is guilty. The outline of the case is simple, though in giving you the details, I will spend considerable time, and I have to call many witnesses before you. Strictly the case of murder against the prisoner is this. On the evening of Thursday, the 10th of*

December 1891, a little girl named Edith Jeal was sent by her father to make some purchases. She lived at Bedford Street Buildings, Brighton and went with her brother Bertram to shops nearby. They bought some chestnuts and put them into Bertram's cap. They also purchased a bundle of firewood. Finally, Bertram went into a shop at the corner of Manchester Row, leaving his sister outside. When he came out, she had disappeared. That was the last Bertram, or the unfortunate father, saw the little girl alive. On Friday, about midday, the body was discovered in a playing field in the east part of the town. I imagine that the defence will not dispute this fact. But if they do, it will not take long for you to conclude that someone led the child to the shed, where she was brutally outraged and murdered. The evidence I shall call before you will show the finding of the body and can leave no doubt whatsoever in the minds of any reasonable man that the little girl was violated by someone and then killed. It might be so to stop the little girl from giving evidence in the witness box against the man who had the heart to perpetrate the outrage on the little girl. Although the body lay undiscovered until Friday, I think there can be no question that the perpetrator committed the indignation and murder the evening before. I shall be calling two medical men who will describe in detail the threatening injuries done to the little girl, injuries which would have killed the little girl in a short time, even if someone had not gone on to strangle her. The prisoner worked in the goods department at the Brighton Railway Company. I will prove that he was the worst for a drink when he left for work on Thursday evening. After leaving the goods yard, a witness named Eliza Dunk saw the prisoner on Sydney Street, near the Railway Station. No one saw the man again until he got to Edward Street, and I might say roughly that all places at which she should identify the man were on the way to the scene of the murder. I might also say they were all on the way to the man's home at Rock Street. In Edward Street, a little girl named Pimm saw the prisoner. Then, the police found him a little further along Edward Street, where a little girl named Alice West, who was only seven years old, spotted him. The court may call her to give evidence to you. However, she was so young she did not appear before the Magistrate. The next witness was one on whom I place a good deal of reliance. He is a policeman who knows the prisoner very well and meets with him on the night of the murder at the bottom of Lavender Street. Another witness will testify that she saw the prisoner standing in Manchester Row. She saw a little girl with a bundle of firewood standing outside a shop, and the man she later identified as the prisoner held out his hand to her, and they walked together into Somerset Street, which was still going in the direction of the murder. In Somerset Street, a woman named Alice Guy saw the accused going toward the scene of the murder, and he was carrying a little child in his left arm. One other witness, Henry Spicer, also saw the prisoner at the top of Chesham Street. That was shortly before the identification of the man as far as the witnesses I shall call before you *were concerned. I should ask if the case should stop there unless those six witnesses are shaken in cross-examination or appear not to be speaking the truth. These witnesses will say beyond doubt that the man in the dock was the man who was with the little girl on that night. They will say that the little girl could only have been the girl that was murdered and that the prisoner, for reasons you will have little difficulty imagining, took the girl along the streets and into the barn in the field where the murder occurred. In a crime of this character, it is not common for anyone to come before you and say, 'I saw it committed'. To the credit of human nature, any person would have prevented the crimes if they were strong enough to prevent such an awful act. If anyone, even too weak, had been present, a man who would have committed such an outrage would probably have the cunning not to be guilty of it in the presence of anyone else. It is, therefore, not to be supposed by you that you would have any direct evidence. Still, I will bring you what is commonly known as circumstantial evidence, which points in only one direction - the prisoner's guilt. This evidence should be as satisfactory as that of any one witness who could come before you and say that they saw the deed committed. That concludes the identification evidence, and no other evidence concerning that night will be heard. There are no witnesses to say what became of the prisoner that night, and even I do not know his later actions. The following day, he went to work as usual, but during the morning, a circumstance happened which is well worth your careful consideration. That man, employed in the dirty work of a cabman, borrowed money from witnesses to have a bath and went away for that purpose. We have no direct evidence from the bathhouse that he did have a bath, but we will call a witness to whom the prisoner admitted that he had a bath and felt better after. If Wood committed the outrage, one could understand his having a bath the next day to remove any traces of that horrible crime as far as he could. That is a question for you. Furthermore, before newspapers published the crime's details, the man in the dock knew of the murder and its location; he spoke freely `of these details to others. It might be that when he was out having a bath, he may have obtained some early information. I do not wish to press it, but there was suspicion about his knowledge of the murder long before his fellow workers at the other end of the town, the opposite end of Brighton to the crime scene, knew of it. There was also a much stronger fact, which amply corroborates the evidence of the witness who says they saw the prisoner going with the little girl to the shed. What purpose did he entice that little girl to the shed? The child was found dead and covered with blood from wounds that were caused before someone killed her. Any man who outraged and killed that little girl, and I am sure you will have little doubt if the same man did both; you would expect to find blood on him. I will bring conclusive evidence regarding the blood stains on the prisoner's garments when the police arrested him. The prisoner's clothing was sent to London and examined by the country's first* *analyst. You will hear his report in detail, showing that there was blood on parts of the prisoner's garments, which you would expect to find if a man committed an outrage, in that horrible way, upon an immature girl of five years of age. I submit that this evidence corroborates that this prisoner is the man who murdered the child on the night in question. This fact is something that the defence will have to disprove. When Detective Jupp arrested the prisoner, he asked him whether he had seen P.C. Tuppen and the prisoner denied it. Asked whether he had been in Lavender Street when the constable bade him a 'good night', he denied that also. He said that he went straight from his work to the North Street Circus; therefore, he was not going in the direction of his home, and his statement was untrue if you believe the evidence of the witnesses who said they saw him going in the direction of the shed. Was this statement consistent with any theory of innocence, or did it not corroborate the evidence which pointed to his guilt?'*

At this point, Mr Day walked over to the solicitor's bench and picked up the letter that George Henry Wood had written at the town hall. He read the various suspicious statements in the document and then continued his speech.

He said, 'As *the case is that of this kind, I will not press it too strongly. It was not a distinct admission; it might mean something other than what I place upon it. But what did the prisoner mean by saying, 'It was all through breaking the pledge?' What did he mean by 'Anything that happened that night was through the beastly drink?' Were these comments consistent with his statement that he had been to the circus all night? That shortly is the case which, with the assistance of my friend, I will lay before you. If I establish the matter beyond all doubt on your part, it will be your painful duty to say that the prisoner was guilty of the crime laid against him. Before calling the evidence, I will quickly allude to one other matter. Since the man's arrest, the gentlemen representing him have requested that the Treasury examine him to ascertain his mental state. Medical gentlemen have now made that examination, and their reports were sent to Mr Gill and the solicitors instructing him. Unless your lordship directs me to the contrary, I do not intend to call those witnesses as part of my case. The law presumes that every man is responsible for any acts he commits until the defence proves the contrary. I will have discharged my duty when I confirm that the prisoner committed the murder. Afterwards, it will fall to my friend Mr Day, if he can, to verify to your satisfaction that the man on the night in question was not responsible for any act he committed. If my friend does make that defence, I will address you again on that matter. At present, it is open to my friend to dispute that the prisoner committed the murder or, if he did so, to prove he was insane when he committed it.'*

This marked the end of the opening statement, and the prosecution's case started in earnest.

Chapter 21: 'A Very Decent Fellow.'

Mr Day called his first witness, Benjamin Sattin, a plan draughtsman for the Brighton Borough Corporation. After entering the witness box, he carefully unwrapped a small set of plans and laid them on the wooden ledge.

Addressing the court, he said, *'I am a draughtsman in the Surveyor's Office in the borough of Brighton and produce these plans which show the scene of the murder. They are correct. The height of the walls shown and the measurements around the walls are also correct.'*

The witness was interrupted by Judge Mathews, who asked, *'Is it a plan for the field?'*

Benjamin Sattin: *'Yes, of the field and the shed. The gate's height is four feet, and the wall varies from four feet to seven feet four inches at the east corner. I have not measured the size of the field, but it would be about 400 by 200 feet. In this field is a shed with brick walls, more of a barn than a shed. A barn would be a better name to apply to it. The barn is about 20 feet by 12 feet. There are brick walls, and it is covered with tiles and is a substantial building. There are houses on the south side. Around the field are Chichester Place, Eastern Road and St Mark's Street.'*

At this point, Benjamin Sattin displayed the plans and pointed out the critical locations of the case. After thanking him for his evidence, the judge released Benjamin Sattin from the court.

The next witness called by the prosecution was Sidney Martin of 1 Station Street, Brighton.

He said, *'I am employed in the Goods Department at the Brighton Railway Company. On the evening of the 10th of December, the prisoner entered the watchman's hut at the Trafalgar*

Street entrance to the Goods yard. He was drunk. He had an oilskin coat on, and I assisted him in removing it, and he put it down. He sat down for a few moments and then went away.'

He was then cross-examined by Mr Gill, who wanted to illustrate George Henry Wood's supposed good character and to show that his drunken state was unusual.

He began, *'Have you known the prisoner for some time?'*

Sidney Martin: *'Yes.'*

Mr Gill: *'Has he been employed by the company for a year and a half or a little more?'*

Sidney Martin: *'Yes, I think he has.'*

Mr Gill: *'I don't know if it is in your knowledge that when he first worked for the company, some difficulty arose about his not being passed by the doctor?'*

Sidney Martin: *'I know nothing of that.'*

Mr Gill: *'Do you know that he was sent to London, at the instance of the company, to have an operation performed on him?'*

Sidney Martin: *'He told me of it.'*

Mr Gill: *'At the time?'*

Sidney Martin: *'No, after he had been to London.'*

Mr Gill: *'From your knowledge of him, was he, during all the time up to within a few days of this matter, a well-conducted hard-working man?'*

Sidney Martin: *'Yes, I always found him a very decent fellow for the position he was placed in.'*

Mr Gill: *'A man who worked full time and was regarded as a good servant.'*

Sidney Martin: *'I believe he was a man who worked very hard.'*

Mr Gill: *'Until this occasion when you saw him, was he a strictly sober man?'*

Sidney Martin: *'I always thought he was a teetotaller, and I could not understand why he was drunk that day.'*

Mr Gill: *'Until you saw him on this occasion, you had no reason to doubt he was a teetotaller?'*

Sidney Martin: *'No, no reason whatsoever!'*

Mr Gill: *'May I take it when you saw him on this occasion, he was very drunk?'*

Sidney Martin: *'He was very drunk.'*

Mr Gill: *'Have you engaged in a conversation with the prisoner?'*

Sidney Martin: *'I have talked to him, and he was rather interested in little things in Canada, where he has been. I always thought he was a very decent man.'*

Mr Gill: *'Did he ever speak to you about fits he had had?'*

Sidney Martin: *'He did not. He showed me his leg, which was very bad, and one or two other things.'*

At this point, Mr Day asked the judge for permission to re-examine the witness. He wanted the jury to hear that George Henry Wood had never experienced fits whilst he was at work and was of sound mind. However, Sidney Martin did make some suggestions to the contrary.

Mr Day said, *'When he spoke about Canada, did he speak intelligibly?'*

Sidney Martin: *'Yes, in one sense, just as we may talk about sowing seeds and what the country was like.'*

Mr Day: *'Have you ever known him to have a fit?'*

Sidney Martin: *'No, I cannot say I have ever known him to have a fit, but on one occasion, I thought he was rather strange. One afternoon I was in the yard at the Cheapside gate, and he stood there and stamped his feet. I do not know if I made any remark, but I thought that man seemed strange. He knocked his feet at the back of the place and then walked out.'*

At this point, Judge Mathews interrupted to clarify Sidney Martin's comments.

He said, *'How long ago did this occur?'*

Sidney Martin: *'A month or two before December. I cannot give you exact dates.'*

Judge Matthews: *'Mr Gill, do you wish this to be taken as evidence?'*

Mr Gill: *'No, I have definite evidence of the man's insanity.'*

Judge Matthews: *'Very well. If you do not want it, it is not evidence.'*

Mr Gill: *'Very well, my Lord.'*

Judge Matthews: *'Mr Martin, what do you wish to tell us?'*

Sidney Martin: *'I went into the yard at about a quarter to three o'clock to telephone for some coal. I went into the watchman's hut, and Wood and Fisher were there. I did not see any standing joke about anything, and seeing him stamping his feet surprised me.'*

Traiton Harriott, the Brighton Station Goods Yard supervisor, was the next witness to appear before the court.

He said, *'The prisoner worked under me for the Railway Company. On Thursday, the 10th of December, he was carting Barley to Longhurst Brewery. I sent him home at twenty minutes to six that evening. He had finished his work. He was wearing Oilskins and his railway clothes under the oilskins. I saw him again the next morning at around six when he returned to work. He did his work as usual on that day. I sent him down to the Sussex Daily News printing works at about 5 am to get one of the carmen for a furniture job. He got back a little after six. I saw him at about 6.30 am on Friday. He said, 'Don't you think a man must be mad to do anything like that? I replied that I did not know what he was talking about. He said, 'Have you not heard of the murder?' I said, 'What murder?' He said, 'The murder of a little girl at Kemp Town.' I said, 'I have not heard anything about it.' The prisoner said nothing further and walked off towards Trafalgar Street.'*

Traiton Harriott was then cross-examined by Mr Gill, who was still trying to show George Henry Wood's '*good character*' and that his alcohol consumption on the day of the murder was unusual.

Addressing the witness, Mr Gill asked, '*How long had the prisoner been working under you?*'
Traiton Harriott: '*About twelve months.*'
Mr Gill: '*Up to this time, was he a quiet, peaceable and well-disposed man?*'
Traiton Harriott: '*Yes very, I always found him so. He was an excellent workman.*'
Mr Gill: '*And a sober man?*'
Traiton Harriott: '*Yes, Sir.*'
Mr Gill: '*You understand him to be a total abstainer?*'
Traiton Harriott: '*I did, Sir.*'
Mr Gill: '*When you saw him at 6 pm or a little after on the tenth, was he the worse for a drink.*'
Traiton Harriott: '*He was the worse for a drink then.*'
Mr Gill: '*What would be his time for going away?*'
Traiton Harriott: '*He would generally leave about nine. Just before Christmas, we work late.*'
Mr Gill: '*Did you send him away that night?*'
Traiton Harriott: '*I did Sir.*'
Mr Gill: '*Was that on account of the condition in which he was?*'
Traiton Harriott: '*That is it, Sir.*'
Mr Gill: '*You thought he was unfit to remain there.*'
Traiton Harriott: '*Quite so.*'
Mr Gill: '*I believe he had been carting to a brewery all day?*'
Traiton Harriott: '*Yes Sir.*'
Mr Gill: '*Had he been engaged in that way for some days before?*'
Traiton Harriott: '*No Sir.*'
Mr Gill: '*Was that the only day?*'
Traiton Harriott: '*The only day, Sir.*'
Mr Gill: '*Was that the first occasion you had seen him under the influence of drink?*'
Traiton Harriott: '*It was the first time I saw him in that way.*'

Mr Gill: *'What time was it the following day when he spoke to you about the murder?'*
Traiton Harriott: *'About half-past six, or within a few minutes.'*

The following person to be called was Eliza Dunk, an essential witness for the prosecution. She had made a statement after seeing a man who matched George Henry Wood's description on the night of the murder, walking with a young child in his arms.

After taking the oath, Eliza Dunk said, *'I am the wife of Thomas Dunk, a railway signalman, and I live at 23 St Martin's Place. On Thursday, the 10th of December, I went through Sydney Street between 6.30 and 6.40. I saw a little girl in the street. A man lifted the girl in his arms. The child screamed out very much. He carried the child a little way and then fell. The child ran up to me, and I took it home. The prisoner was the man I saw with the child, dressed in railway clothes. He appeared to be drunk. On Saturday, I identified the prisoner down at the town hall.'*

Mr Gill: *'When you say drunk, you mean so drunk he fell with the child?'*
Eliza Dunk: *'I do not know whether he slipped or fell because he was so drunk.'*
Mr Gill: *'But he did fall?'*
Eliza Dunk: *'Yes'*
Mr Gill: *'And you say he was drunk?'*
Eliza Dunk: *'Yes.'*

Eleven-year-old Fanny Pimm was the next witness to appear before the court, who had been approached by a stranger on the night of the murder. She said, *'On Thursday, the 10th of December, I was in Edward Street that evening. I went to the sweet shop and saw a man with railway clothes on when I came out. I saw that man afterwards at the town hall on Saturday. On Thursday evening, the man approached me and asked me where I lived. I said, 'Down the lanes.' He then asked me to go home with him. He said no one would interrupt me. I said I was not going, and he said nothing else. The prisoner in the dock is the man I saw.'*

Alice West was the next witness to be called. At just seven, the tiny child could barely be seen over the top of the witness box. After Alice West took the oath, Mr Gill rose to his feet and, incredulously, said to Justice Matthews, *'I suppose my friend Mr Day thinks it necessary for his case to call this witness. Of course, I cannot cross-examine a child like this.'*

Mr Day, unwilling to argue, replied, *'Of course, if your lordship thinks she should not be called, that is fine. Your lordship sees the nature of the evidence.'*

Mr Gill: *'I did not cross-examine the last witness because of her age!'*

Judge Matthews: *'It does not appear there is any question of identity, therefore to a certain point, perhaps the evidence is not necessary to the inquiry. One cannot say how far this little creature knows her responsibility. I think it is not suitable to call her.'*

At this point, Alice West was released from the witness box back into the care of her mother.

P.C. Tuppen was the next witness to appear before the court.

After taking the oath, he said, *'On the evening of the 10th of December, I was at the corner of Upper St. James Street and Lavender Street. I saw the prisoner coming down Lavender Street. He appeared to be drunk. He said 'Good night to me as he passed and I said 'Good night to him. He had on long Macintosh leggings, which came up very high. He wore a blue cloth railway coat, which came down to his hips, and a railway cap. I had known him for about 10 years.'*

P.C. Tuppen was then cross-examined by Mr Gill. With his defence of epileptic mania at the forefront of his mind, he again wanted to remind the jury that his client was intoxicated on the night of the murder.

Addressing P.C., Tuppen said, *'I suppose you knew him before he went to America?'*

P.C. Tuppen: *'Yes Sir.'*

Mr Gill: *'Then you lost sight of him for about eight years?'*

P.C. Tuppen: *'I lost sight of him for a time. I think about eight years.'*

Mr Gill: *'Have you seen him occasionally since his return?'*

P.C. Tuppen: *'Yes'*

Mr Gill: *'This night you saw him, did you see he was drunk?'*

P.C. Tuppen: *'He stumbled just as he passed me, and this caused me to take more notice of him.'*

Mr Gill: *'Would it be correct to say the man was staggering and very drunk? Would it be right to say, 'He staggered as he passed me, and I saw he was very drunk?' I am quoting your own words.'*

P.C. Tuppen: *'Yes, he was very drunk.'*

At this point, P.C. Tuppen was released from the witness stand.

The next witness to be called was Edward Jeal.

He said, *'I live at 8 Bedford Place and am the little girl's father. I remember on the 10th of December, I sent her out with her brother Bertram. That would be at about a quarter past* eight. I sent her to Clark's, the fish shop, to get a bundle of firewood and her brother to Trengrove's to get an egg. He recalled that after about five minutes, Bertram returned home. Trengrove's is about sixty or seventy yards from my house. From what Bertram told me, I went to look for the little girl and searched for her the whole night. I went to the Freshfield Road Police Station and gave information there, and on Friday at about twenty minutes to two, I saw the child and identified her.'*

Mr Gill stated that he did not wish to cross-examine Edward Jeal. Consequently, Judge Matthews was released from the dock, but instead of leaving, he remained in the court to hear the rest of the evidence.

Bertram Jeal was the witness to be called, who repeated the evidence he had previously given at the police court. Afterwards, Mr Day showed him Edith's clothing which Bertram Jeal confirmed had been worn by his sister on the night she disappeared.

Rose Leggatt was the following witness to give evidence appeared before the court. She was another key witness for the prosecution as she said she had seen George Henry Wood holding his hand to a little girl outside Trengrove's grocery shop. After taking the oath, Rose Leggatt repeated the evidence she had given at the police court. She recalled visiting her mother on the night of the 10th of December, and on her way home, she explained that she had noticed a man in Upper Bedford Street who was dressed in a railway uniform.

At this point, Mr Day asked her to look at the prisoner. She briefly did so and then informed the court that George Henry Wood was the man she had spotted on the 10th of December. She explained that she had seen the man put his hand toward a little girl standing outside Trengrove's shop. She said she had witnessed the little girl follow the man to the middle of Somerset Street but had lost sight of the pair afterwards.

Rose Leggatt was then cross-examined by Mr Gill, who was trying to focus the jury's attention on George Henry Wood's intoxication on the night of the murder.

Mr Gill: *'The man you saw was the same man you previously said had pushed against you?'*
Rose Leggatt: *'I never took any notice.'*
Mr Gill: *'Did a man push against you?'*
Rose Leggatt: *'Yes, a man pushed against me.'*
Mr Gill: *'And you say this man was drunk?'*
Rose Leggatt: *'The man who pushed against me was the worst for drinking.'*

The next witness to be called was Alice Guy, who repeated the evidence she had given at the police court. She explained that on the evening of the 10th of December, she had been coming out of her house in Somerset Street between a quarter and twenty-past eight. She explained that she had spotted a man carrying a child who appeared to be crying. She said she did not know the child's age, but it was larger than a baby. She recalled that the child had been wearing a hat.

At this point, Mr Day collected Edith's hat from the exhibit's table and displayed it to the court. After walking to the witness box, he showed the cap to Alice West. After studying the item for a few seconds, she confirmed that it was the same as the hat worn by the child she had noticed outside Trengrove's store. She explained that she shouted to the man, 'Don't hurt that poor little thing, which caused the man to turn around. Alice Guy recalled he had been directly under a lamp and as he turned to look towards her, which gave her a distinct view of his face.

She explained that after this brief interaction, the man had continued walking towards the Royal Sussex County Hospital. After being instructed by Mr Day to look at the prisoner, Alice Guy also identified George Henry Wood as the man she had seen on the 10th of December.

Henry Spicer was the next witness to be called, who repeated the evidence he had given at the police court. He explained that on the night of the 10th of December, he had also seen a man carrying a child at about 8.50 pm. Henry Spicer recalled that the man was walking eastwards along Eastern Road and was only around 150 yards from the playing field where Edith had been found. He described the man as being very tipsy.

However, when Mr Day asked Henry Spicer to confirm that the prisoner was the man he had seen on the night of the murder, he refused. He explained that he could not swear that the man he had seen was George Henry Wood. He also explained that he could not remember what the man or the child was wearing. Mr Gill then conducted a brief cross-examination.

He said, '*You only saw the man as he passed?*'
Henry Spicer: '*Quite so.*'
Mr Gill: '*Even then, you could not see his face?*'
Henry Spicer: '*It was hidden in the child's clothes.*'
Mr Gill: '*But you saw the man was very drunk?*'
Henry Spicer: '*Yes.*'

The next witness to be called was Edward Villiers, who had found Edith's mutilated body on the morning of the 10th of December. He repeated the evidence that he had given at the police court as to how he came across Edith's body. When asked, Mr Gill informed Judge Matthews that he had no questions for the witness.

William Stanford was the next witness to appear before the court. He explained that he had been working with Edward Villiers in Rock Street on the morning of the 10th of December. He recalled that at about 12.30 pm, Edward Villiers had informed him of the murder, and as a result, the two gardeners had returned to the barn where he had observed a child's body lying on the floor, just inside the door on the right-hand side.

He said he noticed a bundle of firewood and several chestnuts lying around the body. Also on the floor was a boy's cap, a small pair of knickers saturated with blood, and a straw hat directly behind the child's head. William Stamford explained that he had sent Edward Villiers to go and inform the police and had found Doctor Humphrey in his absence. Without undergoing cross-examination, William Stamford was discharged from giving evidence.

The next witness called was Doctor Humphrey, who repeated the evidence he had given to the police court about being called to the field by William Stamford on Friday, 10th of December, at about a quarter to one in the afternoon. He recalled walking into the barn and immediately seeing the body of a small child lying dead on the floor. He explained that the child's head was near the east wall of the building and her feet towards the southwest border and that she was clearly dead.

Doctor Humphrey explained that the child's clothes were turned up at the waist, over the upper body, and covered with blood. He remembered that Edith had been undressed except for her feet. He recounted that a pair of blood-smeared knickers were lying far from the body. Doctor Humphrey explained that the child's face was livid and discoloured, indicating that death had occurred from asphyxia. He described how the lower part of the body was very much injured, particularly the genitals.

He informed the court that the spot where the body was found was dark, which meant he could not carefully examine the area or the body. He also stated that when he arrived at the barn, rigour Mortis was well established, which suggested that the child had been dead for many hours. Mr Gill was then cross-examined. Bizarrely, the questions did not relate to Edith's injuries but were aimed at George Henry Wood's mental state.

Mr Gill: *'Did you make the post-mortem examination?'*

Doctor Humphrey: *'No.'*

Mr Gill: *'From what you saw, you would say that the child had been subjected to considerable violence?'*

Doctor Humphrey: *'Yes.'*

Mr Gill: *'Have you seen the report of Dr Saunders in this case?'*

Doctor Humphrey: *'Yes.'*

Mr Gill: *'You have, I believe, made no study of epilepsy?'*

Doctor Humphrey: *'No.'*
Mr Gill: *'And have no experience?'*
Doctor Humphrey: *'I have had experience in ordinary practice.'*
Mr Gill: *'But not epilepsy?'*
Doctor Humphrey: *'No.'*
The Doctor was then dismissed from the dock.

P.C. Pelling was the next witness to be called, who repeated the evidence he had given at the police court. He recalled how he was called to the playing field on the morning of the 10th of December. He explained that the body had been removed by an ambulance and taken to the mortuary and that Edward Jeal had identified the body as his daughter's. He recalled picking up a cap and a bundle of wood once the body had been removed.

Lastly, he conceded that the circus George Henry Wood said he had visited on the night of the 10th of December was in North Street, Brighton, which was a considerable distance from where Edith's body had been found. He acknowledged that if George Henry Wood had been at the circus, he could not have possibly been the murderer.

Mr Gill then cross-examined the witness, still keen to focus on George Henry Wood's state of mind at his arrest.

He said, *'I don't know if you happened to be at the police station when the prisoner was there?'*

P.C. Pelling: *'No, Sir.'*

Recognising that P.C. Pelling was unwilling to support the suggestion that George Henry Wood was of unsound mind, Mr Gill informed the judge that he had no further questions, so P.C. Pelling was released from the court.

The next witness to be called was Martin Marchant, who worked as a cabman at the Brighton Station Goods Yard. He explained that on the 10th of December, he had bumped into George Henry Wood. Martin Marchant explained that the prisoner had asked to borrow 2d. Martin Marchant recalled asking George Henry Wood if he needed the money to buy a pint of beer, to which he had replied that he wanted to take a bath. Mr Gill informed the court that he did not wish to cross-examine the witness.

The response to this witness led Mr Day to address the court. He stated that the following three prosecution witnesses would show that George Henry Wood took a bath on the 10th of December. He informed the judge that due to Mr Gill not cross-examining the previous witnesses, he felt it optional to call the other three.

At this point, Mr Day returned to George Henry Wood's suspicious statement about the murder. He called John Scrase, who also worked at the Brighton Station Goods Yard. He repeated his short conversation with George Henry Wood about the murder on the 11th of December, 1891. Afterwards, he said he heard nothing more about the murder until about 7 pm that evening. Mr Gill then cross-examined the witness. He chose not to dispute his evidence but focused on his client's character.

He said, *'Did you know this man pretty well?'*

John Scrase: *'Yes.'*

Mr Gill: *'And you describe him as a peaceful, quiet and sober man?'*

Mr Day: *'You always found him to be intelligent?'*

John Scrase: *'Yes.'*

The next witness to be called was Albert Fisher, also employed by the Brighton Railway Company. He explained to the court that he remembered seeing the prisoner leaving the goods yard on Friday, the 10th of December, at about twenty minutes to two in the afternoon. He recalled that the two had briefly spoken, and at the end of the conversation, George Henry Wood had stated that he was going down to North Street public baths.

The following witnesses related to the local newspapers and the times that they first reported news of the murder. The prosecution alleged that George Henry Wood had made damning comments about the murder, which he could not have known unless he was involved. In addition, if the prosecution could establish that George Henry Wood had knowledge of the murder on the day after the murder, it would totally disprove his statement about not having any recollection of his actions.

The first of these witnesses to be called was Horace Mockett, who explained that he was the Manager of the Sussex Evening Times. He informed the court that on the afternoon of the 10th of December, his publication's first edition containing any reference to Edith's murder was at 3.15 pm and included a concise account with limited details.

Keen to protect the basis of his defence case, Mr Gill briefly cross-examined Horace Mockett to try and cast doubt over when his publication first carried news of Edith's murder.

He said, *'Had you heard of the murder before that?'*

Horace Mockett: *'Yes.'*

Mr Gill: *'At Two o'clock?'*

Horace Mockett: *'I think it was about a quarter to two; we knew it by two o'clock.'*

Mr Gill: *'Before you knew of the murder, you had heard about it?'*

Horace Mockett: *'Yes.'*

Mr Gill: *'You had heard the body had been found about half-past twelve?'*
Horace Mockett: *'I don't know exactly what time.'*

William Moody, the chief publisher of the Brighton Argus, was the next witness to give evidence. He explained that the paper's first edition, which contained any reference to the murder, was first sold at 3.40 pm, which the jury knew was well after George Henry Wood's initial damning comments.

At this stage, Judge Matthews informed the court that the proceedings would pause briefly. George Henry Wood was led back to the custody cells, and the barristers returned to their chambers. On reflection, Mr Day must have felt that the case was going better than expected. The evidence was damning and, although circumstantial, had painted a consistent and credible timeline that firmly pointed to George Henry Wood's guilt.

The same successes could not be said for the defence's case. Mr Gill appears to have abandoned disproving the evidence against his client. Aside from a few half-hearted insinuations, Mr Gill had not attempted to debunk, let alone discredit, hardly any evidence.
However, there was still a long way to go, and it is clear from the case file that Mr Gill would argue that his client suffered from epileptic mania, resulting from alcohol and lust-induced seizures around the time Edith was murdered.

As referenced in his opening statement, Mr Day was aware of this fact. He knew he could not afford to be complacent. However, he was not overtly concerned and was fully prepared to challenge this aspect of the defence's case.

Chapter 22: *'He knew perfectly the charges against him!'*

After a few minutes, the interested parties re-entered the court, and the proceedings resumed. Francis Simmonds, gatekeeper at the Trafalgar Street entrance to Brighton Station's Goods yard, was called to the witness box. He explained that on the 10th of December, he had been on duty at the gatehouse from two to six pm. He testified that he had not seen George Henry Wood go in or out of the Goods Yard between 4.30 and 5.00 pm.

Francis Simmonds was then cross-examination by Mr Gill, who wanted to discredit his evidence. He was aware that George Henry Wood had informed the police that he had learned of the murder after hearing the newspaper boys calling the headlines after leaving the goods yard during his break.

Mr Gill asked, *'Do you know that the prisoner left the works from 3.30 to 4 pm?'*

Francis Simmonds: *'No, I do not.'*

Mr Gill: *'You do not work at the Cheapside entrance to the works and would not have known if he left through the other gate?'*

Francis Simmonds: *'No, Sir, I would not.'*

The following witness to be called was Detective Inspector Jupp. He informed the court that he had been sent to the Brighton Station Goods Yard on the 11th of December 1891 to interview and arrest George Henry Wood.

He said, *'After I arrested the prisoner on Friday, the 11th of December, I asked, 'Is your name George Henry Wood?' He said, 'Yes.' I said, 'You were in Lavender Street last night at about 8 pm, and he said, 'No, I was not.' I said, 'Do you know Police Constable Tuppen?' and he said, 'I do not.' I said, 'Will you accompany me to the town hall and see Tuppen,' he said,*

'Very well, Sir.' I said, 'Tuppen states that he knows you very well and that you were the worst for a drink when he saw you last night.' He said, 'I was not there. When I left off work, I went straight to the circus. 'I asked, 'Is there anyone you can refer me to who knows you were at the circus last night?' He said, 'No unless the man at the door saw me.' I asked, 'Where are the leggings you wore last night?' He said, 'I will get them for you', and he did so. We then went to the town hall, where he was placed in a row with eleven other men for identification. I afterwards told the prisoner that he would be charged with outraging and murdering a little child named Edith Jeal in a shed in a field near the hospital. He very faintly said, 'No.' He was taken to the cell and, under instruction, removed his clothes. I discovered the flap of the trousers was very wet and blood-stained inside. I also found blood stains on his flannel vest and drawers. His cotton shirt also had large stains, but I could not say what they were. The blood on the flap of the trousers was wet, giving it the appearance of being washed. I mentioned that at the time to the Superintendent. After the clothes were, the clothes were sent to Doctor Stevenson.'

At this point, Inspector Jupp briefly displayed the clothes to the court and continued with his evidence.

He said, '*When the prisoner was in the cell, he seemed dazed, and Superintendent Carter asked, 'Do you understand the nature of the charge?' the prisoner replied, 'Yes, but I don't remember anything about it.' On the Sunday following, P.C. Rampton handed me a letter the prisoner had written to his mother and father.'*

Inspector Jupp read George Henry Wood's letter to his father in full. After this, Mr Gill began his cross-examination. He knew that as a senior police officer, the jury would not question Inspector Jupp's integrity and that any attempt to discredit his evidence would be dimly looked upon by the jury. Instead, Mr Gill focused on George Henry Wood's state of mind during and after the crime.

He said, '*Did he appear dazed when he was at the station?*'

Inspector Jupp: '*Yes.*'

Mr Gill: '*Did he understand what the charge was?*'

Inspector Jupp: '*Yes, he perfectly understood the charges.*'

Mr Gill: '*Did he write the letter before the Judge ordered him to be sent to Lewes or after?*'

Inspector Jupp: '*I think it was on the Tuesday after the murder when he was in the cells at Brighton.*'

Mr Gill: '*Did you know of his having a seizure while he was at the town hall?*'

Inspector Jupp: '*Yes, I heard so.*'
Mr Gill: '*Were you present?*'
Inspector Jupp: '*No.*'
Mr Gill: '*Do you know of the police surgeon visiting him.*'
Inspector Jupp: '*No.*'
Mr Gill: '*You were not present at the time?*'
Inspector Jupp: '*No - others were present.*'
Mr Gill: '*Very well, I will not trouble you about that.*'

Mr Day, who had carefully listened to Mr Gill's insinuations, arose from the barrister's bench and asked the witness some of his questions.

He said, '*Do you believe the prisoner understood the charges against him?*'

Inspector Jupp: '*When I spoke to him on Friday night, he understood me. As far as I could tell, he seemed to possess his senses fully.*'

This concluded Inspector Jupp's evidence. He was released from the witness box but sat with his fellow officers in the main body of the court to witness the rest of the trial.

The next witness was Doctor Douglas Ross, who repeated his evidence at the police court. The court transcripts state that he provided further details about the horrific internal injuries that little Edith had sustained. His testimony is shocking and shows the brutality that Edith Jeal had suffered. Anyone who might be triggered by such accounts should avoid the following paragraphs.

After taking the oath, he explained that he had been called to the Freshfield Road Police Station and, under instruction from the borough police, had conducted a full post-mortem to determine Edith's cause of death.

He said, '*I examined the private parts. There was an extensive tear at the upper part. The peritoneum was torn right through and extended to the anterior bowel wall. There was a purple discolouration on the lower sides of the abdomen on the right. I made a post-mortem examination of the body the next day. The ecchymosis under the scalp corresponded to the bruises outside. The membrane of the brain was very congested, and the veins were distended with dark blood. The brain itself was very congested. The heart's left ventricle was firmly contracted, and the right side was flaccid. The lungs were filled with black blood and congested. The larynx was congested and red, and there was no trachea obstruction. The stomach was normal and contained shrimp and chestnuts. The windpipe was distended. The whole symptoms and condition pointed to death by suffocation, and I believe this was the cause of death. I found a small patch of the intestine denuded of the peritoneum to three-quarters of an inch long to an eighth of an inch broad. That must have been caused by violence. The bowels in the vicinity of it were dark green. The laceration I spoke of earlier extended upwards for about an inch and a half of the abdominal wall. The wounds had blood on them, which showed they had occurred before death. I found another injury on the right side under the skin, which extended about 3 inches and was free from blood. This injury, I believe, occurred after death. A man's person may have caused all these injuries. The rupture of the peritoneum extended up to the anterior wall of the bowel into the peritoneum cavity. It formed an orifice large enough to admit two fingers, and the posterior wall of the vagina was torn entirely through, right up to the neck of the womb. The murderer must have used very considerable violence to have caused these injuries. These injuries would have resulted in death had the child not been suffocated.'*

Mr Day: *'Do you believe that the cause of death was strangulation?'*

Doctor Ross: *'The finger marks on the neck were consistent with strangulation. In my opinion, that is what caused her death. The circumstances I have detailed led me to conclude that the child was violated and then strangled.'*

Mr Day: *'Did you examine the prisoner?'*

Doctor Ross: *'I examined the prisoner on the Sunday following the discovery of the body. I found a slight excoriation under the foreskin of the penis on the right side. I would not expect to find many injuries on the person of a man suspected of causing the injuries to the child.'*

At this point, Mr Gill cross-examined Doctor Ross, which initially focused on Edith's cause of death.

Mr Gill: *'From the post-mortem examination results, I take it generally that the injuries to the child were very atrocious?'*

Doctor Ross: *'Yes.'*

Mr Gill: *'And very great violence was used?'*

Doctor Ross: *'Yes.'*

Mr Gill: *'As to the cause of death, I understand that you say that the marks on the throat indicate that someone had throttled the child?'*

Doctor Ross: *'Yes.'*

Mr Gill: *'That was sufficient to cause throttling?'*

Doctor Ross: *'Strangulation may have been coupled with suffocation by the murderer throwing the clothes over the face and holding them there.'*

At this point, Mr Gill turned his attention to the apparent fits that George Henry Wood had suffered after his arrest. He knew Doctor Ross had attended to the prisoner after his arrest. Ever keen to promote his theory, Mr Gill posed questions allowing the jury to hear about the nature of George Henry Wood's reported attacks.

Mr Gill: *'Did you attend the prisoner at the police station when he was charged?'*

Doctor Ross: *'The police asked that I attend the prisoner on the 20th of December, the last day he appeared before the magistrates. I had just returned home from the police station when the chief constable asked me to see him urgently.'*

Mr Gill: *'Where did you see this man?'*

Doctor Ross: *'On the floor outside the cells of the hall, in the passage.'*

Mr Gill: *'What condition was he in?'*

Doctor Ross: *'I think he was having an epileptic fit.'*

Mr Gill: *'And you attended him?'*

Doctor Ross: *'I stayed some ten minutes with him.'*

Mr Gill: *'And he recovered?'*

Doctor Ross: *'Yes.'*

The Judge, who had been listening carefully, understood Mr Gill's tactics. He was aware that George Henry Wood needed to prove insanity existed if he was going to be found to have had diminished responsibility and began seeking clarity on Doctor Ross' answers.

He said, *'Did the prisoner recover before you left?'*

Doctor Ross: *'Yes, my lord.'*

Mr Gill: *'When you saw him, was he violent?'*

Doctor Ross: *'Very violent.'*

Mr Gill: *'How many men did it take to hold him?'*

Doctor Ross: *'I think there were three constables with him. When I got there, he was better, but they said they had had extreme difficulty before I arrived.'*

Mr Gill: *'Then he was being restrained by three constables?'*

Doctor Ross: *'Yes.'*

Mr Gill: *'He is a man of not strong physique?'*

Doctor Ross: *'I should say he is a very muscular man.'*

Mr Gill: *'I take it from what you saw you did not doubt that it was an epileptic fit?'*

Doctor Ross: *'I had no doubt.'*

Mr Gill: *'Were you informed that he had had other seizures there?'*

Doctor Ross: *'I was told he had another fit about a week before.'*

Mr Gill: *'And of the police surgeon attending the prisoner?'*
Doctor Ross: *'I heard so.'*

Having caused Doctor Ross to admit that George Henry Wood had suffered epileptic fits at the town hall cells, Mr Gill then turned his attention to George Henry Wood's childhood illness.

Mr Gill: *'I don't think you ever attended this man or his family, but you had a brother practising in Brighton?'*
Doctor Ross: *'I had.'*
Mr Gill: *'Do you know of your late brother attending the prisoner as a child two years of age?'*
Doctor Ross: *'I am afraid I cannot answer that. I know he attended the family.'*
Mr Gill: *'But that would be without your knowledge?'*
Doctor Ross: *'No.'*
Mr Gill: *'I suppose in general medical practice, a doctor would not keep records?'*
Doctor Ross: *'No.'*
Mr Gill: *'Have you looked to see whether you could find any record of it?'*
Doctor Ross: *'I have no access to the books.'*
Mr Gill: *'Concerning epilepsy, assuming a child was to have epileptic fits at two years of age, would that seriously affect his afterlife?'*
Doctor Ross: *'It would affect him to a certain extent.'*
Mr Gill: *'In what way?'*
Doctor Ross: *'I should expect to find him weaker in brain power if he suffers from fits frequently.'*

The Judge interrupted again at this point. Unhappy with Doctor Ross's generic answers, he said, *'You could not say that the man would be permanently affected if he suffered from a single fit at two years old?'*
Doctor Ross: *'Not unless I knew how frequently they occurred.'*
Mr Gill: *'Can you say it would be likely to be more serious to his brain power, the effect of having a fit so early in life as that?'*

Judge Matthews, who doubted the plausibility of one fit causing significant brain damage, again interrupted to say, *'After just one fit?'*
Mr Gill: *'Yes.'*
Doctor Ross: *'I could not say of one fit.'*
Mr Gill: *'The effect of his epileptic fit would show his tendency.'*

Doctor Ross: *'I could not say it was an epileptic fit in those days.'*

Mr Gill: *'Well-defined symptoms are touching the question of whether a fit is an epileptic fit.'*

Doctor Ross: *'Yes, but I did not see him then.'*

Mr Gill: *'A child may have the same symptoms, I suppose, as a grown person?'*

Doctor Ross: *'I think an epileptic fit, an attack from indigestion or even worms would have the same character at that age.'*

Mr Gill: *'With regards to foaming at the mouth, biting of the tongue or so forth?'*

Doctor Ross: *'I think so.'*

Mr Gill: *'Do you think a medical man would be unable to form an opinion about that?'*

Doctor Ross: *'I would have to see the fit to say the nature of any fit.'*

Mr Gill: *'Have you any doubt that a medical man can form an opinion about its nature at that age?'*

Doctor Ross: *'I don't think an ordinary medical man can tell the difference between an epileptic fit at that age and a fit from stomach irritation, worms or indigestion.'*

Mr Gill: *'You didn't examine this man yourself carefully?'*

Doctor Ross: *'I examined him on Sunday the 15th.'*

Mr Gill: *'A person having an epileptic fit will, I suppose, while the fit is on, certainly experience a loss of consciousness.'*

Doctor Ross: *'That is so!'*

Mr Gill: *'Do you know whether an epileptic subject would be violent immediately before a seizure?'*

Doctor Ross: *'Not before the seizure. I should expect it afterwards.'*

Mr Gill: *'With regards to foaming at the mouth, biting of the tongue or so forth?'*

Doctor Ross: *'I think so.'*

Mr Gill: *'Do you think a medical man would be unable to form an opinion about that?'*

Doctor Ross: *'I would like to see the fit.'*

Mr Gill: *'Have you any doubt that a medical man can form an opinion about its nature at that age?'*

Doctor Ross: *'As I said, I don't think an ordinary medical man can tell the difference between an epileptic fit at that age and a fit from stomach irritation, worms or indigestion.'*

Mr Gill: *'You didn't examine this man yourself carefully?'*

Doctor Ross: *'I examined him on the Sunday following Friday, the 13th.'*

Mr Gill: *'A person having an epileptic fit will, I suppose, while the fit is on, certainly experience a loss of consciousness?'*

Doctor Ross: *'That is so.'*

Mr Gill: *'Do you know whether an epileptic subject would be very violent immediately before a seizure?'*

Doctor Ross: *'Not before the seizure. I should expect it afterwards.'*

Mr Gill: *'I was going to ask you that momentarily. Would you expect it in the first place, before the seizure?'*

Doctor Ross: *'I have not known it before, but I have after.'*

Mr Gill: *'Do you know as a fact that after the seizure, the fit itself has passed, that an epileptic subject may be in a great state of violence?'*

Doctor Ross: *'I should say they would show violence if they were in a state of epileptic mania.'*

The Judge wanted clarity of this last statement and asked, *'Is that after the seizure?'*

Doctor Ross: *'Yes, after an epileptic seizure.'*

The Judge: *'Doctor Ross, that is not, I think, what counsel is asking?'*

Mr Gill continued, *'My proposition is that after the fit is passed, there may be continuity, an outbreak of violence?'*

Doctor Ross: *'Not always. One man may get an attack of epileptic mania after a fit. Another may be perfectly good. It is the exception to get mania after an epileptic fit, not the rule.*

The Judge: *'Then it is so that the person usually recovers?'*

Doctor Ross: *'Perfectly.'*

Mr Gill: *'And they would be quite sane?'*

Doctor Ross: '*Yes, generally, unless they had mania.'*

Mr Gill: *'This mania is a condition of the mind closely associated with epilepsy?'*

Doctor Ross: '*Yes, closely allied.'*

Mr Gill: *'It may be found in a good many cases, I think, after an attack of epilepsy. I suggest that mania may precede a fit that a definite form of mania may precede a seizure?'*

Doctor Ross: '*I am not an expert. I can only give you my experience.'*

The Judge: *Have you ever known that?'*

Doctor Ross: '*I have not.'*

Mr Gill: *'You, of course, would not have a large experience of epileptics?'*

Doctor Ross: '*As large as the majority of ordinary practitioners.'*

Mr Gill: '*You think mania would be more likely to follow a fit?'*

Doctor Ross: '*That is my experience.'*

Mr Gill: *'You would not be surprised to see an outbreak of great violence follow a fit?'*

Doctor Ross: *'I have known epileptics to tear down a padded room while in a fit.'*

Mr Gill: *'Is it per your experience, or from what you have learned on the subject, that a person may be a perfectly blank as to their previous actions?'*

Doctor Ross: *'Yes, and he is a perfect lunatic then.'*

Mr Gill: *'A person would be a lunatic while the mania lasts.'*

Doctor Ross: *'That is it.'*

Mr Gill: *'And afterwards, the same man might later appear to be quite rational?'*

Doctor Ross: *'No, not just after a fit.'*

Mr Gill: *'Do you mean a person may have a fit of mania and may afterwards be perfectly sane to speak to?'*

Doctor Ross: *'If a man had epileptic mania, I should not expect to find him 'compos mentis' for some days afterwards.'*

Mr Gill: *'This is a matter which is, of course, made a special study by some persons, but you yourself have not made it a special study?'*

Doctor Ross: *'I have not studied epilepsy and am not an expert.'*

Mr Gill: *'How would you describe the mania preceding or following an epileptic fit?'*

The Judge: *'The doctor has not said that he knows of an instance before the fit.'*

Mr Gill: *'Do you know this man has been examined at the instance of the Treasury authorities?'*

Doctor Ross: *'I do.'*

The Judge: *'And also at the wish of his friends?'*

Doctor Ross: *'Yes.'*

Mr Gill: *'You know that?'*

Doctor Ross: *'Yes.'*

Mr Gill: *'Have you seen the report made by Doctor Saunders?'*

Doctor Ross: *'Yes.'*

Mr Gill: *'You know what his position is?'*

Doctor Ross: *'Yes.'*

Mr Gill: *'What is he?'*

Doctor Ross: *'Medical Superintendent of the Lunatic Asylum for Surrey and Sussex at Haywards Heath.'*

Mr Gill: *'Have you read his report generally?'*

Doctor Ross: *'Yes, I have. I agree with some parts, and I differ on some matters.*

Mr Gill: *'Concerning the question of outbursts of epilepsy or recurrence of fits, do you attach importance to the lapse of time between them?'*

Doctor Ross: *'I should attach this importance, that they would be more violent when it broke out after a long interval.'*

Mr Gill: *'Would the effect of drink upon a man who has been a total abstainer be likely to bring on a seizure?'*

Doctor Ross: *'It would possibly bring it on. Debauchery could also bring it on.'*

Mr Gill: *'Either the excitement of drink or the excitement of lust would probably bring it on?'*

Doctor Ross: *'Yes, if a man is predisposed to it.'*

Mr Gill: *'Or both combined?'*

Doctor Ross: *'Or both combined could cause much worse seizures still.'*

Mr Gill: *'How often have you had the opportunity of seeing a man under the influence of epileptic manic or furore?'*

Doctor Ross: *'I have seen many, but I cannot say the number exactly. Possibly one to two hundred, maybe more.'*

The Judge: *'Mania following a fit of epilepsy?'*

Doctor Ross: *'Yes.'*

Mr Gill: *'In your judgement, is it of the greatest importance that a person liable to that should be closely watched?'*

Doctor Ross: *'Yes, he should be restrained or controlled.'*

The Judge: *'This is while the fit of mania is on?'*

Doctor Ross: *'Yes.'*

Mr Gill: *'While the fit of mania is actually on, what do you say should take place?'*

Doctor Ross: *'He should be placed in a padded room.'*

Mr Gill: *'A fit having passed, is it not likely to recur at any moment?'*

Doctor Ross: *'A man who has a fit is always liable to a recurrence of it.'*

Mr Gill: *'You say a man having an epileptic taint and being subject to epileptic mania should be under restraint.'*

Doctor Ross: *'No.'*

Mr Gill: *'How is he to be protected against himself or others?'*

Doctor Ross: *'Some men may be perfectly sane, and some may be violent.'*

The Judge: *'If a man has had an attack of epilepsy, he should always be put under restraint, do you suggest?'*

Mr Gill: *'No, I suggest it would be good for a man to be carefully watched after an outbreak.'*

Doctor Ross: *'If he is violent, then yes. However, I know many epileptics going about and doing their work just fine.'*

Mr Gill: *'And they are still dangerous lunatics?'*

Doctor Ross: *'No.'*

Mr Gill: *'Would they be dangerous lunatics if the fit continues?'*

Doctor Ross: *'They still might have a fit without violence afterwards.'*

Mr Gill: *'But they are liable at any moment to a fit with violence and mania afterwards.'*

Doctor Ross: *'This is so. I speak, of course, of confirmed epileptics.'*

Mr Gill: *How would you describe a confirmed epileptic? How many fits is it necessary for him to be considered a confirmed epileptic?'*

Doctor Ross: *'I do not think the number of fits matters very much. A man may have fits regularly at intervals of a month, two months, or three months. If it went on for years, I would say he was a confirmed epileptic.'*

The Judge: *'And if these attacks were followed by mania, you might consider it necessary he should be restrained?'*

Doctor Ross: 'Yes.'

Mr Gill: *'If there is a considerable lapse of time since a man had a fit, are you of the opinion that he is likely to have a bad fit when he had one?'*

Doctor Ross: *'Yes.'*

Mr Gill: *'From that point of view, would it be better if he fits more frequently?'*

Doctor Ross: *'That is so.'*

Mr Gill: *'The violence is extreme in epileptic fits?'*

Doctor Ross: *'In all bad cases.'*

Mr Gill: *'What do you call a bad epileptic fit?'*

Doctor Ross: *'I am speaking of the after results. A man may have a bad fit without mania or a slight fit and an attack of epileptic mania afterwards.'*

Mr Gill: *'But with regards to the fits only, what would you call a bad fit?'*

Doctor Ross: *'When there is foaming at the mouth and biting off his tongue and convulsions.'*

Mr Gill: *'If a man had convulsions requiring three or four men to hold him down, would that be evidence of a bad fit?'*

Doctor Ross: *'Yes, if the men were necessary, but the best plan is to leave them alone with an attendant to see they do not harm themselves.'*

Mr Gill: *'To protect a man from himself?'*

Doctor Ross: *'Yes.'*

Mr Gill: *'From his own violence?'*

Doctor Ross: *'A man in an ordinary epileptic fit is not dangerous to others.'*

Mr Gill: *'Do you agree that between 25 and 30 is a dangerous time in the life of a man with epileptic taint?'*

Doctor Ross: *'My experience is that this is about the usual time when epilepsy develops itself with more violent attacks.'*

The Judge: *'And more frequent?'*

Doctor Ross: *'I did not say more frequently. The man is in the full vigour of health then. He is the strongest and most subject to excitement.'*

The Judge: *'Have you any doubt that an epileptic subject, when not under the influence of either the fit or the mania, may be a perfectly rational, intelligent person?'*

Doctor Ross: *'Quite so.'*

Mr Gill: *'I think you told me you agree with the proposition that while the mania was on after the fit had passed, the patient would be unconscious of his actions?'*

Doctor Ross: *'He might or he might not. I would not say so in all cases. He might know what he was doing, although he was perfectly insane.'*

Mr Gill: *'There are a great many lunatics who know perfectly well what they are doing?'*

Doctor Ross: *'Yes.'*

Mr Gill: *'Do you think a man may be so drunk as to be unconscious of what he is doing?'*

Doctor Ross: *'Yes, I do.'*

The trial, at this point, paused for lunch. After the short break, Mr Day re-examined Doctor Ross for the prosecution, who wanted to clarify some of his previous answers relating to epileptic mania.

He said, *'How do you distinguish between epileptic fits and epileptic insanity?'*

Doctor Ross: *'I distinguish between epileptic fits and epileptic insanity. I observed nothing in the prisoner to indicate his suffering from epileptic insanity. It would not be possible for a man suffering from an epileptic fit to carry a child for a quarter of a mile. The first symptom of epilepsy would be the man falling down. He becomes quite helpless. I did not see the prisoner seized with the epileptic fit. I saw him some quarter of an hour after he had fallen down in the police cells. He was unconscious at the time I saw him. He was foaming at the mouth, and there were convulsions. It is very possible as well for a man to simulate a fit. When I have seen the prisoner at other times, he seemed perfectly in possession of his senses.'*

The Judge: *'Was there anything to show he was a confirmed epileptic as far as you could see?'*

Doctor Ross: *'He had not the appearance of a confirmed epileptic, to begin with.'*

The Judge: *'Are there any other indications?'*

Doctor Ross: *'No, you're Lordship.'*

Mr Gill: *'Would you not expect a confirmed epileptic to be of weak physique?'*

Doctor Ross: *'Not necessarily.'*

Mr Gill: *'I may take it among your epileptic patients; many of them are going about their ordinary avocations in life?'*

Doctor Ross: *'Yes, I see a great number of them. I had a housemaid myself for four years who was an epileptic.'*

Mr Gill: *'There was a question I should have asked you before on the other part of the case. Could you tell from examining the little girl's body how long she had been dead?'*

Doctor Ross: *'Quite. Seventeen hours, as Rigour Mortis had set in.'*

This marked the end of Doctor Ross' extensive evidence, and he was released from the witness stand, no doubt to his relief. Any hopes held by Mr Gill that he could successfully argue that George Henry Wood's illness legally made him irresponsible for his actions must have, at this point, completely diminished.

Doctor Ross doubted whether George Henry Wood suffered epilepsy as a child. He also disputed that the fits George Henry Wood had suffered since arrests were likely due to alcohol withdrawal. Damningly for the defence, Judge Mathew's interjections suggest that he also agreed with the prosecution.

The final prosecution witness to be called was Doctor Thomas Stevenson, Home Office Analyst. After taking the oath, he told the court, *'On the 14th of December, I received a parcel of clothes from Detective Jupp. A coat, trousers, drawers, and shirt were sent to me for inspection. There were smears of blood on the coat and on the edge of the right pocket, both inside and outside. There were also two on the front left of the coat and below the left pocket. On the trousers, there was a very large, still moist smear inside the front turn-down flap. Smears of blood were on the outer side of the pocket, to the left and a little below the neckband, at the front. On the Oxford shirt, there were two smears of blood to the left and a little below the neckband at the front. The undershirt or vest had blood on it in several places. These were on both the inner surface and the bottom edge. On the drawers, there were five stains of blood. The flannel vest had been wetted and rubbed, and the trousers flap's inner side appeared to have also been washed. It was wet but still sticky with blood. The blood was mammalian. The stains on the inner side of the trouser flap were not probably more than four or five days old, and the rest of the blood might have been of the same date, but certainly, all of it was less than a fortnight old. I examined them chiefly on the 14th of December and 15th.'*

Doctor Stevenson was not cross-examined and was released from the stand, which concluded the case for the prosecution.

Chapter 23: 'A Frenzied Man'

Mr Gill rose to his feet, took a deep breath, and began the case for the defence. He started by delivering a lengthy opening statement.

Addressing the court, he said, *'You're Lordship and the gentleman of the jury. You will have gathered from what has occurred; several other witnesses are unavailable to give evidence which may assist you in coming to the proper conclusion in this case. Before I indicate the nature of that evidence, I might say a word or two about my position in representing the prisoner. Firstly, can I draw your attention to the nature of the crime the prisoner is charged with? The prosecution has suggested that the child was outraged by this man and, afterwards, murdered. The case put forward by the prosecution is circumstantial evidence, which you must consider to conclude that the prisoners were the man responsible for the act of outrage and murder. You will have gathered from the prisoner's statement and the letter he wrote to his father that he says he has no recollection of his movements after tea time on Thursday, the 10th of December. He states his mind is a complete blank regarding it, and he cannot recollect any circumstance. Though the crime has been brought home to his feet, he is unconscious of any criminal act he might have committed. That being his position concerning the matter, I cannot deal with the witnesses in cross-examination. I am not in a position to defend a man charged with murder who has his faculties. This is very different from a man who can give such information to allow his counsel to test the accuracy of the evidence presented by the prosecution witnesses. I cannot suggest something that would show that they were mistaken. I am practically placed in the same position as the man himself. I have nothing to discredit those who give evidence in the matter. I take their proof, and I do not question it. Some issues I have asked about are outside the case, but as to what they say they saw upon the evening in question, I accept it, and you must judge it for what it is worth. But, gentlemen, the evidence is circumstantial, a class of evidence that, to some extent, is dangerous to act upon. The case has no direct evidence, but it simply and solely relies on inferences drawn from specific issues. Of course, you must not lose sight of the fact that this man on trial does not offer any explanation. But remembering that, he says he cannot remember anything for reasons included in his letter. Now, gentlemen, it is a case of circumstantial evidence, a case of the most terrible character, a case of the most atrocious nature, a subject too horrible to contemplate. Suppose the man who was guilty of it was sane. The details of the case from the very description of it, without one particle of explanation outside the crime itself, must suggest that the man who did it, whoever it was, must be bereft of his senses. It must have been a man without any particle of feeling that you would imagine being in the mind of any ordinary being. It is a crime revolting, horrible, and unnatural, and if you look at the details of it, you find that the more you examine it, the more horrific, abnormal and revolting it appears. However, this man stands accused of committing such a crime; therefore, he has to answer. You are trying him here for murder, not for the offence of having carnal knowledge of the child, though this is an incident of the case. Even if you conclude this man was conscious during the felonious act, you still have a second question to consider. If this man committed the murder but was irresponsible for his actions at the time, must this man answer with life as a responsible being? Gentleman, apart from the murder itself, one cannot help but think when you hear of a man having carnal knowledge of a child of five years of age, a little mite as you know, the child would be, seeing, as you have seen the older brother whose head hardly came up to the top of the witness box. Remember, he is nine years of age, and you will remember that the murdered child was a child of such tender years. Is it possible to believe that a sane man committed such an act? It is an unnatural offence that a rational man could not be guilty of. Any man possessing his ordinary faculties could not commit such a crime. But be of no doubt that someone committed such an act upon that child that night. It was a crime accompanied by extraordinary violence, an offence followed by the child's killing, but a killing under what circumstances? A killing as it appears, with a ferocity which would indicate that it was the act or the acts of a frenzied man. It was not a case of a man killing a child to destroy evidence. A sane man might have done this after strangling and smothering the child as described by the doctor. The marks indicate sufficient violence on the neck of the child to destroy life, and if that were the motive influencing the man at the time, his act would have been intelligible. But that is not what has happened. The doctor who did the post-mortem and other witnesses proved that with extraordinary ferocity and unprecedented violence, horrible injuries were inflicted upon the body of this poor little child, little more than an infant, when alone in that place. For the man I represent here, I ask you to have in your mind when you consider the question, the awful nature of the crime itself, the description of the crime, and other associated circumstances. If you're satisfied beyond all reasonable doubt that this was the man who committed the crime, you have to consider another question, which I shall submit to you. You will have to decide whether you believe these were the actions of a man who was irresponsible for his actions and had no control over himself. Was this man a victim of mania at the time of the act? If this is your belief, he should not end his life on the gallows. Instead, this man should be forever shut up in some place to prevent him from making mischief to himself or anyone he may encounter. My friend, Mr Day, almost unconsciously spoke with the surprise that a man might be guilty of such a crime. He said the crime was 'inhuman'. It was inhuman. You would not expect a man in control of his senses to be guilty of it. But, gentlemen, it is rightly said that when a man takes a life, and it is brought home to his feet, he is responsible. He is presumed to be sane until the contrary is proven. The accused is responsible for establishing to the satisfaction of a jury that he was not accountable for his actions. It would not be a conclusion that you would regret. It would not be a conclusion that you should be unwilling to arrive at for the sake of human nature that Mr Day speaks. This man was, in fact, irresponsible, and what he did was under the influence of mania and as one bereft of his faculties. Gentlemen, let's consider what we know beyond the post-mortem and injuries sustained by the child. Outside the evidence given by the gardener who first saw the child and, with good reason, did not interfere with it and spoke of the terrible injuries. Outside of these facts, what else have you heard from the prosecution about this man on trial? The Crown's witnesses said the prisoner had worked for the Railway Company for some time. You have it as fact, incidentally proved by one of the witnesses who had known him for ten years, that he had apparently gone away for several years and that he had seen him frequently during the past eighteen months to two years. You have the railway servants telling you that from the time he was in their service, he was a well-conducted, hard-working, sober and inoffensive man. Therefore, you have his life accounted for the whole time he was in their employment, up to the afternoon of the crime. This man has got the best character considering his circumstances. All that could have been given in this man's favour has been. He is said to be a harmless, inoffensive, well-conducted and sober man. However, that day, for the first time, he was said to be under the influence of drink. On that afternoon, a man who has known him over the past twenty months said he was so drunk that he was incapable of taking off his coat, having given way to temptation after obtaining a drink on that day. We may suppose that this happened because he was engaged in carting from the station to some brewery for the entire day. Between 6 and 7 pm, this man, previously a teetotaller was so intoxicated that he could not take off his coat and was sent home from work. Having got off his coat, he sits down and remains for some minutes in the hut where he was, then leaves the premises of the Railway Company. Remember, he says that from a time earlier than that, he did not know his movements in the sense of any recollection. I asked the doctor whether a man could be so intoxicated that he could be unconscious of what he was doing. I wondered if a man could do various actions he may not recall afterwards. No doubt such a condition may be arrived at, and my lord will direct you upon the aspect of the case as far as this man's condition arose from drink. I also introduce drunkenness for another reason, which I suggest was relevant to the crime. In some of the questions, I asked Doctor Ross whether alcohol could bring about the epileptic seizure this man suffered from that night. But whether this was the case or not, it will not be necessary for me to argue elaborately to decide responsibility concerning drunkenness. There are differences of opinion on the subject. One hears the statement that drunkenness is no excuse for crime, and that is a statement that is generally accepted. Still, when a man must form in his mind some definite intention, it is essential that the accused's condition be included in it and should have weight in consideration of the case. The man became drunk, not with the view of committing a crime, but due to abstinence for a considerable time. His temperance meant he quickly fell under the influence of the drink, so much so he reached the point of unconsciousness of action. How far this fact has on the question of intention is a matter for my lord to direct you. As I have said, I introduced that for another purpose, not solely to raise the condition of the man's mind but to suggest that the man had a recurrence of epilepsy that he was at any time liable to suffer. Is it impossible to believe that an epileptic seizure occurred and a man committed the crime during the furore before or after it? Once the fit had passed off, the same man inflicted those terrible injuries upon the child. Now, gentlemen, I got from the police constable as he stated that when he charged this man, the prisoner said he had no recollection of the evening of the crime. The witness for the prosecution describes him as appearing dazed. You know that this man was an epileptic subject, or you know the defence will prove it because you already have the evidence of the witness for the prosecution. Doctor Ross saw him under the influence of an epileptic fit. The police called him instead of the police surgeon because he was the nearest medical man at the time. Doctor Ross states that he does not doubt that the prisoner was under the influence of an epileptic seizure. Gentlemen, there is no more difficult question for those dealing with crime than the question of insanity. When it is suggested that a man that committed a crime has an inflicted mind, it is often considered with the greatest possible suspicion. As an advocate, I do not have any right to express myself. However, when the question of insanity is introduced, it is undesirable for close inquiry into the matter. Rightly so, allowances are given to witnesses that have to answer such questions, which find themselves at the court's disposal and have to express an opinion on the subject. Of course, happily, I trust you do not know insanity personally. I trust it may never be brought home to you by anyone belonging to you. What a calamity the curse of epilepsy is for a family. But for all I know, there may be a man among you who has realised what a cruel visitation it is when it does occur. Now Gentlemen, as far as I can, I propose to prove to you that this man has been subject to epilepsy for his entire life. Doctor Ross has told you that if there is a period of a man's life in which he is most subject to epilepsy if he has the epileptic taint, it is between the ages of 25 and 30. This man is 29 years old, so you have him at a period of life where if the taint is in him, it is most likely to produce the worst possible results. Epilepsy you will only know of from what you heard from the witnesses. It is a terrible malady closely allied to insanity. It is a form of insanity. It is not extraordinary to find several members of a family suffering from the condition. When an individual at some point in his life has epilepsy, I suggest it will likely affect them for the remainder of their days. And though it may be challenging to establish that a young child is affected by epilepsy, I will, as far as I can, show you what the condition was as a child. Having spent his life there, his father, a respectable tradesman in Brighton, has to go through the ordeal of seeing his son tried for murder. However, he is a necessary witness and is required to lay the foundations for you to come to, what I submit, is the humane and natural conclusion in this case. I hope you will find this man irresponsible at the time of the crime. Therefore, I shall get as much evidence from his father as possible. Gentleman, I will tell you exactly what this man's life has been like. He is 29 years old. When the prisoner was about two years old, he suffered from fits of some kind. His father will tell you what he saw and say that his child was a patient of Doctor Ross, the brother of the witness that testified earlier today. However, I regret to say that this man is dead and, therefore, I am incapable of calling him. He and other gentlemen in general practice do not keep records of particular cases they attend, having many to look after. However, the prisoner's father will tell you that the late Doctor Ross told him that his son would not survive due to the state of his head. The father will also tell you that this child had one particular fit, apart from other convulsive fits, when he foamed at the mouth and bit his tongue severely. This is as near as we can get evidence that the prisoner is an epileptic subject. The question of time elapsing between one fit and another is, I venture to say, unimportant. It is unnecessary to confirm epilepsy because sufferers experience fits every hour or every day of the week. A person may have epilepsy, a dangerous epileptic, even though a considerable time may elapse between one seizure and another. That child, commencing his life in that way, a way, I say, which would likely affect him for the remainder of his life. Fits which weakened his brain and were most damaging to him, a curse to him, as he grew up in Brighton. He joined the Navy but returned home in less than a year because of a malformation of the chest and the itch he* caught in service. After he returns home, his friends find another occupation for him on a farm. There he remained for less than a year. His employers tell his parents he has had a fit, and he returns home. After a short time, he travels to America, where he remains for seven or eight years. Then, due to the communication with his father about his condition, his father found the means to fund the prisoner's ticket back to England.

Of course, it is challenging to get the case satisfactorily before you. The prisoner is not in a position to call skilled witnesses or seek witnesses from as far away as America. It is said that the law is equal to the rich and the poor, but though that may be true to a certain extent, a man is in an infinitely better position by having the command of money to place a case of that kind satisfactorily before you. This man's case is imperfectly placed before you, as you would expect, considering his financial means. But as well as I can, incomplete as it may be, I will put as much information as I have managed to gather before you. You know that this man gave an account to his parents saying that his mind was blank concerning that night, and he is in no better position to instruct the solicitor his father employs to defend him. He can tell no other story than what is in that letter. He does not know the occurrences of that night, so what would be the position of those instructed to represent him? What would be the position of any person wishing to advise him on what course he should take? It is challenging to understand. You have heard the evidence. You learned that this man, while in the cells of Brighton Police Station, had repeated epileptic seizures of the most violent possible character. These attacks were so fierce that it required three of four men to hold him, and the police had to call for their surgeon. What would naturally occur under those circumstances? The witnesses' depositions tell of a crime with such horrific events, and knowing that they continued to have fits whilst on remand, he continued to suffer from those fearful epileptic seizures and, as he has described in his letter, his mind whilst under remand. You would say the greatest experts should consider the state of this man's mind on the matter because they should be at the service of every individual who requires them. Still, such efforts to find an expert so that we may know whether this is to be treated as a criminal responsible for his conduct, an expert to determine on the day of the crime whether the man was irresponsible were made. I say it would occur to any one of you that the proper thing to do would be to get from that man some story of his life, to let him give some account of his movement during that night, to let us know something of his life, and of how the prisoner passed his time when he was out of the country. There is a means of getting some information about his life in America. However, there is no means of bringing witnesses to the court. We cannot test his statements about his time in Canada and communicate with the people he named - people who would give truthful answers and have no motive to say anything but the truth. Some inquiries of this kind did take place to no avail. You *will suppose, too, that you will have some account of the state of the prisoner's mind up to the time he committed the crime. You should have no difficulty learning that he was employed at Brighton, working hard, abstaining from drinking, and conducting himself well. It is easy to understand from his family how he passed his time. This young man was engaged to be married. He had spent no money other than repaying the sum his father had advanced to bring him home from America and acquiring furniture for the room where he intended to live with the girl he was to marry. He speaks of this person in his letter, the letter of a man whose mind is off balance. He says there, however, of the girl he hoped to marry at Easter. So you have the man leading this right kind of life and looking forward to a respectable life. This man, who had had no seizure, was looking forward to a considerable time before anything would recur. But what unhappily occurs? This terrible misfortune occurs, this horrible incident, of his having the temptation of going to a brewery on this day, of his getting drink. However slight, still enough to deprive this man of his senses and to bring home this result, that in that drunken state, if you believe he was the man, bring him to the condition that walking about, he was unconscious of what he was doing. And what effect would these actions have on a man prone to epileptic seizures? An outbreak, of course! For a long time, this man led a respectable life in every way. What would be his state of mind when he does this insane and unnatural thing, satisfying the cravings of his unnatural lust upon that infant child? What would be the state of such a man's mind, a man unconscious as the result of drink, a man with lust, if you please? When of all times in that man's life, with the epileptic taint so strong in him, when, if not then, would he be likely to be seized with an epileptic fit of the worst possible character, and either before or I care not whether before or when recovering from a fit, be guilty of acts of automaton, unconscious acts, of violent acts, shown by the evidence, which had committed on the body of that mite of a child? You know that even occupying a police cell, he was subject to more than one fit. Do you suppose that the fits that were witnessed by the police Surgeon, by Doctor Ross, or by the policeman were, notwithstanding the interval that had elapsed since the last fit, feigned or epileptic? Would you have any doubt upon this material fact, that upon the night of the 10th of December, placed in the position in which the case for the prosecution seeks to place him, everything is favourable, everything makes it likely that at that moment the man shall be the victim of a seizure of this terrible character? Gentlemen, consider these observations and suggestions, consider whether they commend themselves to you, whether they are reasonable, whether they are based on such material as it is possible to place before you, and if you had to form your own opinion on them, without further assistance what you would say concerning it. I will assist you as far as possible by giving you the opinion of at least one man with special knowledge of the subject. I propose to call before you this man's father, the constables and such evidence as I can get for the prosecution, and the warders who saw him when he was awaiting trial. You will remember that I invited you to put yourself in the place of those representing this man after a committal trial and think of the material they could collect. This was accomplished via communications with reliable persons in America. Several communications were also made to the authorities at the request of the prisoner's friends to ask that a person selected by the Home Office should have the opportunity of forming an opinion on the subject. I hope the authorities choose those well qualified to discharge their duties. My friend, Mr Day, appears for the Treasury authorities today, and I have the honour of appearing for them elsewhere. It is supposed that they select competent men, and he is the man chosen for the particular duty they desire to discharge. Doctor Saunders, the chosen expert for the defence, is ideally qualified to speak on these matters. He has had under his charge numbers of persons suffering from this terrible disease of epilepsy. He would have frequent opportunities for forming an opinion on the consequences of epilepsy. His experience tells us that many persons with this taint commit criminal acts, criminal in themselves, but are not treated as criminals because they are regarded as irresponsible. He has been supplied with all the material available to form an opinion. I don't complain that he did not give evidence for the prosecution. In some cases, that is the course that is adopted. I don't say in every case, and I will take it upon myself to call him. He has seen the prisoner on more than one occasion. Regarding his opinion on this subject, this man has practical experience and excellent knowledge from studying books. This man is in contact with the matter on which he expresses his opinion, and you will have the opportunity of hearing that opinion. Doctor Ross has had the opportunity of reading that report, and with some of it, he agrees, and with some of it, he does not, but I say that the opinion of a man with special knowledge is of great importance. I think it is unlikely I will address you again in this case. It is not a part of my friend's duty, nor would he be disposed to do it, to struggle for a verdict in this case. He put the facts fairly before you, nor will he attempt to work for an adverse judgement unless he feels the need to do so. True, Doctor Saunders is my witness; he is my witness in the sense that I called him, but my friends select him with all the fairness which characterises the authorities in all their business. His report is at my disposal, and I understand that another specialist has examined the prisoner. He has given me the opportunity of calling Doctor Saunders. Therefore I will examine the other specialist on the matter to see if he expresses an opinion as to whether the man was responsible for his actions that night and could judge right and wrong. These are the observations I make for you. The issue is not whether this man will go free due to your verdict. All I am asking is that you say that he is guilty of the crime, but when he committed it, he was not responsible for his actions. All that means is that this man goes away from the world and is protected against him and others. He will lead a life of seclusion among other men who have committed crimes where it has been found that the condition of the mind was such that they should not be held responsible. When a person is considered a lunatic or subject to mania, it is not a subject for reproach but a subject for pity. I ask that the disgrace is not brought upon those connected with this man because disgraceful it would be if he committed this terrible crime as a conscious, responsible person. I ask you to find that he was not accountable. It is awful to have a verdict returned against him that he has executed such an act as this. Still, it will be some satisfaction to those connected with him to know that although it was the jury's opinion that he did commit the act, he did it when he was not master of himself and was not responsible for his actions. This revolting crime can be understood if you decide it was committed by a frenzied man whose actions were beyond his control. I am obliged for your attention and will proceed to put the evidence I have intimated before you.'*

This marked the end of the defence's opening statement. Mr Gill had laid out his defence strategy to the jury and began to call his witnesses to prove his case.

Chapter 24: The Medical Evidence

The first witness to be called for the defence was George Wood Senior. Addressing the court, he said, *'I am George Wood, of 11 Rock Street, Kemp Town. I am the father of the prisoner. He is twenty-nine years old. He was born in Brighton. I remember an illness he suffered when he was about two years old. Doctor Harris Ross attended him. He examined the child and stated that we should never raise him because of the compression of the brain he was suffering from. I remember one occasion, especially when he had a fit. This happened before we sent for Doctor Ross. We had a Hospital letter and were going to take him there that morning, but we sent for Doctor Ross because of the fit. It was a different kind of fit from what he had before. He foamed at the mouth and bit his tongue through. Doctor Ross attended him for some time, and he got better, but often, an evening afterwards, he would wake up screaming with a vacant manner, and it was some time before we could bring him to. He was a thin and emaciated child. He continued in this delicate state until he was eight or nine. He had scarlet fever. He got better and first went into errand boys' places. Then he went on to the ship St. Vincent, the Coastguard in our district. I was living at Black Rock, Brighton, close to the sea, which gave him the idea. He went on the ship, but in a short time, he was discharged for chest malformation. He also suffered from the itch he contracted on board the ship. He afterwards worked on a farm close to Brighton. He then enlisted in the 1st Battalion of the West Surrey Regiment. He stayed in the army for 239 days and was discharged with varicose veins. He came home again, and after that, he went to America. He remained there for nearly eight years. During the time he was there, I frequently heard from him. I had letters from Mr Goulding from America, and he also had some conversations with me about my son. Money was found for him to come home, and he came home. After he came home, his first employment* was at the Gasworks while the strike was on in London. He burst one of the veins in his legs and came home, and afterwards, he worked for the Brighton Railway Company. He worked for several weeks before being sent to London for an examination. An operation was performed on him for his varicose vein. Afterwards, he resumed his work at the Railway Company. He worked with them up until the time of his arrest. He used to be called at five am and had to get to the station at 6 am, and he worked all day through. Sometimes he came home as early as half-past seven or eight, but sometimes it was after ten before he left the yard. While working there, he conducted himself well, and I had no reason to complain. During that time, he was undoubtedly a sober man, according to my knowledge. While working, he had repaid from time to time the money sent to him to bring him back from America. He had nearly paid it all off. He was making the last payment the week he was arrested. He was courting a young woman and would marry her at Easter. I communicated all the information I had regarding my son to Mr Ayres, the solicitor, who has been acting in the matter.'

Having given his evidence, George Wood Senior was cross-examined by the prosecution, who were keen to minimise George Henry Wood's reported condition and its impact on his state of mind. The prosecution, aware that George Wood Senior would say anything to save his son's life, was keen for his words not to sway the jury.

Mr Day: *'How often have you seen your son in a fit?'*

George Wood Senior: *'What fit?'*

Mr Day: *'Have you seen him in a fit since he was eight?'*

George Wood Senior: *'No.'*

The Judge: *'He had only spoken of one fit when he was two?'*

Mr Day: *'Who is Mr Goulding who called upon you?'*

George Wood Senior: *'A Reverend gentleman from Canada.'*

Mr Day: *'Was he the chaplain of a gaol in Canada?'*

George Wood Senior: *'He was.'*

Mr Day: *'Did he visit you concerning moving your son from a gaol in Canada back to England?'*

George Wood Senior: *'We had previously exchanged letters on the subject.'*

Mr Day: *'I think he was convicted of horse stealing?'*

This question hit a nerve with George Wood Senior, who still could not bring himself to accept that his son knowingly murdered and sexually assaulted a small child. After pausing briefly, he curtly replied, *'No doubt under one of these fits!'*

Nonetheless, Mr Day had forced George Wood Senior to admit his son had a criminal history, which he knew would resonate with the jury. Having completed his task, Mr Day informed Judge Matthews that he had no further questions for the witness. At this point, the witness was discharged from the court.

Mr Ayres, George Henry Wood's principal solicitor, was the next witness to be called.

He said, *'I am from the firm Messrs. Prince and Ayres of Middle Street Brighton. At the instance of the prisoner's father, I have conducted the defence in this matter. Having received certain information from the father, I obtained a statement of his life whilst abroad. Upon receiving that statement, I communicated with several persons abroad by letter and received answers. I supplied the Treasury with copies of the letters I wrote, the answers I got, and the prisoner's statement. Some time ago, I requested that some expert should have the opportunity to examine the prisoner to inform the case. For that purpose, I supplied them with all the material in my possession, stating who the people who wrote the letters were and stating that Mr Goulding was a prison chaplain.'*

Mr Day informed the Judge that he did not wish to question the witness. Consequently, the Judge dismissed him from the witness box.

The following witnesses to appear before the court were the police constables who had guarded George Henry Wood at the town hall cells. The purpose of calling these witnesses was to prove to the jury that George Henry Wood was prone to seizures and that they were severe in nature.

P.C. Harris was the first of these witnesses to give evidence.

He said, *'I am P.C. Harris of the Brighton Borough Police, and I had the prisoner in my custody at the town hall. Whilst under my care, he had fits. The first, I think, was on the 22nd of December. He was very violent, and it took four of us to keep him steady on the ground to stop him from injuring himself on the floor. P.C. Rampton was there. I describe his condition as extremely violent. On that occasion, we did not send for a doctor. I think it was on the 30th of December that he had another fit of the same kind. Upon that occasion, he was extremely violent and showed extraordinary strength. We were astonished at a man possessing such strength. I think five constables were holding him at that time. I was present when Doctor Rogers saw him. I was not present when Doctor Ross saw him.'*

P.C. Geale was the next witness to be called. After introducing himself, he said, *'I have seen the prisoner fit outside the cells and in the private room at the Brighton police station. I was* one of the constables who assisted. I think I said I did not believe a man could have such strength. He was extremely violent.'

The next witness to be called for the defence was Doctor Rogers, who said, *'I have been a surgeon to the police force in Brighton for 20 years. On the 22nd of December, the Chief Constable called me to see the prisoner at the police station. I was asked to attend to the prisoner who was apparently having epileptic convulsions. The first attack was very severe, and he had a second attack while I was there. I have not the slightest doubt it was an epileptic seizure. In the evening, I saw him again, and he seemed calm. I saw him twice afterwards, but not in any fits. The seizure was a violent one.'*

Mr Day then cross-examined the witness, still keen to dismantle the insanity defence.
Mr Day: *'When he recovered from them, he appeared to be in a sane state of mind? Is that correct?'*
Doctor Rogers: *'He was in a muddled state of mind.'*
Mr Day: *'You said when he recovered from them; he appeared to be in a sane state of mind?'*
Doctor Rogers: *'Yes.'*
Mr Day: *'Can you be mistaken about these fits being of an epileptic character?'*
Doctor Rogers: *'I do not think so.'*
Mr Day: *'What were the outward indications?'*
Doctor Rogers: *'There were strong convulsions, the skin was red, and he foamed the mouth and struggled convulsively.'*

The following witness to be called was George Albion Read, a Lewes Prison warden guarding George Henry Wood since his remand. The defence wanted to illustrate to the jury that George Henry Wood's fits had continued after he was sent to Lewes prison. Conveniently, these attacks occurred shortly before George Henry Wood's appearance at the Court of Assize, which seems serendipitous, to say the least, considering the same situation appeared at his court appearances in Canada.
He said, *'The prison authorities have employed me as an attendant upon the prisoner. I have remained with him twelve hours out of twenty-four. He is under constant supervision. He has had three seizures whilst I have been with him. He has been in the infirmary ward since. The first seizure occurred on Sunday, the 7th of April, in the evening. When I arrived on the 4th, Governor Crickett told me he had had a fit the night before. At about 7.45 pm, he was exercising, walking up and down the ward, and suddenly fell. I went to him at once. He was*

lying on his side. His face was red, his back arched with his legs drawn up. After, he shot them out and pulled them up. I put him on his back, loosened his neck, and gave him water, which made him come around. He complained of his head at times, not just previous to this. Then, on the 12th of February, he was lying on the bed reading with his face downward and his head towards the foot of the bed. Without any warning whatsoever, he rolled off the bed onto the floor. I used the same means on that occasion, and he came around. I called for assistance; I called someone in to see. His face was red. On the 25th, he sat in a chair with two arms in front of the fire. His tea was brought in, and instead of going for it himself, he asked me to get it, which I did. I said, 'Are you not going to have your tea?' He did not answer me, so I concluded it was another attack. He did have a fit, so I applied water and brought him around. He has complained of his head occasionally and said it has ached.'

Mr Day then cross-examined the witness, keen to cast doubt about his medical expertise.
He said, *'Have you had any experience with epileptic patients?'*
George Albion Read: *'No special experience, but I have seen people in fits.'*
Mr Day: *'Was there any foaming at the mouth?'*
George Albion Read: *'No, Sir.'*
Mr Day: *'Or biting of the tongue?'*
George Albion Read: *'No.'*
Mr Day: *'Did you tell Doctor Sheppard the fits were of a slight nature?'*
George Albion Read: *'They were slight. There was no struggling or anything of the kind. He was very soon out of them.'*
Mr Day: *'Can you tell if they were epileptic or not?'*
George Albion Read: *'I don't know. I am not a doctor.'*
Mr Day: *'Has the Prison Surgeon ever seen him in one of these seizures?'*
George Albion Read: *'Not with me, Sir.'*

The next witness to be called to give evidence would be the defence's star witness, and would either make or break the case against George Henry Wood. Doctor Charles Edward Saunders confidently walked into the witness stand carrying his report. However, his confidence would be shaken by Justice Matthews, who was already satisfied with George Henry Wood's guilt and completely unwilling to accept any suggestions.
After taking the oath, Doctor Saunders said, *'I am a member of the College of Physicians and Medical Superintendent of the County Asylum. I have made a special study of the subject of insanity, and, apart from experience at the Asylum, I have made a study of epilepsy and have*

had large numbers of epileptic subjects under my observation continuously. At present, I have at least 100 under my observation, and I have studied the writing of others on the subject. After I was instructed by the Treasury to see the prisoner in this case, I saw him on two occasions. I was supplied with the depositions in the case and several other documents. I was given information about the seizures at Brighton Police Station, the evidence of Doctor Rogers, and the police evidence. I saw the documents from Canada but I am unsure whether I saw his father's statement. When I saw the prisoner, I examined him. He appeared to be perfectly rational. In my opinion, that is not inconsistent with him being an epileptic subject. Epileptic subjects may suffer from mental unconsciousness without a convulsive fit. I know Doctor Savage as an authority on the subject of epileptic insanity. The mania sometimes associated with epilepsy may precede epilepsy or take the place of the fit, but more commonly, the patient becomes violent after the fit of convulsions and unconsciousness. I have seen many cases where the person has been exceedingly violent and raving mad after the fit.'

At this point, Justice Matthew stopped writing his notes and frowned. Unhappy with this later comment, he said, *'Doctor Saunders, when has the prisoner been raving mad?'*

Doctor Saunders: *'Practically raving mad.'*

Mr Gill: *'In that condition, can a man commit great violence of the most purposeless kind?'*

Doctor Saunders: *'Certainly. The furore was a common occurrence of epilepsy in asylums at all events. Sometimes they might be in the state for only a few hours when they would practically recover from their condition before the fit. Epileptics are constantly kept under observation in the Asylum, but they are not put in a padded room except under peculiar circumstances.'*

Mr Gill: *'To protect them against themselves or other people?'*

Doctor Saunders: *'Both. Some epileptics fit very frequently, and others have considerable intervals. Assuming a man has a tendency to epilepsy, the drink would likely bring on a bad seizure. This would be especially true if the man had abstained from drinking for a while. Lust would also be very likely to bring on a seizure. At all events, statistics in the case of criminals showed that epileptics were more liable to attacks between 25 and 30 than at any other age.'*

Mr Gill: *'In your judgement, may an epileptic subject be guilty of great acts of violence without any recollection of a thing having occurred or being conscious?'*

Doctor Saunders: *'I believe so.'*

Mr Gill: *'Concerning the injuries inflicted on the child, would you say the violence on the body was more consistent with the conduct of an epileptic or a person in his sense?'*

At this point, Judge Matthews again interrupted and said, *'Mr Gill that is a question for the jury!'*

Doctor Saunders: *'I am familiar with the Broadmoor statistics. From these statistics, it appeared that of the total number of lunatics detained, 7 per cent were epileptic subjects, and of those charged with the crime of homicide, 11 per cent were epileptic.'*

Mr Gill: *'They were suffering from an epileptic form of insanity?'*

The Judge: *'Epilepsy is not insanity!'*

Mr Gill: *'What is the difference between epilepsy and insanity?'*

Doctor Saunders: *'I do not know.'*

The Judge: *'That is a very proper answer.'*

Doctor Saunders: *'Having made this examination and seeing the prisoner twice, and having these materials before me, I furnished a report in accordance with instructions.'*

Mr Day: *'The material before you included statements by the prisoner himself?'*

Doctor Saunders: *'Quite so.'*

Mr Day: *'Upon which you acted in forming your opinion?'*

Doctor Saunders: *'I do not think I was influenced by that because, after all, his statements were only of a general character as to his life history.'*

The Judge: *'You acted on them so far as they went?'*

Doctor Saunders: *'At the same time, I had other information, and it would be difficult to say how far I acted on what he said and what I had previously known.'*

Mr Day: *'Were you also actuated by the atrocious nature of the injuries inflicted on the little girl?'*

Doctor Saunders: *'In a measure.'*

Mr Day: *'Did you assume for the purpose of your opinion that the prisoner was a confirmed epileptic?'*

Doctor Saunders: *'I did. That is an epileptic; I do not know whether it is a confirmed one.'*

Mr Day: *'As to the hundred patients in your asylum, it is not a home for epilepsy, but an asylum for mad people?'*

Doctor Saunders: *'Yes, people of all sorts of insanity.'*

Mr Day: *'People are confined there because they are mad and not because they have epileptic fits occasionally?'*

Doctor Saunders: *'Yes, they are confined because they are mad.'*

Mr Day: *'Do you draw any distinction between an epileptic seizure and epileptic mania?'*

Doctor Saunders: *'Well, you need not necessarily get mania when you have an epileptic fit. In that sense, I do draw the distinction.'*

Mr Day: *'Is there anything, in this case, to indicate that the prisoners suffered from epileptic mania?'*

Doctor Saunders: *'Not at all from personal observation. Nor would there be in any case.'*

Mr Day: *'If you saw the patient with mania on him, would it be indicated?'*

Doctor Saunders: *'Yes.'*

Mr Day: *'I suppose I may put it the other way. From what you saw, he did not suffer from epileptic mania?'*

Doctor Saunders: *'No, nor mania of any form.'*

Mr Day: *'It is not unusual for mania to proceed with fits of epilepsy?'*

Doctor Saunders: *'No, I do not think it is. Not an outburst of violence at all events.'*

Mr Day: *'But such as to render a man unconscious?'*

Doctor Saunders: *'Yes, we frequently know when people are going to have fits by their behaviour preceding the fit. That is a very common experience.'*

Mr Day: *'It is common knowledge that epileptics are to be met within all walks of life, carrying on their business?'*

Doctor Saunders: *'Yes.'*

Mr Gill: *'Did that affect the opinion you formed?'*

Doctor Saunders: *'Not as to his epilepsy or his responsibility as an epileptic.'*

Mr Gill: *'With regard to being influenced by any statement made by the prisoner, did you form your opinion, whatever it was, upon matters outside?'*

Doctor Saunders: *'I do not think his statement influenced my mind in the least.'*

At this point, Mr Gill informed Judge Matthews that he had completed his case. The final witness to be called was Doctor Edgar Sheppard, who was only called by Mr Day to give evidence following a request by the Judge himself. He entered the witness stand

After taking the oath, he said, *'I was formerly, for 20 years, Medical Superintendent of Colney Hatch Criminal Lunatic Asylum. I have examined the prisoner in the case. I saw him last Monday. I found him relatively calm and collected, and he talked coherently. He was naturally depressed by the position in which he found himself. He told me he did not recollect anything about the circumstances that brought him to that position. I examined his head. There is a slight scar on the vortex of the scalp, which was a little tender on pressure, and it may be said that the conformation of his cranium is not a good one. It is very narrow and compressed at the side and has a high-arched palate, which is associated with the conformation of the skull. He was perfectly himself and not insane by any means. I heard that on that night, he was in a state of intoxication. All the documents and evidence were supplied to me by the Treasury, and*

I have heard the evidence was provided to me by the Treasury, and I have heard the evidence of Doctor Saunders. There is much in his evidence that I do not agree with, but I also do agree with a great deal.

Mr Day: *'Can you tell me what you agree with?'*

Doctor Sheppard: *'I would prefer to be asked questions singularly.'*

The Judge: *'Will you give us your views on mania associated with epilepsy?'*

Doctor Sheppard: *'Epilepsy may and does occur very frequently, without any mania associated with it. I think that is contrary to what Doctor Saunders said.'*

Mr Gill: *'Not at all. He said so most distinctly.'*

Doctor Sheppard: *'He said so distinctly, did he? That is not what I took for his evidence.'*

Mr Gill: *'Do you agree mania may precede an epileptic seizure?'*

Doctor Sheppard: *'It sometimes does.'*

Mr Gill: *'And that it may follow an epileptic seizure?'*

Doctor Sheppard: *'Much more likely.'*

Mr Gill: *'May a person after a seizure be guilty of extraordinary acts of purposeful violence?'*

Doctor Sheppard: *'Unquestionably.'*

Mr Gill: *'And they are frequently?'*

Doctor Sheppard: *'Yes.'*

Mr Gill: *'Excessive violence?'*

Doctor Sheppard: *'Yes.'*

Mr Gill: *'Ferocious violence?'*

Doctor Sheppard: *'Yes.'*

Mr Gill: *'Do you think epileptics suffer from uncontrollable impulses?'*

Doctor Sheppard: *'Well-established epileptics leading dissolute lives very often do.'*

Mr Gill: *'Are there cases of epileptics who would occasionally be irresponsible and at other times perfectly rational?'*

Doctor Sheppard: *'Quite so if they are well-established epileptics.'*

Mr Gill: *'What point have you got to arrive at before you establish it well?'*

Doctor Sheppard: *'A person must be frequently observed to have a series of fits at various times.'*

The Judge: *'Followed by what?'*

Doctor Sheppard: *'Followed by maniacal excitement and aggressive acts.'*

Mr Gill: *'And great violence?'*

Doctor Sheppard: *'Yes.'*

Mr Gill: *'You have heard the description of Doctor Ross. I think that would be one violent fit, would it not?'*

Doctor Sheppard: *'There was a violent fit undoubtedly, followed by an act of lust.'*

The Judge, who appears confused by these comments, said, *'Mr Gill, which fit are you speaking of now?'*

Mr Gill: *'I am speaking about the one Doctor Ross was called to see at the police station.'*

The Judge: *'But Doctor Ross did not witness the attack. He clearly explained that he was called in after the attack.'*

Mr Gill: *'The fit I spoke of that Doctor Ross saw was after he had been in custody for about 20 days. This episode could not have arisen from his leading a debauched life, you know. After that interval, you have a fit, a violent fit of epilepsy. I wish to convey to the court that a man with epilepsy may have a long rest period and no fits at all. However, when he is guilty of any excess, either intemperance or lust, it may be followed by a series of epileptic fits, especially if he is epileptic. Although there has been repression for several years, he may have a severe series of epileptic fits. That is what I want the jury to hear. That would help you conclude that the man was a real epileptic. It would help me conclude that acts of excess, which he has recently been guilty, had reproduced a condition that had existed before. A man with a tendency to epilepsy, having abstained from drinking, gives way to it and, if you please, to lust simultaneously. Would that probably bring about an epileptic seizure?'*

The Judge: *'Subsequently?'*

Doctor Sheppard: *'Subsequently, exactly, after any deviation from the right course.'*

The Judge: *'How long after?'*

Doctor Sheppard: *'It might be immediate or after some days, and it might last for a considerable time.'*

The Judge: *'Don't you think it is in the highest degree probable that it would be immediate from the exciting influence?'*

Doctor Sheppard: *'It is in some cases.'*

The Judge: *'Can you tell me what would satisfy you that a man is a confirmed epileptic? How many violent fits must he have to qualify as a confirmed epileptic?'*

Doctor Sheppard: *'I had better give it in a negative sort of way. Say if a man had been without fits for two years, I could not call him an established epileptic. I should say if he had antecedent epilepsy, it would be necessary to be more cautious in his mode of living if he wanted to prevent a recurrence.'*

The Judge: *'Because latent epilepsy might burst forth at any time?'*

Doctor Sheppard: *'If he was guilty of excess.'*

The Judge: *'And might with all the greater violence from having been dormant for so long?'*

Doctor Sheppard: *'I don't think so. I am sure from my personal experience that is not so.'*

Mr Gill: *'Even under the exciting influence of drink?'*

Doctor Sheppard: *'That is not so.'*

Mr Gill: *'You have heard the description of his attack at the police station that it took four men to hold him down. Would this be an epileptic fit?'*

Doctor Sheppard: *'Unquestionably.'*

Mr Gill: *'A very violent one?'*

Doctor Sheppard: *'It seemed to be so.'*

Mr Gill: *'You have heard of the seizures described by Doctor Ross, Doctor Rogers, and the police constables?'*

Doctor Sheppard: *'I have.'*

Mr Gill: *'He was getting near a confirmed epileptic at that time?'*

The Judge: *'But that was after the crime?'*

Doctor Sheppard: *'This is subsequent to the event which produced that. The question as to the moment when a man may have an epileptic fit is a matter of absolute uncertainty.'*

Mr Gill: *'I suppose you attach importance to men making a special study of this subject and will agree with me that ordinary men don't know much about it?'*

Doctor Sheppard: *'I am quite sure they don't.'*

Mr Gill: *'It requires special knowledge?'*

Doctor Sheppard: *'Undoubtedly.'*

Mr Gill: *'What is known about the condition is in fact, not very much?'*

Doctor Sheppard: *'No. I don't think people have gotten much ahead of it.'*

Mr Gill: *'Even with your skill, it would be difficult for you to say at what moment an epileptic subject would have a dangerous outburst?'*

Doctor Sheppard: '*Unless I knew his antecedents, it would be complicated.'*

Mr Gill: *'Presuming the prisoner committed the act with which he is charged, you would think he was unconscious.'*

Doctor Sheppard: '*Yes, but not from epilepsy. He would be but from intemperance.'*

Mr Gill: *'I will take it from you what I wish to establish, that in your opinion, he was unconscious at the time?'*

Doctor Sheppard: *'I will give you reasons afterwards. I think it was very likely he was.'*

The Judge: *'On what grounds?'*

Doctor Sheppard: *'You may meet with intemperate men in the street, unconscious of what they are doing or where they are going.'*

The Judge: *'You were asked as to this particular occurrence. Knowing all the circumstances, how does it occur to you that he would be very likely unconscious?'*

Doctor Sheppard: *'Because the man was very drunk, according to the evidence, and especially if he had an epileptic tendency, likely to commit an act of that kind.'*

Mr Gill: *'Drink acts with special violence on epileptics, does it?'*

Doctor Sheppard: *'I think it does.'*

Mr Gill: *'Would you say it would give way to aggressive acts by such a subject, a ferocity that would suggest insanity?'*

Doctor Sheppard: *'I do.'*

Mr Gill: *'Considering the evidence, would you regard this as a case with many complications?'*

Doctor Sheppard: *'Undoubtedly.'*

Mr Gill: *'You had the descriptions of the fits at the time you made the report?'*

Doctor Sheppard: *'Yes.'*

Mr Gill: *'And you were to some extent influenced by the descriptions of these seizures?'*

Doctor Sheppard: *'Those described to me were not of a severe character evidently.'*

Mr Gill: *'Therefore, you did not, in fact, have described the seizures at the Brighton police court?'*

Doctor Sheppard: *'I don't doubt the violence of those for a moment.'*

Mr Gill: *'You don't doubt they were perfectly genuine?'*

Doctor Sheppard: *'Certainly not.'*

Mr Gill: *'May I take this from you? Didn't you have a description of those seizures given to you when you made your report?'*

Doctor Sheppard: *'I know all about them from the evidence put before me.'*

Mr Gill: *'The police evidence, for instance, do you know whether it had been taken?'*

Doctor Sheppard: *'I spoke to Doctor Ross, and he told me of the violence.'*

Mr Gill: *'That is what I want to establish.'*

The Judge: *'Were you sent to make this examination by the Treasury?'*

Doctor Sheppard: *'Oh, yes, my lord.'*

Mr Day: *'You have told us that intemperance may bring on a seizure. May a great shock also bring on a seizure?'*

Doctor Sheppard: *'Undoubtedly.'*

Mr Day: *'Would the shock of a charge of this kind bring on a seizure in a man with epilepsy?'*

Doctor Sheppard: *'Yes.'*

Mr Gill: *'As to the fits you have heard described by the warders as taking place in the gaol, do you consider these true epileptic fits or not?'*

Doctor Sheppard: *'They may have been true epileptic fits, moderating after great violence. They were the last fits he had.'*

Mr Gill: *'Can one have an epileptic fit without foaming the mouth?'*

Doctor Sheppard: *'Oh dear, yes.'*

The Judge: *'And do you regard these fits as serious or casual?'*

Doctor Sheppard: *'If you mean the subject's future, I should say that if he leads a temperate life, there is no reason why he should not become free of them. It is a matter of doubt. I don't give a positive opinion.'*

Doctor Sheppard's evidence was the final blow for the defence. Whilst he had acknowledged that he likely suffered from epilepsy, he refused to confirm that this was the cause of the violence George Henry Wood had inflicted on Edith Jeal. Doctor Sheppard had refused to agree that George Henry Wood had any type of mania. Worse still, he had pointed to alcohol as the cause of any unconsciousness George Henry Wood might have experienced on the 10th of December.

Doctor Sheppard's evidence marked the end of the prosecution's case. All that remained for the jury to hear was the closing arguments and the Judge's case summary.

Chapter 25: *'May the Lord have mercy on your soul'*

Mr Gill then gave his final address to the court. He knew this was his last opportunity to save his client from a death sentence. Given the strength of the evidence, he must have realised that there was little chance that the trial's outcome would benefit his client. Still unwilling to stop fighting, Mr Gill delivered a final appeal to the jury.

He said, *'I shall not address you as to the facts of the case. There is evidence upon which you will have to decide a verdict with the assistance of Mr Day, me and his Lordship. I invite you to consider the evidence's accumulated force, putting it all together. We are dealing with a subject about which people know very little. I found that to be the case with the last witness called on behalf of the Crown. Indeed, if a subject on which those who have studied the topic know very little, it might well be that doctors who have not given their full attention to epilepsy and insanity do not know much about it. Therefore, we must use the material they have supplied us with and give due weight to the opinions they have formed. It would be desperate if a man's life were surrendered due to differences of opinion as to the state of his mind. When the issue is as severe as it is in this case, it is a terrible responsibility. I don't say this to unnerve you in any way. Still, it is a responsibility you must be alert to when deciding which of the two medical experts' opinions, who agree on many points but disagree on others, you believe. I don't suppose that my friend, Mr Day, will suggest that any evidence put before you of a medical character would lead to any doubt of the prisoner's guilt. One sometimes hears of people in good positions, addicted to criminal acts, which are explained away by supposing they suffer from indefinite, indescribable complaints. This is not a case where it is suggested that the answer to the prisoner's charge is 'marked epilepsy.' That is not put forward here, and it is a subject, happily, I have not got to deal with. Take the evidence of the father as to the* man's life. Do you have any doubt that he is simply telling the pure truth without the slightest exaggeration? What a wretched life this man has had up to the present time to the commencement of his career. The illness described to you caused that tremendous fit when he was a child, different from the other fits that he had before. A fit of such a character that blood poured from his mouth and foam gathered on his lips. The nature of that fit prevented him from being taken to the hospital. A fit which occasioned Doctor Ross' late brother to be sent for. A fit brought from him, the latter, and the expressed opinion that he would never be reared due to the formation of the child's head. Happy, it would have been for him if he had never been so that he might never have known this moment! This is the earliest account you have got of the fits. Do you suppose there is any exaggeration in it? How does his life after this episode corroborate that? He remained delicate and weak until he reached seven or eight years. Then he seemed to get better but had two or three situations in which he had to leave. Then he goes to sea. Not only does he have a narrow form of the head, but he is discharged for malformation of the chest. He goes home and tries to work again. He joins the Army but is invalided out of his regiment. As time goes on, he goes away to another country. Regarding evidence from America, producing witnesses on that point is quite impossible. It is quite out of the question. But weigh the value of the evidence you have heard, evidence which comes from the Crown, the police and persons who are witnesses for the prosecution to all intents and purposes. What opinion do you have of this man's life? Remember the earlier years of his life. What has he gone through during that time? Then after he returns home, he lives the peaceful, quiet, respectable life of an honest man. He works early and late, getting the best possible character from his employers. No man is to have the advantage of saying, 'I was drunk, and in my drunkenness, I did some act of violence.' There are cases of men who frequently get drunk and commit acts of violence whilst under the influence of drink. Indeed, they should not acquire any benefit as a result of that. There is no such case here, and no human being would suggest that this man got drunk to commit a crime to bring on an epileptic seizure. He was living this respectable life up to the 10th of December. Until that unfortunate night, you have heard nothing contradicting the prisoner's statement that he had no recollection of what had happened that evening from the time he left his work. His mind is perfectly blank upon it. He is seen during the evening by a police constable who saw him so helplessly drunk that he was staggering. He describes him as being very intoxicated and staggering. Unfortunately, the constable could not take him into custody for being drunk, escort him home, or do something. But there he is, in the condition described by the constable, who must have known that he was in an altogether peculiar condition. The best possible evidence from the people who saw him daily during the two years he was employed at the railway yard shows the man was a total *abstainer. Now, what was it that happened? No human being can tell. This is a case of circumstantial evidence on the part of the prosecution. It is also circumstantial evidence on the part of the defence if you please. You are invited to conclude that this man committed the act. I invite you on circumstantial evidence, if not direct evidence, to conclude that this man was under an epileptic seizure that night. His epilepsy, having lay dormant, was brought out by excitement, drink, and, if you please, by insane lust when he committed the crime. This was the first of a series of epileptic seizures. What took place afterwards points to what has occurred. Doctor Sheppard, who was called, says he believes this man was unconscious from drinking. You have heard Doctor Saunders' opinion on whether he was out of a drink or epileptic mania, and you can form your own opinion. The opinions you will have gathered are that the man was unconscious, and it is the opinion of one of the doctors that this unconsciousness was caused by drink. How is that arrived at? Upon what material is it based? Doctor Sheppard suggests that the epileptic seizure this man had days after his custody arose from the sudden shock due to the charge against him. However, it is not conclusive whether the unconsciousness occurred from mania following epilepsy or preceding it because we are in the dark as to which is more probable, whether mania would follow or precede epilepsy. No doubt one would conclude that the first epileptic fit was when Doctor Ross was called to see the prisoner, and another would no doubt come to the conclusion that the first epileptic fit, which had been lying dormant in that man, came out through drink and lust at the time of the crime. That man had a series of epileptic seizures and, in the mania following those epileptic seizures, was guilty of brutal acts of purposeless violence. The violence is consistent with the unconscious state of a man who has undergone an epileptic fit. Doctor Sheppard does not doubt that at the Brighton police court, in the cells, that man had fit after fit of the most severe character. How is it to be decided in a court of justice? Many things can be resolved in a court, such as questions of contract and the law laid down with the greatest possible nicety upon many questions. But how can any competent evidence tell us when a man is a confirmed epileptic? How can it tell us when a man is liable to fits when he is a mere epileptic? Doctor Sheppard, who sees hundreds of these subjects, says he needs to find out where the dividing line comes in. I put it to him on the evidence of Mr Rogers, the police Surgeon, and Doctor Ross, both persons in no way influenced to say anything favourable about the prisoner unless it was correct as far as they could judge. What was the theory that it was an epileptic fit of a strong character that possessed him? How many points did the Doctors agree upon? How fine the line upon which the Doctors disagreed is not the main point, but in the first place, are they both correct in saying the prisoner is stating the truth when he says that he was unconscious and knew not what took place that night? Do you have any doubts about that? Do you believe the medical men have formed the proper conclusion? I have established that he was unconscious of his actions and the victim of this curse with which some people are visited. What value do you attach to the whole case's history, from when the charge was made to when he is watched day and night in prison? The Prison Doctor discovered that he had a seizure and sent him to the Infirmary. From that day to this, an attendant has watched over him as they do at Broadmoor and other places where lunatics and epileptics are confined. This is done to prevent them from injuring themselves or others. I beg of you to give all the weight to this evidence that your conscientiousness thinks it deserves. Remember in weighting it the sources from which it comes. Doctor Saunders is not a man I have sought to put before you. I have not chosen him. At the enormous expense, the prisoner's friends are not bringing a great specialist or skilled man to express an opinion. Remember, too, that the evidence I have put before you is obtained from those who have acted for the prosecution. It is the mind of a Doctor selected by the prosecution who, from his great experience, is likely to form the best opinion on the matter. It is not asking you for much. It is the mind of a man selected by them who, from his great experience, is likely to form the best opinion on the matter. It is not asking you for much. It is not a great boon to a man. I said it was unfortunate that he survived the attack in his youth. For many men, it would be better to die a felon's death upon the scaffold than to be shut up in a criminal lunatic asylum. Still, appealing to this man, I ask you to say that this crime was not the act of a sane man and that you have enough material to justify this conclusion. Your mind would tend to think that a man possessing his faculties would not justify such a verdict for a moment. Weigh it, I ask. Give it all the consideration it deserves. Make as much of it in favour of the prisoner as you can. If you are satisfied beyond all doubt that there is substantial evidence in the case that the man committed the crime, I am not in a position to respond to the man's statement. He remembers nothing. But suppose you arrive at the point that you are prepared to fix him with the commission of this crime on this substantial evidence and say he is guilty on the indictment. In that case, I ask you to say in addition to the verdict that although he is guilty of the act charged in the indictment, you believe he was irresponsible when he committed the deed.'*

Mr Gill had vigorously argued his case, which lacked any tangible input from his client and had used every possible defence available to him. Whilst he did not deny that George Henry Wood had committed the crime, he had reminded the jury of mitigating factors which he hoped would dissuade the jury from finding George Henry Wood guilty of his actions.
Next, the court heard the final statement for the prosecution. Mr Day, who was feeling quietly confident and had far less to be concerned about, made a much briefer address to the court.

He said, 'Mr Gill has suggested three defences. Firstly, the man is not guilty based on the facts. Secondly, drunkenness. Thirdly, insanity was the cause. If you turn your mind only to the question of insanity, it was a waste of time to ask them to find that the prisoner had not committed the murder. If Mr Gill thought that the prisoner was not guilty of the murder, he would have cross-examined the witnesses at greater length and would not have talked about insanity. In respect of the statement made by the prisoners to the effect that he was at the circus, if this were true, there would be no difficulty in proving it, and it would have been a good defence. However, no attempt has been made to prove it to be true. As to drunkenness, as his Lordship will tell you, there could be no answer to the criminal charge. Now let's deal with the suggestion of insanity. The defence suggests that when the prisoner strangled the girl, the prisoner did not know it was wrong. They must find that he was irresponsible in his actions. Let's see what evidence there was in support of this. The defence called the father, but what did his evidence amount to? The father's evidence instead went to disprove epilepsy. The prisoner was in the navy and was not discharged for epilepsy but for chest malformation and itch. He was then released from the Army due to varicose veins. Mr Gill called no witnesses to prove that he had a seizure while at home, and no one was called from the works at which he was employed. If he had been in the habit of having seizures, would some persons not have been called to prove it? The facts seem to go against the prisoner more than otherwise. The fact that the prisoner had been regularly at work for some time before the murder was almost conclusive that he did not have epilepsy. The fact that he went to work the morning after the crime proves that he had no seizures during the night. Was there any slither of evidence from the defence that this man had a seizure that night? Before the jury can find a verdict that he was not responsible for his actions, you must have some evidence of his condition that night. Although you will pay the most significant attention to the scientific experts on the question as to whether this man was sane on that night, you have to consider what was found in the shed. The bundle of firewood and the chestnuts were found in the hut near the body. Is it reasonable to suppose the prisoner had a fit while carrying the child? If he had, the child would have struggled to get away and dropped the wood and the chestnuts. In conclusion, the sole interest of the Treasury is that justice should be done. I submit that there was no evidence that the man on the night in question had an epileptic fit or that this man was insane on the night of the murder. I ask you to find the verdict upon the evidence, and it remains with you to do your duty.'

This marked the completion of both the cases for the defence and prosecution. The final speech made to the jury was by the Judge. Unfortunately for George Henry Wood, it was obvious that he was far from convinced by the defence's claims and used this opportunity to make his feelings known again.

With the utmost solemnity, Judge Mathews said, '*Gentlemen of the jury, it is entirely unnecessary to remind you of the gravity of the case. It is painfully impressed upon the minds of everybody in court. You have been told more than once of the responsibility resting upon you. Your great responsibility is administering the law, and you have no other duty. You have to pronounce the questions submitted to you following the law, and this is not very controversial in this case, and there your responsibility ends. Now, what is the defence that is offered to the prisoner's charge? The first suggestion is that you ought not to be satisfied that he was the man by whose hand this unhappy little girl lost her life. This suggestion is made by the learned counsel for the prisoner, who defended him so ably, energetically, and ingeniously. However, he was not able to cross-examine any of the witnesses because of his client's position, who had no recollection of what had occurred and could give him no information of any kind. Gentlemen, if this unhappy prisoner was not the man who carried this child and murdered her, where was he on the night in question? He should have no difficulty in informing you all. You see how complete the chain of evidence is. The prisoner left the railway works on the night of the 10th of December and was under the influence of drink. He was not so drunk that he could not walk away, and we could follow him until he had got a considerable part of the way home. Under the influence of drink, he seemed to come under an influence that often follows a diabolical temptation. If you believe the evidence called before you and the statements have not been challenged in any way, you will see he took up two little children. One he took up in his arms and was going away with it when he fell, and the child was taken away by a woman who saw this. Further on, he met a policeman who had known him for years, and the policeman noticed he was under the influence of drink, though he was able to walk away. He was seen shortly afterwards, close to the shop where the poor little child was standing, with a cap filled with chestnuts and a bundle of firewood. He was seen stretching out his hand to her. Shortly afterwards, he was seen by another man going in the direction of the field with the child in his arms. For what purpose? Do you, as reasonable men, doubt that even under the influence of mania of any sort, he came under the horrible temptation to abuse a child? And, then, what happened subsequently? The following day the child's body was found outraged, as you have heard, an outrage that must have been perpetrated if the intention attributed to him was carried into effect. It is impossible for a man of his age to abuse the child without inflicting terrible injuries upon her. It is evident that the child must have been injured by a vigorous man in the way it was. The following morning the body was found with terrible injuries upon it. What follows? The suggestion is made that the man did not recollect anything that occurred on the night in question. This is, of course, an effortless way of answering the charge of an atrocious crime, a crime so atrocious he has no recollection of what occurred! That is what is said of him now, and the whole of the defence rests on that. The evidence of epilepsy and mania, which the defence gives as the alternative, is rested. The next day he sees a policeman. Before seeing the policeman, he had spoken about the murder, but not much was made of that. When he meets the policeman, the policeman asks him a few questions. What are the answers? Not, 'Something happened last night, and I have no recollection of what it was.' The policeman asked if he had met a constable who knew him. He said he had not. He said that he had not been in the street mentioned. He was asked where he had been. What was his answer? He replied that he did not have the slightest recollection. This answer was that of a conscious man that must give the best explanation he could, and the reason was that he had been to the circus. Then he was asked whether he could provide the name of anyone who had seen him at the circus. He replied, 'No, except perhaps the doorkeeper.' He must, if possible, get away from the locality in which he knew the crime had taken place, a crime of which he knew. Although the point has not been brought forward, he had before mentioned to a fellow workman about this outrage and this murder. Then the Inspector took him to the police station, and his clothes were examined. As you would expect, if such a crime as this had been committed, there were indications that have been spoken of. His garments were smeared with blood, as you saw was the portion of the child's clothing, from which you can infer the condition of the rest of the garments. When all that is shown and established, what must be the conclusion of any reasonable man under the circumstances? Are you confident that this is the man whose hands committed the crime? Are you satisfied that it was this man that outraged the child? The only further evidence necessary to refer to in this part of the case is the letter that he wrote afterwards to his family. Judge whether it was not the letter of a man who, though he said he knew nothing about it, had presented to his mind the position in which he was placed. Now we come to what has been called the real defence in the case. Now, Gentlemen, the law is perfectly clear on this point, on this defence of insanity. We're not here to discuss the wisdom of the law. If the law is wrong, it would have been set right long before this. The law has not been altered for many, many years. The defence of insanity cannot be successfully set up unless the jury is satisfied, with the evidence offered on the part of the prisoner, that he did not know that the act he did was calculated to produce death. Or if he knew it would, he did not know it was wrong. The theory of uncontrollable impulse to do what is wrong may be discarded at once. Doctors have tried to set it up, but everyone that does wrong under the circumstances may be said to do it under an uncontrollable impulse. If he knows what he is doing is contrary to the law of the land and to the law of God, he is responsible for what he does. It is idle to talk* of uncontrollable impulses. It is not suggested in this case that there was an uncontrollable influence. The defence is of a different character and is totally new, so far as I understand it. It is said here you ought to come to a conclusion that this man was a raving madman at the time he committed the crime. This, it was argued, is because he was subject, and has been subject since his charge, to attacks of epilepsy. The evidence offered ought to satisfy you that this man was furious and in a state of mania at the time when this was perpetrated, and not merely that when he was a child of some two years old, had a fit, and since this charge has been brought against him has had a series of epileptic fits. What is the view of Doctor Saunders upon the subject? He suggests to you that this man was in a state of epileptic mania when he attacked the child. Was he in a state of epileptic mania when he took the child up in his arms? Was it mania that led him to the child to this lonely field? Was it mania that induced him to go into the shed, or did he go there so that he might not be seen? What do you think is the true explanation of this matter? Then it has been said mania led to the murder, and the murder followed the outrage. But did the mania begin when he took the child there, or if not, when did the mania begin? It is suggested the mania came upon him in the interval between the outrage and the murder because he is not being tried for the outage. What evidence is there? How is it possible or reasonable to suggest that, upon any fact that has been laid before you? The child was strangled. Why? The man who committed the awful outrage would readily be tempted to go further. How was he to get rid of this child? Was he to leave the child there to linger after his attack? He sees nothing in the world but to stop the poor child's cries and destroy the evidence against him. Was that the explanation, or was he under the influence of mania due to epilepsy? Now gentlemen, about this defence which has been set up, observe the extreme humanity with which the law is administered in this country. When these epileptic fits were noticed, the man was in custody. There was a succession of them, not preceded or followed by mania. These were ordinary passing attacks of epilepsy, rather serious seizures in themselves and were followed by a speedy recovery for the most part. The prisoner recovered after cold water was sprinkled on his face. An application was made by the unhappy father of the man to have the case investigated, and two distinguished medical men were called in so that you may have the full information on the subject. The two prominent men called here are Doctor Saunders and Doctor Sheppard. They do not agree. You are asked to conclude that there was raving madness which made this man unconscious, according to the evidence of Doctor Saunders. But what has he told you that you didn't know before? The counsel for the prisoner explained that very little is known about the subject. Doctor Saunders tells you that in his experience with certified lunatics, there are many instances in which the lunatics have epilepsy. He says in such cases, mania may precede or may follow epilepsy. Do you think that *if Doctor Sanders was asked to certify this man as a lunatic because he had an attack of epilepsy in his youth, he would have done it? Do you think if he was called in to certify him a lunatic after those conversations concerning what he expressed as to his opinions of his sanity, he would have done it? What evidence has he laid before you that at the time this deed was done, there was any mania to speak of? What is the use of telling you the condition of lunatics under his observation and charge? The question for reasonable men is whether you can apply any of that information, which was hardly worth his while to give, to the particular facts of this case. I ought to read it to you, and let us see what it all amounts to.'*

The Judge then read Doctor Saunders' full report to the jury and then continued.

He said, '*Doctor Saunders infers that because a man is an epileptic subject, he is not legally responsible to the court of justice for a crime he may have committed. He is an epileptic subject because he has had epileptic attacks since the case arose. Was he unconscious when he carried the child through the street? Was he unconscious when he went to the shed? Was he unconscious when he outraged the child? Is that what the Doctors wish to infer? How does it help us in this case that mania may precede or follow a fit? The common result of an epileptic seizure is a complete loss of all control and power over anything. Does that help us in this case? He says, 'After a seizure or fit, the patient may be raving mad.' This is quite true, but what is the conclusion about this man? There was a seizure. When? There was a fit. When? He was raving mad. When? Doctor Saunders said the atrocious character of the crime influenced the prisoner. If the atrocity of the crime is to be the answer, how is society to be protected? Apparently, a man committed a most atrocious crime, and when he is called to account, he says it is so atrocious he could not be in possession of his senses. That is not the law. You have to administer the law as I told you. The atrocity of the crime is no defence. Atrocious crimes are committed by people who know perfectly well what they are doing.'*

At this point, the Judge read Doctor Shephard's report to the jury and continued with his statement.

He said, '*The shape of the prisoner's cranium is not inconsistent with a rational being. Before the crime, the prisoner was employed by the Railway Company and considered a good servant. He was able to give an intelligent account of his life in Canada. There is the case, and an awful case it is. You will not need further word from me. I have told you your duty, which is to administer the law if you believe this unhappy man knew what he was doing when he committed the outrage on the child. If he knew what he was doing when he attempted to outrage the child and carried out that attempt, you ought to find him guilty. If you think he was in a state of mania and did not know what he was doing, did not know he had got the child in his arms, did not know he was taking the child to the field, did not know he went to the shed, did not know any of those things were wrong, you will find that he was insane when the crime was committed. You know what your duty is, and I have no doubt you will perform your task.'*

Having completed his speech, the Judge directed the jury to retire. The jury arose from their bench, silently vacated the courtroom, and entered the adjacent deliberation room to discuss the case privately. After only eight minutes, the jury re-entered the courtroom and retook their seats. The Clerk of the Arraigns arose and addressed the jury.
He said, *'Do you all agree upon a verdict?'*
The Foreman: *'We do, Sir.'*
The Clerk: *'Do you find the prisoner guilty or not guilty?'*
The Foreman: *'Guilty.'*
The Clerk: *'And that is the verdict of you all?'*
The Foreman: *'Yes, Sir.'*
The Clerk of the Arraigns then arose. He turned to George Henry Wood and solemnly said, *'Prisoner at the bar, you stand convicted of the crime of wilful murder. Have you anything to say for yourself why the sentence of death should not be passed upon you?'*
In a low and faint tone, George Henry Wood replied, *'I have nothing to say.'*
Judge Mathews tapped on the neatly folded white gloves on the desk beside him. Underneath laid a neatly folded black cloth cap. The Clerk of the Arraigns approached the bench, took up the black cap, placed it on top of the Judge's wig, and returned to his seat. The chaplain arose from his seat and stood adjacent to the bench.
Judge Mathews turned to the accused and said, *'George Henry Wood, I have no wish to add anything to your awful position by words of reproach. You have been convicted properly by the jury of a most atrocious crime. I advise you to make good use of the time you have left and look for mercy where it may be extended to you. I have now to pass the sentence of the law. You will be taken back to the place from whence you came, and thence to the place of execution, and there to be hanged by the neck until you shall be dead, and your body to be buried in the precincts of the prison, and may the Lord have mercy on your soul.'*

At this point, George Henry Wood began to sway and appeared to faint, which caused immense excitement within the court. He was immediately removed from the dock and taken down to the holding cells beneath, with the sentence still ringing in his ears. The Judge then adjourned the proceedings until the following morning.

The entire case took only six hours to reach its conclusion. Afterwards, the court quickly cleared, apart from two police constables and an elderly man, who crouched on a seat below the public gallery near the dock. With eyes filled with unspeakable sadness and desolation, George Wood Senior remained in his seat, silently praying for his son.

A short while later, the' Black Maria' transported George Henry Wood back to Lewes House of Correction. Despite being incarcerated on two previous occasions, his treatment on this occasion was to be completely different. The strict rules for condemned prisoners were distinct from those that applied to other classes of prisoners. After reaching the prison, he was taken straight to the condemned cell on the ground floor of the right wing.

Here, he was completely isolated and hidden from the wider prison population. The prison chaplain had unlimited access to the condemned cell and could visit whenever the prisoner requested his attendance. No external visits were permitted unless ordered by the Visiting Justices.

Significant concern existed about condemned prisoners escaping or harming themselves whilst awaiting execution. Consequently, four prison wardens in pairs would guard those awaiting execution 24 hours a day. George Henry Wood was allowed to attend chapel. However, during the service, he was placed in a secluded nook to prevent other prisoners from setting eyes on him.

Outside the prison, interest persisted in surrounding the case. On the day following the murder, a further broadside ballad was published in Brighton about George Henry Wood's trial at Lewes. The lyrics are as follows:

The man who did the Brighton murder,
And outraged the poor little child,
The have sent him from the world forever,
To a murderer's grave, he is consigned,
The hangman now has done his duty,
Within the dismal Sussex Gaol,
For his victim, full of childish beauty,
All feeling people did bewail.

Wood that killed the child at Brighton
To eternity has just been hurled.
The law has justly punished the right one,
For his crime, I'm sure disgraced the world.

The little girl you well remember,
With her brother was shopping in the town,
She had hardly seen five mid-summers,
Ere by this villain, she was struck down.
Her murderer held a good position,
Working on a railway line,
But 'tis said that in a drunken condition,
All thought or care did he resign.

By the magistrates committed,
At Lewes Assizes, he was tried,
I am not guilty there, he pleaded,
But his guilt he could not hide.

Tho' defended by clever counsel,
Useless it soon proved to be,
He was sentenced to die on the scaffold,
And now he is in eternity.

His innocence, he still protested,
Although he was condemned to die,
A petition for him was presented,
Though we can't tell the reason why,
How could he expect a pardon,
For doing his unnatural crime,
He hid her body in the garden,
But her blood was on him all the time.

They bound him on Tuesday morning,
And led him forth to meet his death,
The sun and the heavens were adorning,
The gaolers hardly drew a breath,
The chaplain read the burial service,
And the last prayer for him did give,

The hangman touched the fatal lever,
And the Brighton murderer ceased to live.

Chapter 26: *'And for this, petitioners will ever pray'*

After George Henry Wood's conviction, various Brighton tabloids published Doctor Saunders' report in full. Commentators questioned the criminal guilt of an individual prone to epilepsy and the fairness of the death sentence George Henry Wood had received. Increasing public interest led to editors dedicating vast columns of their newspapers to the debate - should George Henry Wood be executed, reprieved or placed in a lunatic asylum indefinitely?

Seizing on this opportunity, George Henry Wood's friends and family prepared a petition to submit to the Crown, to try and stop the death sentence from being carried out. On Saturday, the 9th of April, the petition was released to the public and began to gather signatures. The petitioner's letter reads:

'To the Right Honourable Henry Matthews, Q.C, M.P., Her Majesty's Principal Secretary of State for Home Affairs. The humble petition of us, the undersigned inhabitants of the Borough of Brighton here with:-

That on the 8th of April, at the Sussex Assizes held at Lewes, George Henry Wood, an inhabitant of Brighton, was charged with the wilful murder of Edith Jeal on the 10th of December 1891, was found guilty, and sentenced to death. While preparing the prisoner's defence, communications occurred between his solicitors and numerous persons who had known him when he was in America.

Replies were received, and copies are sent herewith. At the request of the prisoner's solicitors, the solicitor to the Treasury submitted a statement of the prisoner's life, together with copies of the said letters from America, and other documents (copies of which are sent herewith, showing that the prisoner is an epileptic subject), to Doctor Saunders, the Medical

Superintendent of the Sussex County Lunatic Asylum at Haywards Heath, and instructed him to examine the prisoner and report upon his mental condition. A copy of Doctor Saunders' report is sent herewith.

In addition to Doctor Saunders, the Treasury, on behalf of the prosecution, caused the prisoner to be examined again. His mental condition was reported upon by Doctor Sheppard, a copy of whose report is also sent herewith.

At the trial, the first-named medical expert and the other medical gentleman gave evidence. A verbatim report of the trial is sent herewith, the result of which medical evidence is to create great doubt in the minds of your petitioners as to the legal responsibility of the prisoner, in respect to the commission of the act he has been found guilty of committing.

Your petitioners, therefore, humbly pray that you may be able to advise Her Majesty to commute the Capital Sentence passed upon the prisoner into one of detention as a criminal lunatic during Her Majesty's pleasure. And for this, petitioners will ever pray.'

While George Henry Wood's defending counsel repeatedly referenced the Manitoba letters during his trials, the jury never heard their full contents. Now that the trial was over, George Henry Wood's solicitors, who were keen for the public to hear the letters in full, sent copies to various Sussex-based media outlets, which published them in their entirety.

As detailed in previous chapters, the Manitoba letters stated that George Henry Wood had suffered from repeated attacks of epilepsy. This generated further sympathy from some quarters of the public, who believed that his condition meant he was not responsible for Edith's murder. In an attempt to try and persuade the authorities to grant a reprieve, these readers also submitted their own letters to the press. These individuals felt that the execution of a man who was potentially insane was cruel and unjust.

The first letter's author did not supply their name but titled themselves '*Humanitas*'. Their letter reads as follows:

'*I trust your sense of fairness to give me room to appeal to my fellow townsmen on behalf of this most unhappy man, who lies under sentence of death in Lewes Gaol. I have just signed this petition to the Home Secretary, praying for a commutation of the capital sentence on the grounds of the condemned man's responsibility when he committed the awful crime of which he was convicted. If anything I say may induce others to affix their names to the petition, my purpose in troubling you with this letter will have been served.*

In signing the petition, I found myself in good company - in the company of medical men of the highest standing, of humanitarians, of those who belong to the higher civilisation, of those who shrink from the staining of their souls with the brutalising lust for a fellow creature's blood. I cannot bring myself to hope that the petitioners' prayer will be answered, but for all that is right to protest against the capital sentence being carried out in defiance of the expert medical evidence given at the trial. I argue that Wood should not be executed for the following reasons:

Because the law recognises that punishment should be so inflicted as to act as a deterrent and not be given in mere vindictiveness, and as not one man, probably in ten million (or, one would like to think a hundred million), has ever, thank God, the slightest desire to murder and mutilate children, an example which shall act as a deterrent can scarcely be required. Because the evidence of the highest available authorities in cases of mental disease is distinctly in favour of the accused's responsibility.'

'Humanitas' then quotes vast sections of Doctor Saunders' medical report to justify his thoughts and opinions before continuing to argue for a reprieve.

He then writes, '*Now I ask in all seriousness - Could any thinking human man, having read this clearly expressed an emphatic opinion of one of the highest medical authorities obtainable, stand aside in smug indifference while the common hangman was strangling Wood? If Doctor Saunders had been a nobody, one's anxiety would not have been so keen. But he is the Medical Superintendent of the Sussex County Lunatic Asylum. This position would also prove him to be a specialist in mental disease of high standing, and he is known to be a man of great intellectual attainments.*

Moreover, the report from which I have been quoting was not drawn up for the defence, and it was furnished to the prosecution at the request of the solicitor to the Treasury, a fact which intensifies the importance of the report, though Doctor Saunders is not a man to make a one-sided statement whoever might be his employers. Nor can it be doubted that he has all the great medical authorities on his side; most assuredly, he has the witness of our common humanity that this man was insane when he murdered Edith Jeal

As to the Judges summing up, that, no doubt, was against the theory of epileptic insanity; but the legal mind seems incapable of grasping the idea of insanity save in the case of a person who has done some criminal act five minutes after escaping from a Lunatic asylum. It seems to me that Doctor Saunders has a broader, truer, and more just and human method of looking at the matter. For my part, I would accept his opinion as to a person's state of mind in preference to the opinion of any judge on the bench.

It appears to me, Sir, simply to come to this - either that this expert medical evidence is not worth the paper on which it is written, or else that, granting its reliability, granting, as surely most calm-minded men must grant, that it is the unbiased opinion of a distinguished specialist, then we can't get away from the conclusion that the hanging of this man will be a terrible miscarriage of justice.

I might add a third ground of protest, namely that the slaughter of a fellow mortal in cold blood is anti-Christian (although the clergy do read the Burial Office over his living body). Still, I don't know that would be any good, seeing that there are not any Christians left to argue with, but an interesting point has occurred to me somewhat in this connection. Let us suppose that 50,000 adult persons are interested in this case.

Now being a good deal among people and hearing what is being said, it seems to me not an unfair calculation that some 40,000 of these persons would decline to raise a hand to save this man from the scaffold. Just think of the brutalisation of so many minds, all thirsting for this poor mad creature's blood! For you cannot, under any conceivable circumstances, you cannot say that it is noble for one man to wish for another man's death. Higher civilisation will have none of this. Christianity says it is damnable.

Humanitarianism tells us that it is a relic of the brute-beast savagery and blood-lust in man. How anyone can refuse to sign the petition after the publication of Doctor Saunders' report is more than I can understand. 'Granting', says Doctor Saunders, 'The fact that the man is an epileptic' - and the fact is indisputable - 'His irresponsibility for the deed he committed may be strongly affirmed.'

On the 12th of April, Prince and Ayres briefed the Sussex Daily News on the petition's progress. They explained that the petition had received signatures from twenty leading medical practitioners in Brighton and its surrounding districts. The names included Doctor Saunders of the Sussex County Lunatic Asylum and Doctor Rogers, the police surgeon who had treated George Henry Wood after his arrest.

In addition, the ongoing publicity generated signatures from approximately seven hundred members of the public, clergymen, and solicitors. By the 13th of April, Prince and Ayres announced that the number of signatures had reached 1000. While they would have preferred to wait a little longer, Prince and Ayres knew the Easter holidays were fast approaching. They knew that judges and other officials would be on holiday and unavailable to intervene if they did not act soon.

Therefore, on the 14th of April, they submitted the petition to the Office for Home Affairs. They also published notices informing the public that they could still sign the petition and should contact their offices at Middle Street, Brighton, should they wish to do so. Whilst the case for a reprieve gained momentum in some quarters, in others, there was anger from others. These individuals also wanted to make their opinions known publicly and did so via the press. Some of these included direct responses to *'Humanitas'* demands and sympathies. Others went further and directly ridiculed Humanitas' position.

These letters were initially published in the Sussex Daily News but, due to the continuing interest in the case, were republished by other outlets. The first letter was written by an unknown author who signed off as *'Sanitas'*. His letter is as follows:

'Humanitas will, in my humble judgement, be a great pity in the interests of justice. Humanitas appears to be sincere in what he says, but extraordinary things have, as we all know, been said and done by people whose motives have not been called into question. In my opinion, his letter is most ill-advised and calculated to do a great deal of mischief in getting sympathy for this abominable murderer.

If he is a father himself, I would like to ask him how he would like one of his children to die as Edith Jeal did. He writes airily of the 'brutalisation of so many minds all thrusting for this poor mad creature's blood.' This is only one of his wild statements, which he has not taken the trouble to substantiate.

My experience with people like 'Humanitas' is that they are very fond of making groundless assertions. Why does he not tell us what grounds he bases his plea for mercy in this case? I expect he cannot do so; his whole letter is nothing but an appeal to that sentimental portion of the community which is always running after notorious criminals, trying to make them out to be insane, drooling over them, and turning them into heroes and heroines. We have seen this in previous cases, and now it is the turn of the Brighton murderer.

Besides, I deny that Wood is insane. Epilepsy is not insanity, and if it is, how does 'Humanitas' account for so many persons subject to epileptic fits going about their usual invocations? What I want to know is, if Wood was insane when he committed this crime, how was it he managed to take the poor child to a quiet shed where no one could see him at his horrible work, and how was it that he left the murdered child there, and went home as usual, and, when arrested, said he had been at the Circus?

Many of your readers would like to have this question answered by 'Humanitas' if they can. I contend that it is insulting to persons who, unfortunately, are subject to epileptic attacks to call them insane. 'Humanitas' may say this is the 'Higher Civilisation'. I call it 'Higher Sentimentality.'

A second letter was published on the same day by an author known only as 'Common Sense', whose letter is as follows:

'I am a constant reader of your paper, and, having had many years of experience in a large County Asylum in Middlesex, I write to ask if you can explain how it happened that if Wood was the very 'dangerous epileptic patient' he is represented to be, he was not placed under proper restraint?'

A further letter was written by '*Justice*', who wrote:

'Much is being said and written in favour of a commutation of the sentence passed on criminal Wood, now in Lewes Gaol, and although I am averse to capital punishment as a rule, under any circumstances, I cannot bring my mind to think that the act of this crime should be viewed as the result of uncontrollable will. I have witnessed a great many instances in which individuals, under the influence of drink, expose their true and natural character, and I think, in this case, the fellow had been intoxicated, and his natural disposition showed itself. I do not profess to be an expert in matters affecting the brain, but I am not altogether ignorant of the vagaries of human nature and consider the verdict in this case strictly just.'

The Easter weekend came and went, but the Home Office issued no decision concerning the reprieve. Still incarcerated at Lewes Gaol, George Henry Wood must have been praying that he would be saved from the gallows. Whilst there was silence from authorities, the public continued to debate what should happen. On the 16th of April 1892, 'Humanitas', having read the responses to his original letter, once again wrote to the Sussex Daily News. His letter reads as follows:

'It seems to me that 'Sanitas' gives away his whole case for the judicial strangling of this most unhappy man. I do not suppose that if an angel were to come from heaven, he would be able to convince such men as 'Sanitas' of the barbaric shamefulness of the bowl that they are setting up for this poor creature's blood.

    In the Dictionary of Medicine, edited by Sir Richard Quain, M.D., you will find, under the heading of 'Epileptic Insanity', these words: 'Those familiar with epileptics know that the majority do not know, or at least an imperfect idea, of their misdeeds, such a state of unconsciousness being the chief characteristic of epileptic insanity generally.' The humane thing to do is to keep Wood away from the world forever.

We all, I suppose, agree that he is unfit to be at large; but to execute such a man would be an act of barbarity unworthy of a civilised people and would be in defiance of the clearly stated opinions of medical experts. Can 'Sanitas' or anyone else believe for a single instant that these medical men would have signed the memorial to the Crown had they not had misgivings about the prisoner's sanity? If ever a murderer deserved to die, this man did, if he is sane. But he is not!'

Another response was published, this time by an author known as '*A sympathiser with the bereaved*', who agreed with '*Sanitas*'. The letter says:

'If a man in a fit of passion kills another, he (as a rule) is condemned and executed. But one who ill-treats a little helpless child, whose tender years would claim out protection, is pleaded earnestly for. Surely he must deserve his just punishment for such a sin!'

The following letter published was from a resident of Worthing. The author, known as *'Mother'*, wrote:

'I am surprised at the people of Brighton signing a petition in favour of the commutation of the death sentence. The verdict was right and just, and if ever a man deserved hanging, Wood does. Wood was not mad enough not to try and hide all traces of his guilt. He might have been mad drunk, but are we to get up a petition for and pity a wicked fellow who drinks until he is mad enough to commit any dreadful crime, even taking the lives of our dear one?'

The final letter published on the 16th of April is interesting. The letter was written by an author known only as *'Barrister'*, which reads as follows:

'If the idea that Wood was 'irresponsible' for his crime on the ground of being a confirmed epileptic had recommended itself to his fellow workman, is it not tolerably certain that the latter would have contributed to his defence? Yet I am informed that none of them did so?'

This author was correct. Not one of George Henry Wood's colleagues had testified that he had experienced seizures before, on the day, or after the murder. On the contrary, multiple witnesses testified that George Henry Wood had carried out his work duties ably and competently.

In addition, no acquaintances or family members had testified that George Henry Wood suffered from epilepsy, aside from George Wood Senior, who could only testify to witnessing a single fit that happened when his son was a young child.

Consequently, the authorities and many sections of the wider community were unwilling to accept that George Henry Wood was insane. Instead, they attributed his actions on the night of the murder to alcohol consumption and his perverted needs.

Meanwhile, *Humanitas*, who clearly felt strongly about the case and was unhappy with the criticism his previous letters had received, sent a further letter to the Sussex Daily News on the 16th of April, 1892. The letter reads as follows:

'I ask those who disagree with me to discuss the matter without becoming desolate. It is most disappointing to find people discussing the profoundly solemn and momentous question of this man's sanity or insanity with so much flippancy, so much recklessness of statement, and so many personal animosities against myself, as though I were the criminal pleading for my own life and not, as I simply claim to be the friend of this most unhappy and, as I contend, most afflicted fellow-creature.

When I find such an array of expert medical testimony on the side of the theory of Wood's responsibility, I am compelled to relieve my conscience by protesting with all the carnitines in my power against the execution of this man. It is entirely beside the question for your correspondents to heap abuse on me for entering this protest.'

The editors added another letter to the late edition of the paper, written by an author known only as 'Considerate.' This author also expressed regret about the views of *'Sanitas.'* The letter reads:

'Sanitas appears to treat the whole affair as a joke and further accuses your correspondent 'Humanitas' of 'appealing to that sentimental portion of the community.' I would ask, is it better to appeal to that which is higher in man or that lower spirit of vengeance? He constantly denies that Wood is insane and that epilepsy is not insanity. In doing this, he falls into the error of making wild statements without taking the trouble to substantiate them.

Meanwhile, an anonymous letter was sent directly to Henry Matthews, Secretary of State, on the 13th of April, 1892. The note is fascinating, and its contents suggest that the author knew the Wood family. It gives some insight into the Wood family and suggests that George Wood

Senior had not been completely honest when he testified to his son's *'good character'* at the Sussex Assizes. The letter is as follows:

'Sir,

As you are just now being inundated with letters and petitions concerning the life and actions of the Brighton murderer, I think it is only fair that you should know one or two little incidents of his life that every worker at the Brighton Railway Works is thoroughly conversant with, but that does not seem to come out either in evidence at the trial or in any printed matter that has appeared up to the present.

First, we have read over and over again why he came home from Canada but never why he went to Canada. Well, about fourteen or fifteen years since he was working here in the works as a factory lad and having a thieving propensity, he took it into his head to do a little housebreaking on his own account. So one morning, on his way to work, he broke into a shop selling sweets and tobacco. Afterwards, he appeared at the works well loaded with the produce of his little fling. There are men working here now who unknowingly had a share of the plunder.

The police got the scent of the matter, and he was taken and awarded one or two months in Lewes Gaol. I forgot just now, but you can easily find out the Brighton police knowing full well the facts, which can easily be verified hence his visit to Canada.

Now, as to his total abstinence, well, Sir, it is and has been a sham, and his father knows full well it is a sham. His uncle has followed him into public houses and endeavoured to do his best to keep him from disgracing himself and his family by his drinking propensities under cover of total abstinence.

I am not writing you this to do him any harm, for I am on the most intimate terms with his family, but I do think it wrong that you and the public should be deceived and imposed upon by a family professing such intense piety and profound religious principles. This matter you can easily prove for one of his uncles is a policeman here in Brighton and one a postman, both I believe and know are very steady and very much respected. I have decided to let you know this in the interests of justice.

Yours, a lover of truth.'

The letter was received and read by Hamilton Cuffe, Assistant Solicitor to the Treasury, on the same day, who forwarded the letter to the Office for Home Affairs along with a note that highlights the letter's main themes, the letter reads as follows:

'Sir,

The statements in this letter are:

- The reason for the convict going to Canada 13 or 14 years ago was that he was convicted of housebreaking and stealing and served a sentence in Lewes Prison.
- That his total abstinence was a sham.

Is it worthwhile to get a police report on these statements? So far as they go, they would tend to show that the convict is a criminal and not a lunatic

H.C 13.4.92

Secretary of State, Henry Matthews replied on the same day, stating that he did not think further evidence was necessary. However, on the 14th of April 1892, in light of the ongoing press attention, he sent a telegram to Charles Matthew, Justice of the Assize, to ask whether he felt further medical evidence was required. The judge replied on the same day as follows:

'Sir,

In reply to your letter in regards to the convict George Henry Wood, I say that I concur with the opinion that any further medical inquiry in the case is not called for. The view taken by the jury as to the mental condition of the prisoners at the time when the murder was committed seems to be correct.'

J. P. Mathews.'

On the 22nd of April, 1892, Reverend Wilkinson, Chaplain at Lewes Prison, briefed the press. He informed the reporters that he had visited George Henry Wood in the condemned cell daily. He explained that the condemned prisoner had maintained that he had no recollection of the crime. He stated that George Henry Wood had initially begged to see his mother but had accepted that this was impossible due to her ill health.

On the 25th of April, Henry Matthews sent an early telegram to Prince and Ayres at Middle Street. He explained that he was unwilling to grant a reprieve, but as customary, he did not elaborate on his reasoning. He informed the solicitors that the law must take its course and that their client would be hung at 9 am the following morning.

Mr Ayres had the unenviable task of informing George Henry Wood's family of the response. He immediately composed a sympathetic letter and delivered it by hand to Rock Street.

Meanwhile, back at Lewes Prison, George Henry Wood awoke early and, after breakfast, attended the chapel. The Secretary of State's decision was received shortly after, and Captain Crickett was tasked with delivering the news to the condemned cell. George Henry Wood was said to be inconsolable as he was informed that he would be hanged at 9 am the following day.

With the execution fast approaching, George Henry Wood was permitted to receive a visit from his father, uncle and younger brother. In 1892, family members and convicts were separated by two rows of iron bars and a three-foot wide walkway patrolled by prison warders. This prevented any physical contact between family members and added to the distress that the visit caused.

The authorities described the meeting as very painful, as you would expect, given the circumstances. Throughout the meeting, George Wood Senior repeatedly asked his son if he had anything to confess. As a man with deep-rooted religious views, he urged his son to admit his guilt and pray for forgiveness. Even at this late stage, George Henry Wood continued to play dumb.

He said to his distraught father, *'If I had remembered anything, you would have heard it long ago.'*

As the visit concluded, George Henry Wood gave his father a letter for his mother, which apparently contained similar sentiments. George Henry Wood wept bitterly as George Wood Senior and his other children began to leave. It is impossible to feel any sympathy for George Henry Wood. However, you can only imagine the anguish of his family.

Outside the prison, having learned of the Secretary of State's decision, local press representatives began to assemble. Captain Crickett emerged from his residence and briefly addressed the press. He explained that George Henry Wood had been guarded around the clock since his trial. He said that the prisoner had been extremely calm and had not given any trouble.

Meanwhile, some members of the public were still concerned about the looming execution and refusal of the Home Secretary to interfere. Letters objecting to the decision continued to be received by local newspapers. A final letter from *'Humanitas'* letter was printed in the late edition of the Brighton Argus on the 25th of April 1892. The letter reads as follows:

'Wood, tomorrow morning, will be dragged forth into God's sweet fresh air and strangled in cold blood. A minister of the Gospel of the Prince of Peace will go through the accursed mockery of reading the Burial Service over a living man's body. The solemn testimony of the experts in mental disease, testimony given at the prosecution's request, not of the defence - will

be ignored. All that is most savage and debased and depraved in the human heart will, I hope, be satisfied by this most Christian and most ennobling spectacle of the deliberate strangling of a fellow creature. I also hope that my critics will now be satisfied. The gentle ladies and gentlemen in the columns of the Sussex Daily News have been screaming at the pitch of their voices for the blood of this poor, afflicted fellow mortal - dancing on him, as it were, while he lay on his deathbed. Oh yes, they should feel thrilled and Christian-minded on Tuesday morning at nine am when they reflect on what will be carried out within the walls of Lewes Gaol. Well, Sir, I do not envy them their happiness.'

Chapter 27: Behind the Scenes

Publically, the authorities appeared satisfied that George Henry Wood was entirely culpable for Edith Jeal's murder. However, behind-the-scenes concerns about his impending execution had been rumbling on since the trial concluded.

On the 9th of April 1892, Judge Charles Mathews wrote a letter to the Office for Home Affairs to inform them of George Henry Wood's trial's outcome. The letter included the case file, witness depositions, Judge's notes and a trial account. The package was received by Hamilton Cuffe, Solicitor to the Treasury. After studying the extensive file, he sent a telegram to the Office for Home Affairs with his opinions on the case. His summary clearly shows that he felt that the trial's outcome was just. The letter reads as follows:

'As regards the prisoner's guilt, there is no question it was an atrocious case of outrage and murder of a little girl of 5. The prisoner, a railway servant, was drunk and was seen to take up one little girl and try to carry her away, but he fell, and she managed to escape. He then spoke to another little girl and tried to induce her to accompany him. Finally, he met the little girl, five years old, took her over fields to a shed, outraged her with brutal violence and strangled her.

There are questions as to the prisoner's sanity. It seems clear that some years ago in Canada, he suffered epileptic fits but had been free from them for at least two years before the crime. Since he has been in custody, he has had five fits - one of them very severe (see Doctor Rogers's evidence). The other three were in prison and were very light and short. Apart from these fits, the prisoner has shown no symptoms of insanity either before or after the crime.

Saunders, Superintendent of the Haywards Heath Asylum, thinks Wood was insane and irresponsible when he committed the crime. He founds his opinion mainly on

1. *The frightfully atrocious nature of the injuries he inflicted, which he thinks is consistent with the action of an irresponsible man*
2. *Statistics about the number of criminal lunatics who have epilepsy.*

I think he fails to make anything like a case. The whole character of Wood's proceedings (trying to carry away one little girl, inducing another girl to go with him and then leading away the girl Jeal and carrying her over fields to a shed) is wholly unlike the irresponsible and unconscious actions of a person with epilepsy.

Doctor Sheppard disagrees with Doctor Saunders' opinions. He rejects the suggestion that the crime was committed due to the uncontrollable impulse of an irresponsible epileptic and thinks that if the prisoners did not know what he was doing; it was not because he was insane but because he was drunk.

The jury had both doctor's reports before them and found the prisoner guilty without hesitation. The Judge, it may be gathered from his summing up, considered the prisoner fully responsible.

Charles Edward Troup 9.4.1892.

Charles Edward Troupe forwarded the letter and associated files to Edward Leigh Pemberton, Assistant Under-Secretary of State, who read through the files and discussed the case at length with Henry Matthews, the principal Home Secretary. Afterwards, Edward Pemberton sent an official response on the 11th of April, 1892. His letter is as follows:

'Dear Cuffe,

As to whether or not the prisoner is a 'confirmed epileptic', the correspondence sufficiently shows that he had several epileptic fits in Canada, one of them accompanied by mania. Since his commitment, he has had 5 of the same fits. He had no fit for more than two years before the murder.

Nonetheless, it may be affirmed from the evidence that he was liable to epileptic fits. After a long period of abstaining from liquor, he had given way to drink for about a week. In light of this, I may say that if he had a fit on the night of the murder, it should not be surprising.

But what evidence is there that he did have a fit? None! What evidence is there to point to this contrary view? He attempted to entice a first little girl, then another and finally succeeded with a third and carried her over fields for a quarter of a mile to a barn where he would be hidden from observers and outraged and murdered her. These facts suggest that the man's actions were not acts of the unconscious epileptic but of a mere criminal – a drunken criminal, but still a criminal.

Again, an epileptic committing violence in a fit is not only unconscious of it at the time but has no recollection of it afterwards. That is why the prisoner pretended the picture he gave was manifestly false. He knew of the murder the next day before anybody else did. He took the precaution of having a bath to wash all of the marks of the murder and outrage from his person. He falsely told a policeman that he had been to the circus.
Doctor Saunders' report is most unconvincing. I presume you will ask the Judge whether he considers that further medical evidence is needed.

Edward Pemberton'

On the 12th of April 1892, Doctor Saunders, who appears to have been unhappy with his treatment at the Assizes, wrote a lengthy letter to the Secretary of State outlining his concerns about George Henry Wood's guilt and reaffirming that he was irresponsible for his actions. His letter clarifies that he felt that the Judge had misdirected the jury and did not fully understand what he meant by 'epileptic unconsciousness' and how it linked to insanity. Although not published, the letter was leaked to the press, who described it as being 'far more elaborate than the first report'. The letter is as follows:

To the Right Honourable: Henry Matthews, Q.C., M.P. Principal Secretary of State for Home Affairs

Sir,
May I beg the favour of your attention to the following letter I sent you undercover to the Hon: H. Cuffe. Having been instructed by the Secretary of State to inquire into the sanity of the above-named George Henry Wood, I think it is incumbent on me to point out to you that the question of the prisoner being a confirmed epileptic, or the reverse, was one on which the learned Judge who tried the case laid much stress, on which he was wholly misinformed.

It justified me, fully justified me, in my opinion, of the man's irresponsibility. It may assist you in considering the evidence (as we may call it, out of a court of law) on this head, if, in the briefest possible way, 'Ipsissima Verba', of the various deponents to the man's epileptic state while in Canada, which prove that so far from Wood having had no fits, since the infantile convulsions which his unhappy father spoke of in the witness box, until after the murder, that he had while under close observation during a period of three years, repeated, sometimes daily attacks of epilepsy.

The doctor in charge of the penitentiary at Stony Mountain, Manitoba, writes, 'George Henry Wood, confirmed here as convict no 15 during 1887, 1888 and 1889, was repeatedly under my care as surgeon of this penitentiary. He suffered from repeated attacks of epilepsy, some more severe than others, when admitting him to the hospital would be necessary.

The total number of days in the hospital, during the period of his imprisonment, was for nine days convalescent and unfit for duty 94.' The warden for the same gaol corroborates the above and adds, 'whilst here he was well behaved and received all the remission of time he could obtain.' A gaoler at Portage la Prairie writes, 'I consider him a character not responsible for his actions and should certainly not be out of some place of keeping.'

Of course, I had not had the opportunity to elaborate in the witness box any opinion on the condition of the mind in epilepsy. I want not to be thought of to speak disrespectfully of the Judge if I say that his notion of a person with epilepsy was a man who fell and, after a few convulsive kicks, got up and went about his business as if nothing had happened, with his mind clean and unclouded.

Epilepsy is a profound disorder of the brain finding expression for the most part in violent explosive force, but just as definitely interfering, for the time being, with mental power, as any form of insanity. In the way the learned Judge spoke to the jury of unconsciousness, I felt sure that they must have had present only in their minds, the kind of unconsciousness which would popularly be associated with persons unable to move their limbs, much less to walk and perform complex acts.

This is not the actual unconsciousness (If I may be allowed the explanation), which I had in my view when I said that epileptic acts in an unconscious way, under uncontrollable impulse. The minds of all epileptics are more or less warped. They are liars, cruel, jealous and deceitful. In many cases, the mind completely gives way, and they have to be restrained in leg irons.

I have already signed a memorial, praying that you, in fluent terms, give your consideration to the unheard facts of the case, but I have returned to add that these personal remarks pursue my position in the matter.

I have the honour to be, Sir,

Your obedient servant. C. S. Saunders, M.D. Medical Superintendent.'

The letter was forwarded to Henry Matthews on the 14th of April, accompanied by the following memorandum:

'The points on which the doctor lays emphasis are:

1. *That there is evidence that Wood is a confirmed epileptic.*
2. *That epilepsy does not mean merely falling in a fit but is often accompanied by well-marked mental derangement, sometimes amounting to permanent insanity.*

What he does not show is that, in this case, the prisoner ever showed any insane symptoms before or after his fits or at any other time or that there is any reason to support that when he committed the crime, he was suffering from a fit.

Cuffe.'

The Home Secretary, Henry Matthews, replied the same day with the following response:

'To that, the nature of this report, one has only to ask one question, whether, at any time during the two years before the murder, it would have been possible to certify this man as a lunatic and place him under permanent control - clearly not, from the evidence!'

On the 13th of April, a further memorandum was sent to Judge Mathews, asking whether he felt that any additional medical reports should be sought before the execution took place. The Judge replied as follows:

'In regards to G.H. Wood under the sentence of death. H.M. Prison, Lewes.

Sir,
In reply to your letter regarding the convict George Henry Wood, I concur with the opinion that any further medical inquiry in the case is not called for. The view taken by the jury as to the mental condition of the prisoners at the time when the murder was committed seems to be correct.

Justice C. H. Mathews.'

Despite the ongoing publicity, as described in previous chapters, it appears that Judge Mathews was still convinced that George Henry Wood should hang. However, this confidence was shared by only some stakeholders. On the 14th of April 1892, Walter Bartlett, the Under Sheriff of Lewes, was informed by Captain Crickett, Governor of Lewes Gaol, that George Henry Wood had suffered another seizure.

As the appointed Under Sheriff for Lewes, Walter Bartlett was responsible for ensuring that the execution was carried out. Unsure of what to do if George Henry Wood experienced further seizures on the day of the execution, he wrote to Edward Leigh Pemberton, Under-Secretary of State, asking for guidance. His letter is as follows:

'Sir,
I think it is right to inform you that George Henry Wood, under sentence of death at Lewes, has, since his conviction, had a fit (whether of an epileptic or hysteric nature, I do not know). I am apprehensive lest he may, on the way, have another. I shall be very much obliged if the Home Secretary has any recommendations for the course I might adopt should such a contingency arise.
I am, Sir, your obedient servant,
Walter Bartlett, Under Sheriff of Sussex.'

Edward Leigh Pemberton sent a memorandum to Troup asking that he respond. His letter is as follows:

'Mr Troup,
Make this letter official. Mr Pemberton will inform the Under-Sheriff verbally that in the improbable event of the convict being taken with an epileptic fit when on the scaffold, it will be the duty of the High Sheriff of Lewes to suspend the execution and to apply to the Secretary of State for instructions. Please also ask the Prison Commission to obtain a medical report on the alleged fits since George Henry Wood's conviction and the state of his health. If he has another fit, it must be reported to the Home Office.

Edward Leigh Pemberton.'

Mr Troup, after receiving the response, complied immediately with the requests. He wrote a brief note to the Prison Commission the same day asking for the nature of George Henry Wood's fits to be established. He also urged that future fits be reported immediately to the Office for Home Affairs. He also sent a telegram to Walter Bartlett asking that he visit his office on the 20th of April 1892 at noon. It is unclear why an in-person meeting was necessary. It may be that the Office for Home Affairs wanted to ensure that instructions relating to such a serious matter would be understood correctly.

On the 15th of April, Captain Crickett sent a brief medical report to Edward Leigh Pemberton. The report was compiled by Richard Turner, Prison Surgeon at Lewes Gaol, who also appeared to be sceptical of the authenticity of George Henry Wood's seizures. His report reads as follows:

'This prisoner, after being found guilty of murder and sentenced to be executed, fainted away in the corridor of the Assizes convict cells due understandably to the strain of his trial and its verdict on the 7th of April 1892. As might be expected, he was very much depressed during the next 24 hours.

On the 9th of April, having been sent by car to attend to him at his cell at Lewes Prison at 7 am (Saturday). I was told that G.H. Woods was in a fit, and I went to him immediately. I found him throwing himself about in his cell on the floor like a hysterical woman, but there was no rigidity of the limbs or convulsion of any kind, foaming at the mouth, or biting of his tongue. His eyes were tightly closed, and his teeth were not clenched.

He resisted a spindle of cold water in his face (which brought him to on a few previous occasions in 10 minutes) by lying on his face and putting his arms on his face. I examined the pupils of the eye, and they were sensitive to light. He came too in about 10 minutes. When I arrived, the attendants attempted to lay him on the bed, but he asked to lie on the floor. He said he became faint and rolled himself around on the floor. After a bit longer, the man stood up and sat on the chair in the cell. This fit was a hysterical one that is exaggerated, if not feigned entirely, certainly not epilepsy, due to the prospect before him.

He has been quite rational since his remand on the 15th of December 1891. He has always been calm, rational and of sound mind. Physically, with the exception of varicose veins in his leg, he has fair health. He had all the appearance of a man who had been drinking for some time before.

I am, Sir, your humble servant,
Richard Turner.'

The report was forwarded to Henry Matthews, who, at this point, was still considering issuing a reprieve. After reading the information, he sent a memorandum simply stating, *'Seen. H. M.'* At this point, the Treasury and Home Office authorities must have felt a sense of relief. They had sufficient evidence to suggest that George Henry Wood's fits were either feigned or hysterical in nature. Insanity had been disproved both in court and by the subsequent medical evidence. The execution would be carried out in line with the laws of the time, and all those involved could retain a clear conscience.

However, things were not going well at Lewes House of Correction. George Henry Wood had reportedly experienced another fit on the 19th of April 1892, just 7 days before the execution was due to be carried out. The four death wardens immediately attended to him, and Richard Turner, the medical officer, was called to assess his condition.

After George Henry Wood recovered, Captain Crickett demanded that the four wardens and Richard Turner write statements about the episode. The following day, Captain Crickett forwarded the statements to the Prison Commission, who, in turn, sent them on to Edward Leigh Pemberton, Under Secretary of State. The letter was received at the Office for Home Affairs the next morning. Richard Turner's second report reads as follows:

'Sir,

I have the honour to report for the attention of the Secretary of State in the Home Department that George Henry Wood, under sentence of death, is reported by the attendants in charge of him, had a similar kind of fit to the ones he had whilst waiting for trial. The prisoner was lying down at 7.30 am after reading his books when he was believed to be asleep. He was lying face down and lying on his hand. His eyelids were closed; he had no convulsions, no foaming at the mouth and lay perfectly still.

Whilst in the attack, he was laid on a mattress on the floor of the cell as previously directed by me. No personnel restraint of any kind was required. His attendants, Warden Read, Counstick, Brown and Occasional Warden Shear, saw the fit. Their reports will accompany this letter.

George Henry Wood is of perfectly sound mind and has been since he came here on the 15th of December 1891. Being a non-resident, he has only once been seen by the prison's medical officer in an actual fit.

I am Sir, your humble servant.
Richard Turner.'

The four wardens' reports are included in the case file but repeat the same facts. Therefore it seems pointless to detail all four here. The most detailed account was written by George Albion Read. His statement is as follows:

'George Albion Read, an attendant, was with George Henry Wood and Mr Coustick, an attendant, on the 18th of April 1892. Wood had been reading while sitting on a chair for a considerable time. At about 7.30 pm, he asked if he had been reading too much and complained of pains in his head. He moved from the chair and lay down on his bed. I thought he had gone to sleep, but not feeling satisfied, at about 7.45 pm, I attempted to rouse him but found I could not do so.

I concluded it was another attack. According to Doctor Turner's instructions, I placed him on a bed on the floor and watched him see that he did not hurt himself. He was, however, reticent and did not move his hand or foot. There was no tongue biting, but a little movement came from his mouth, but I could not positively say what it was. I was relieved at 5 pm by Mr Shears and Hudson (Mr Brown, Warden, also coming in), and he had not recovered and was still lying on the bed.

Mr G Read.'

Captain Crickett explained in a covering letter that George Henry Wood had slept well the following night and appeared in good health when he woke the following day. Hamilton Cuffe, Director of Public Prosecutions, received the letters on the 20th of April and was sceptical of their contents. His patience was running out with the case, as shown in the following memorandum to Edward Leigh Pemberton on the same day. It reads as follows:

'Was it a fit or not? Hardly an epileptic fit! No convulsion, foaming at the mouth or grinding of the teeth. Legs were said by the warders to have been still, but that might be simulated. The doctor did not see him in a fit. He has only seen him once in a fit out of five. Nor does it appear that the fit was reported to the Governor.

Aside from four unskilled wardens, no one will give the Secretary of State any help regarding whether these fits were real or feigned. Surely this should not be! Send a telegraph to the Governor stating that it is of the utmost importance that the Secretary of State should have a decided medical opinion on whether these fits are real or feigned. The medical officer has only witnessed one, which needed to be a sufficient guide for him to pronounce decisively.

Request that immediate arrangements be made for having either the medical officer or his assistant deputy continuously at the prison day and night so that the prisoner may be seen and reported on every occasion of a similar seizure. Any seizure should also be reported immediately to the Governor and the medical officer.'

The urgent telegraph was sent the same day to Lewes House of Correction. Richard Turner and his deputy made themselves available around the clock so that they could form an opinion as to whether any further *'fits'* were epileptic or not. Serendipitously, George Henry Wood did not suffer any more seizures. Whether this was because he did not suffer any further attacks or, alternatively, ceased simulating fits due to the constant presence of the medical officer will never be known.

Despite this, Captain Crickett appears to have been anxious about the impending execution and sent a further telegram to the Office for Home Affairs. The telegram reads as follows:

'Sir,
Who should I telegraph, the Under Secretary of State or Prison Commission, if Wood is seized with a fit at any time on Monday next or particularly Tuesday Morning?'
I am, Sir, your obedient servant,
Captain Crickett.'

The telegram was received by Edward Leigh Pemberton, who passed it to Henry Matthews, Secretary of State, who replied immediately, requesting that someone be available on the day of the execution. On the 25th of April, the eve of the execution, Captain Crickett sent a further telegram to the Prison Commission and Office for Home Affairs, which stated, *'The prisoner Wood is in fair health today and has had no further attacks.'*

Chapter 28: Arrangements for the Execution

The Office of the High Sheriff is the oldest, continuous, secular office that works under the crown. Each county within England and Wales has a High Sheriff, and although their role has changed, the position has receded and evolved. The position is still current but dates back to Saxon times, when the Shire Reeve, as the High Sheriff was then known, was responsible for collecting taxes under the King's authority.

They also had law enforcement powers and could summon *posse comitatus*, the full force of the county, to pursue perceived felons within the county they presided over. One of the more unsavoury requirements of the High Sheriff was to ensure that capital punishments were carried out in a timely and efficient manner. This was usually managed by the county's undersheriff, who acted as a deputy to the High Sheriff.

Immediately after the verdict, Captain Crickett, Governor at Lewes Gaol and the Under-Sheriff of Lewes, William Bartlett, were informed of the sentence. In turn, Captain Crickett sent a telegram to the Prison Commission, who in 1892 controlled English prisons, to alert them of the sentence. In return, they returned the statutory *'execution pack',* which contained the official list of approved executioners. Having received appropriate training and vetting, the Treasury deemed these individuals competent to perform judicial hangings. This list was held and regularly updated. Anyone deemed inappropriate or incompetent was immediately removed.

Captain Crickett sent the list to Walter Bartlett, Under Sheriff of Lewes, who was tasked with selecting an executioner. After reviewing the list, Walter Bartlett wrote to the Office for Home Affairs advising that he had chosen the principal executioner, James

Billington, to perform the execution, which was scheduled to take place on the 26th of April, 1892.

Subsequently, an official invitation was sent to James Billington requesting his attendance at George Henry Wood's execution. The invitation included the executioner's fee of 21. 2s. In addition to this fee, executioners could claim reasonable expenses. This did not extend to accommodation as executioners were lodged in convict cells, with little adaptations to the conditions provided to prisoners, probably to their displeasure. This arrangement reduced costs and prevented any alcohol consumption by the executioner, which was a significant concern for the authorities.

A few days later, James Billington wrote back, accepting the invitation. In 1892, The Office for Home Affairs and Prison Commission urged county sheriffs to appoint an assistant executioner. This practice would allow the assistant to obtain experience and provide assistance in the case of multiple executions, which were not uncommon. However, in the case of George Henry Wood, it appears that no assistant was recruited.

The Governor, Captain Crickett, was tasked with the necessary equipment and ensuring its functionality. Unlike other prisons, Lewes conducted very few executions; consequently, the gaol did not have permanent gallows. Execution equipment was stored in bulk at Holloway Gaol and could be ordered by smaller prisons. These items included: the rope, pinioning apparatus and a cap made from an approved pattern.

On the 17th of April, Captain Cricket ordered the necessary equipment, which was delivered a few days later. After the executioner's box arrived at Lewes, a senior warden examined the equipment for damage but found none. He lubricated the ropes and pinioning straps with petroleum ointment and then moved them to the cold basement of the gaol to ensure they remained flexible. The gallows and execution shed were also transported from another Gaol. Although it is unclear if they came from Wandsworth or Holloway Prison, they, too, arrived several days before the execution date.

Once all the necessary equipment was in place, Captain Crickett discretely approached local contractors to erect the scaffold. Recruiting someone to carry out this dreadful task was not always easy. On one occasion, John Every, who owned the most prominent iron founder in the area, was approached to see if he would be willing to construct the gallows. However, he deeply opposed the death penalty and refused to undertake the work. Luckily for the authorities, someone else accepted the contract and, shortly after, began constructing the grisly apparatus.

The closeness of the condemned cell to the gallows probably meant that George Henry Wood was aware of these activities, which likely increased his sense of dread as the day of reckoning fast approached. The High Sheriff was invited to inspect the equipment when the work was finished. During this visit, Walter Bartlett witnessed senior wardens testing the apparatus, with sandbags used in place of the condemned prisoner.

James Billington had been told to arrive before 4 pm on the eve of the execution to view the condemned prisoner and be provided with the victim's age, condition, build and stature. These details were essential for calculating the correct length of rope from the table of drops to allow the prisoner's quick and humane death.

The need for decorum and good conduct was continually impressed on executioners and their assistants. Executioners and their assistants would receive a memorandum of conditions at every judicial hanging. This booklet detailed the appropriate conduct expected during and after executions. The role was cloaked in secrecy, and any public interviews were prohibited. To ensure executioners followed these rules, the Office for Home Affairs withheld their fees for two weeks after an execution was carried out.

Anyone who was known to break these rules would automatically forfeit the payment and any expense claims. Prison Governors also bore responsibility for the professionalism of any execution in the prison they managed. In case they forgot their responsibility, the execution pack contained a memorandum to Prison Governors written by Godfrey Lushington, the Chairman of the Prison Commissioners. The memorandum reads as follows:

'Whitehall, the 7th of October 1885

Sir,
I am directed by the Secretary of State to acquaint you that on several occasions, his attention has been called to the proceedings, before and after execution, of the person employed as executioner, which appears to have given rise to grave public scandal.

The Secretary of State thinks the danger of repetition of such occurrences would be much diminished if it could be arranged that, on the occasion of every execution, the executioner should reside in the prison where the execution takes place. The Secretary of State has, of course, no authority to control the movements of the executioner, who is engaged and paid solely by the Sheriff, as the officer responsible exclusively for the carrying out of the execution.

Still, as you are aware, the Secretary of State has already given instructions that quarters should be provided for the executioner in prisons whenever the Sheriff wishes him to reside there. He thinks that it is desirable that in future, when it is known that execution is about to take place in any prison, the Governor should be instructed at once to communicate with the Sheriff and inform him that, if he desires, the executioner will be provided with lodging and maintenance in prison, and that in the opinion of the Secretary of State, he should, in engaging the executioner, make it compulsory that he should sleep there so long as he may remain in the place where the sentence is to be executed, and indeed on the night proceeding the execution.

The Sheriff should, of course, understand that this matter is one entirely for his discretion but that the Secretary of State, while not wishing to interfere with his responsibility, desires him to be informed of his opinion that grave public scandals may be avoided by insisting on this as a condition in the engagement of the executioner.

I am. &c.
Godfrey Lushington
The Chairman of the Prison Commissioners.'

These concerns stemmed from one individual, Bartholomew Binns, who appeared on the approved list of executioners between 1883 and 1884. Between these dates, he carried out eleven different executions. Initially, he was praised for his work, but as his career gained momentum, his inefficiency and poor conduct caused several public scandals.

Bartholomew Binns was known to frequent public houses before and after executions, and officials reported that he had attended executions whilst under the influence of alcohol. To make matters worse, the authorities received word that he had given interviews to members of the public and had publicly displayed his execution equipment. Whilst these acts were considered inappropriate, this was not the worst of his behaviour. Bartholomew Binns oversaw at least two 'bungled' executions, leading to scrutiny and condemnation in the national press, further embarrassing the government.

The first incident occurred on the 3rd of December, 1883. Bartholomew Binns had been invited to execute Henry Dutton after he was convicted of the murder of his Wife's Grandmother. When Bartholomew Binns arrived at Kirkdale Prison, Liverpool, on the eve of the execution, the Governor suspected that he was drunk but took no action. Henry Dutton was slight in stature and weighed only nine stones. Bartholomew Binns calculated a drop of seven feet five inches, which resulted in a prolonged death.

Spectators at the grisly execution said Henry Dutton violently struggled after falling through the trapdoor. His body spun around several times and twitched convulsively for eight minutes before he took his last breath. After the execution, the traumatised Governor who had witnessed Henry Dutton's slow and painful death sent a telegram to the Office for Home

Affairs to share his concerns about Bartholomew Binn's competency. He denied being drunk at the time of the execution and attributed the botched nature of the execution to the new rope he had used. Unfortunately, no action was taken by the authorities.

On the morning of the 10th of March 1884, Binns again attended Kirkdale Gaol. On this occasion, his victim was 18-year-old Michael McLean, who was sentenced to death for murdering a Spanish Sailor earlier the same year. Michael McLean was short and frail, yet Bartholomew Binns allowed a drop of over ten feet. Despite agreeing that the actual length needed was nine foot six inches, the official table of drops suggests a.

Michael McLean's death was instantaneous at his inquest, but the Governor of the Gaol, Major Leggatt, said that Binns was drunk on arriving at the gaol the day before the execution. He described Bartholomew Binn's conduct as questionable and recalled that he acted by the 'rule of thumb'. The jury at Michael McLean's inquest questioned Bartholomew Binns. He admitted being in a 'stupid sleep' but denied being drunk. This was contradicted by reports from the attending journalists, who testified that Bartholomew Binns had visited a Public House near the gaol and had consumed a significant quantity of alcohol.

After the inquest, the county's Under-sheriff sent his concerns to the Office for Home Affairs and the Prison Commission. Bartholomew Binns appeared utterly unphased by the situation. Later that day, he was spotted in several public houses where he showed off his execution ropes and straps to patrons. When he reached the train station to journey home, he was reportedly *'very far advanced in liquor'*. Much to the embarrassment of the authorities, he also gave several private interviews about his profession locally.

The authorities were worried that the reports suggesting malpractice would reopen the debate about capital punishment. As far back as 1884, opponents to capital punishment would seize upon any executions considered 'botched' to further their cause. Even officials who supported capital punishment publicly stated they had grave concerns about the nature of these two deaths.

In September 1884, the Court of Alderman decided to no longer retain the services of Bartholomew Binns as Public Executioner, and his name no longer appeared on the official list. Even after his dismissal, he continued to attract the attention of the press, much to the embarrassment of the authorities.

Chapter 29: *'In the midst of life, we are in death'*

As dawn broke on the morning of 26th April 1982, the heavy rain which had relentlessly fallen upon Lewes during the previous night slowly began to clear and was replaced with bright and warm sunshine. As the temperature rose, dense fog and sweet spring freshness diffused through the entire area, thus reminding its town's residents that winter was over.
As George Henry Wood awoke to the realisation of his sentence, fear and regrets must have filled his mind. As he glanced out of the infirmary window, he must have recognised that his fate on the gallows was now inevitable.

Many people began to assemble outside the gaol, and as the morning drew on, the number rapidly increased. Many of these macabre spectators waited in the open space before the prison. The remaining group climbed on top of the grass bank at the southwestern corner of the gaol. This bank was known to be the closest accessible position to the execution pit, but the tall perimeter wall prevented anyone from seeing the act itself. The bank's position also allowed a clear view of the flagstaff onto which the black flag would later hang. Directly opposite the gaol's frontage were several carts and other vehicles laden with people eager to witness the lifting of the death flag. Despite the crowd's size, they were described as mournful, respectful and, on the whole, orderly.

Nonetheless, ever fearful of public disorder, three Lewes police constables under the charge of Superintendent Osbourne were positioned outside the gaol to deter inappropriate or unfitting behaviour with the occasion's solemnity. As soon as the reprieve was denied, several press representatives were invited to witness the execution, including three from Brighton. These journalists worked for the Argus, the Brighton Herald and the Brighton Gazette. These individuals were expected to be present at the hanging so that after, they could report the gruesome details to their eager readers.

The three men agreed to travel together and met at Brighton Station's gates around 7.25 am. After entering the station concourse, the group boarded the early morning train. At 7.30 am, the steam train began the short journey east. As the steam train sped through the picturesque countryside, talk of the execution filled the carriages. People animatedly discussed the nature of George Henry Wood's crime and debated the sentence's fairness.

The journalists later reported that they heard minimal sympathy for George Henry Wood's situation and overheard many people stating that he deserved the punishment he had been given. However, they did report that compassion was expressed toward George Henry Wood's parents, George and Margery, who were likely back at 11 Rock Street, clock-watching and imagining the horror of their eldest son's final moments.

Meanwhile, the early morning train pulled into the Lewes station. Large groups of passengers disembarked and quickly made their way across the platform, through the exit and onto the road. Here, different segments of the morning commuters separated and followed different routes through the town. The three press representatives followed the section of the crowd that was heading for the gaol as they walked up Station Street to the main road that led directly to Lewes Prison.

As they walked, the journalists stopped and interviewed members of the public but reported a complete lack of excitement in the town. Having failed to obtain any answers that would complement the sensational story they hoped to write, the journalists continued. They arrived at the prison just after 8 am and continued the long drive until they reached the entrance. After being welcomed by the gatehouse warder, the press representatives handed over the Home Office-issued papers required to enter the prison. The papers had previously been reviewed and signed by the Under-sheriff, Walter Bartlett, who was responsible for all aspects of the day's events.

After these checks, Warder Richardson came out and greeted the journalists and immediately led them through the little wicket gate in the frontage of the prison, which allowed access to a courtyard. Here they remained for the next twenty minutes. With little else to do, they studied the area. The group quickly spotted the Gaol's Chapel on the first floor of the central building, identifiable through a stone belfry. The structure housed the chapel's bell, which would sound out the haunting funeral knell, minute by minute, during and after the execution.

As the journalists continued to wait to be taken to the gallows, Warder Richardson gave an account of George Henry Wood's final days. He explained that the condemned man had attended mass on the previous Sunday, where he had intently listened to the administrations of the Reverend B. Wilkinson, the resident chaplain of the gaol. He also informed them that the Reverend had visited George Henry Wood every day since he had received his sentence and that the two had developed somewhat of a close friendship.

Their conversation was interrupted by activity just inside the porter's lodge. The gatehouse warder set up a small table near the door and rested the official visitor's log on its surface. The journalists were asked to enter their details so that the High-sheriff had records of anyone entering or leaving the gaol.

Meanwhile, two prison wardens in plain clothes emerged from the entrance leading to the chapel and passed the waiting reporters as they made their way out of the gaol. The reporters were informed that the two men were the death wardens who had guarded George Henry Wood during his last night. The journalists spoke to the pair, who explained that George Henry Wood had passed a good night, although his mood was sombre.

The warders stated that he awoke very early, washed and dressed, and appeared calm and self-possessed. Breakfast was brought to the infirmary by the catering staff at an early hour, as was usual, and on this day, it consisted of coffee, bread and butter, and an egg. However, as you might expect, George Henry Wood had no appetite and ate very little.

Reverend Wilkinson arrived at the gaol at a quarter to eight as he had promised George Henry Wood the day before and immediately made his way to the infirmary to tend to his subject. As he entered, he found George Henry Wood, who was reportedly calm and composed at this point. Immediately, Reverend Wilkinson began to pray with the prisoner. Afterwards, the Reverend took out his Bible and read portions of the scripture aloud.

Suddenly, George Henry Wood interrupted the protestations to ask that the Reverend read Hebrew, John 14 and a section of chapter xvii. A few minutes into the reading, George Henry Wood, who had now lost his composure, interrupted the Reverend and exclaimed tearfully, '*My time is short.*' As the minutes passed, George Henry Wood became increasingly restless and began pacing across the stone floor, his hands twitching nervously at clutching his sleeves.

After the Reverend finished his ministrations, the prisoner asked him to get him a pen and paper to write final letters to his family and acquaintances. Sitting at the plain deal table in the infirmary cell, he began writing a sincere farewell to his parents. He also left messages to people he felt had supported him while imprisoned. Finally, he asked that his apologies be sent to Edith's parents for his acts.

Throughout this time, Reverend Wilkinson repeatedly asked George Henry Wood if he had anything to confess and urged him to repent. However, as indignant as ever, the distraught condemned man repeated that he recalled nothing.

George Henry Wood's demeanour became increasingly unstable as the fatal hour approached. He repeatedly fell to his knees, prayed for forgiveness and wept bitterly. He also begged Reverend Wilkinson to remain with him until the end. As a man of God, Reverend Wilkinson could think of nothing worse and feared what he might observe on the gallows. However, such was his sympathy for the anguished man before him; he reluctantly agreed.

At 8.45 am, the chapel's bell began to sound out the funeral knell at one-minute intervals. The infirmary cell was near the chapel; therefore, George Henry Wood must have been in no doubt that his death was imminent.

Meanwhile, outside the gaol, the waiting crowds continued to grow in number and became loud and animated. However, the haunting bell's toll and what it signalled caused a deathly silence and stillness to pass through the group. The schoolmaster, Mr Baxter, entered the courtyard of the reporters, who were still patiently waiting, and asked that they accompany him to the committee room.

As they made their way, the journalists observed several gentlemen emerging from the Governor's residence, which was directly opposite. The group included Captain Crickitt (Governor), Under-sheriff (Walter Bartlett), Medical Officer (Richard Turner), Deputy Medical Officer (James Slack) and Prison Surgeon (Henry Crickitt).

These officials walked to the condemned cell where George Henry Wood was sitting. The Governor had moved the prisoner from the infirmary a few minutes previously due to its closeness to the gallows. Shortly after, the Chief Warder of the Gaol, Mr Farr, asked the reporters to follow him. They walked eastwards and passed through several enclosed yards within the gaol. On the way, they noticed four warders stationed outside an open door that led to the prison's east wing.

The death wardens were tasked with accompanying George Henry Wood to the gallows to witness his final moments. This could not have been easy for them. As previously stated, executions were infrequent at Lewes, and this was likely the first time they would see a man hung. In addition, the wardens had guarded George Henry Wood 24 hours a day since his conviction. It was not uncommon for these death wardens to develop relationships with condemned prisoners and sometimes feel pity and sorrow at the end.

The reporters continued walking through the final yard until they passed the last, which led into an immaculately kept grass-covered exercise yard adjacent to where Brighton Road branches off to Chailey. As the group made their way into an exercise yard along the path bordering the area, they immediately spotted the black-painted wooden crossbeam enclosed in a three-walled wooden shed in an attempt to disguise it. Despite these efforts, it was unmistakable as the apparatus of death. A new rope hung around the beam, connected to another stout scaffold cord, dangled a few inches down.

Earlier executions had been carried out on a high scaffold supported by a platform. As the executioner released the trap doors, the prisoner would descend below, suspended by his or her neck. However, condemned prisoners were often distraught and barely able to walk. It was also not common for them to faint on the way to the gallows, which forced them to be dragged or carried.

In 1885, the authorities decided that expecting condemned prisoners to climb stairs in their last moments was inhumane and requested that gallows be constructed at the ground, thus removing the need for stairs. Lewes House of Correction had followed this trend, and consequently, the previously described shed stood above a brick-lined pit that opened at ground level and descended approximately 12 feet below. A flight of stone stairs allowed access and enabled the retrieval of the body after the execution. Two heavy oaken doors covered the mouth of the execution pit. Leather strips hung on either side of the crossbeam, allowing the wardens to steady themselves as they held the prisoner in his final seconds.

Adjacent to the execution pit, the reporters observed a thick buckled leather strap lying on the ground, which James Billington had placed there earlier that morning. The authorities had enforced the mandatory use of leg straps within executions during the latter part of 1856 following the botched execution of William Bousfield. William Calcraft, the principal executioner, had conducted the judicial hanging at the time. However, in the days leading up to William Bousfield's date with death, William Calcraft received several death threats, and the usually confident William Calcraft became highly nervous.

At the moment of the execution, William Bousfield walked from Newgate's condemned cell to the execution platform directly outside the gaol in front of two thousand public witnesses. After an unnerved William Calcraft completed his final checks, he stepped to one side and released the bolt. However, instead of remaining at the gallows as customary, Calcraft, who lost his nerve, ran off. William Bousfield was dangling below the platform and slowly suffocating from the noose. Without his executioner, he raised his legs and balanced himself on the mouth of the trapdoor.

William Calcraft's assistant gave William Bousfield a firm push which caused him to descend for the second time. However, within a few seconds, he again regained his original position above the drop. The vast crowd, who at the start of the execution had been entirely silent, initially gasped and moaned but quickly began to boo, hiss and curse at the officials.

The officiating chaplain, utterly horrified by the spectacle before him, went and found William Calcraft and forced him to return to the scaffold.

Initially, William Calcraft appeared dazed and unsure of what to do. However, he eventually regained his composure and threw himself around William Bousfield's legs, forcing the prisoner to fall with some force and causing the hanging to end. The bungled execution caused immense public outrage, and leg bindings were made mandatory.

Meanwhile, at Lewes, the nervous waiting journalists continued to study the prison's exercise yard. As they did so, they noticed a set of little stone squares cemented onto the flint along the boundary wall near George Henry Wood's grave. These small markers bore the initials of previously executed prisoners and their death dates.

As the journalists continued to study the area surrounding the gallows, they noted another disturbing and ominous sight. Dead opposite the gallows, the warders had dug a grave and placed several wooden planks over its opening to disguise it. However, the tomb's position was clearly visible from the pathway that the execution procession would walk, and it is likely that in his last moments, George Henry Wood recognised his grave.

A few minutes before 9 am, after hearing movement outside his cell, George Henry Wood again fell to his knees and began to pray. The waiting crowds outside the prison, aware of the time, were by this point waiting in silence, and the only sound that occasionally interrupted the muteness was whispering. Late arrivals and distant voices were the only sound that interrupted the stark stillness around the gaol. At a few minutes before 9 am, Reverend Wilkinson asked for the final time if George Henry Wood if he had anything to say, to which he silently shook his head.

At precisely 9 am, without warning, the executioner and several other officials entered the condemned cell. James Billington immediately began pinioning George Henry Wood's arms to his waist at the elbows with a long leather strap. The prisoner could still raise his lower arms, shook hands with the Governor, and said, *'Goodbye, Sir. You have been very kind to me.'* He turned to others in the room and thanked them for the compassion they had shown him. The Governor gave a covert signal, and the sad procession started moving towards the gallows.

The reporters adjacent to the scaffold watched as the group emerged from the condemned cell's entrance. Reverend Wilkinson led the procession with *'great pity and sadness'* and began reading the burial service. Despite his best efforts, his words at times were completely overpowered by the prison chapel's tolling bell.

Immediately behind the Reverend, George Henry Wood was flanked by Warder Sprinks and Warder Keel on either side. With concerns about an epileptic episode still fresh in the official's minds, Warder Webb and Brown followed behind to provide extra strength if George Henry Wood caused any problems or passed out. Next in the group was the executioner James Billington, followed by the Governor, Prison Surgeon and other officials. George Henry Wood was bare-headed. The journalists noted that he was wearing the same attire he had worn at his trial.

As the procession continued their journey, George Henry Wood walked with a firm step and held his head erect, ever arrogant to the end. At this point, George would not have been able to see the gallows but undoubtedly must have been experiencing significant anxiety and apprehension.

The morbid black spectacle came into their view as the group reached the broader end of the yard. The sight caused George Henry Wood's facial expression to immediately change. He began breathing more quickly, and his complexion became pale. He briefly glanced across at the three reporters as he reached the gallows, but his face remained expressionless. Even at this point, George Henry Wood always continued walking forward until he was positioned immediately under the cross beam. James Billington turned his prisoner by the shoulders so that he was facing the rear of the shed and had his back to the small group of spectators.

Warders Sprinks and Keel, who had been given clear instructions by James Billington earlier that day, stepped onto the wooden trapdoors. Afterwards, they positioned themselves on either prisoner's side to steady themselves grasped at the support ropes hanging from the gallows. Once in position, they each placed a hand on George Henry Wood's upper arm for support.

George Henry Wood, by this point, appears to have accepted his death and was highly composed. With the prisoner position, Reverend Wilkinson positioned himself on the grass and continued to read the burial service. However, as a supporter of abolishing capital sentences, he turned his back on the scaffold.

Recognising that everyone was in the correct position, James Billington quickly grabbed the leather strap from the ground and secured them around George's legs. While this final pinioning occurred, George quietly repeated, *'Lord, Jesus, receive my spirit.'* James Billington placed the noose around George's neck and adjusted it. He pulled the white cap from his pocket and drew it over George Henry Wood's head.

Reverend Wilkinson, who was still loudly reciting the burial service, said, *'In the midst of life, we are in death.'* James Billington performed a brief final check to ensure everything was correct, stepped to the side and firmly pulled the lever. The heavy oaken doors parted, and George Henry Wood descended into the pit below. His death occurred instantaneously, and such was the drop's force; the rope did not sway. In most instances, the fall from the scaffold caused instant death by dislocation of the vertebrae. However, it was common for the body to experience spasms after death. Therefore it was customary for the bodies to be left in position for one hour before removing them.

After being informed that death had occurred, the three ashen-faced journalists cautiously crept to the mouth of the pit and studied George Henry Wood's lifeless body. They noted that the white cap had slipped on one side of the convict's head, and his eyes which could be seen, were closed. They reported that George Henry Wood's face appeared somewhat distorted, and he had an abrasion on the right side of his face.

At the point of George Henry Wood's death, the loud thud of the oaken doors echoed through the silent prison grounds. This ghastly message was passed from warden to warden until it reached Deputy Engineer Elliott, who stood at the main entrance. At 9.15am, he slowly hoisted the black '*death*' flag, which informed the waiting crowd the sentence had been carried out.

The waiting crowds appeared deeply affected by this grim symbol. Men held their heads in horror, and many women began to cry. Conversations quickly started, and many recalled hearing the rattling thud of the falling trap doors. However, many of those present promptly lost interest and left the area, and by 9.30 am, the area was completely clear.

Having completed his grim duties, James Billington exited the prison and went to the Railway Station to catch the 9.30 train to London. After precisely one hour, the warders descended into the execution pit and cut George Henry Wood's body from the execution rope. After washing the corpse, they carefully carried it up the stone stairs to ground level.

Although George Henry Wood's death had been court-ordered, the law stated that an inquest still had to occur. Consequently, the warders placed George Henry Wood's body into a plain wooden coffin and put a small piece of wood beneath his head for support.

Knowing that the Coroner's jury would view the body, the warders attempted to position the body appropriately. However, despite their best efforts, George Henry Wood's dislocated neck gave the body an unnatural appearance. The pair then carried the body to the infirmary ward at placed it onto a pair of wooden trestles at the centre of the room, which had been placed there earlier that day.

At 10.30 am, the Coroner's jury arrived at the prison. After signing in, they were escorted from the gaol's gatehouse to the committee room. The group comprised twelve notable Lewes residents. The records show that the group consisted of Councillor James Pelling (Foreman), Mr William Nathaniel Barnard, Mr James Sands Blackett, Mr Phillip Burtenshaw, Mr William Watkin Dutton, Councillor Joseph Robinson Hardwick, Mr Owen

Harvey, Mr William Likeman, Mr Charles Morrish, Mr Thomas Rickey, Mr Edward Rusbridge and Mr Henry Tucker.

As soon as the group arrived at the committee room adjacent to the Governor's house, and were seated around a large wooden table. The three journalists were then moved to the room to observe the final stages of the proceedings.

After officially opening the inquest, the Coroner said, *'The body of George Henry Wood now lies in Her Majesty's prison, and it is for you to find, which means he came to his death after hearing the evidence.'*

The Foreman: *'Nearly all the jurymen have asked me if we can view the scaffold?'*

The Coroner: *'That is a matter you must ask the Governor. I have no jurisdiction to let you into the prison or any part of it except by permission of the Home Office. If the Governor allows you to see it, you might.'*

The Foreman: *'But we know it is done very frequently?'*

The Coroner: *'Nonetheless, it is a matter for the Governor to decide.'*

The Coroner then requested that the jury follow him to the infirmary to view the body. The group complied with the request and filed out of the room. After a few seconds, the group reached the room and entered. Once inside, they silently surrounded George Henry Wood's coffin. In whispered, the group discussed the corpse's appearance and pointed out several visible marks indicating a violent and sudden death. Some jurymen had attended George Henry Wood's trial and commented on his changed appearance.

For obvious reasons, George Henry Wood was given no access to razors since his conviction, and as a result, he had grown a substantial beard which some commented had also changed his appearance. They also noted that the condemned prisoner had also lost considerable weight since his sentence, which had also changed his facial features.

As the group continued to study the body, they found it was cold and had somewhat of a serene expression. The deceased's uninjured arms lay limp at his sides, and his hands fully open, allowing the jurors to see his heavily tattooed wrists. The face was pale but bore no injury except his left cheek, which had developed purple speckling due to Livor Mortis.

These findings led the jury to conclude that death was instantaneous without suffering. The Foreman once again requested that the jury be permitted to view the gallows. However, the Governor explained that he had no authority to allow them into the gaol and asked that the jurors return to the committee room.

The first witness of the inquest to be called was the Prison Governor, Captain George Crickitt.

He said, *'I am the Governor of H.M Prison at Lewes. The body the jury has just seen is that of George Henry Wood, aged 29, a railway porter formerly of Brighton. He was indicted and convicted of the murder of Edith Jeal and was sentenced to death by Mr Justice Mathew at the Lewes Assizes on 5th April 1892. He was duly hanged this morning at 9 am in my presence, the Under Sheriff, the surgeon, a Congregational minister Mr Wilkinson the deceased belonging to that sect, and the prison officials. The certificate required by the statute has been signed.'*

The Coroner: *'Has the judgement of death been duly and legally carried out?'*

The Governor: *'Yes, Sir.'*

The next witness to be called was Richard Turner, the prison's medical officer.

He said, *'I am the surgeon to Her Majesty's prison and observed the execution of George Henry Wood.'*

The Coroner: *'Were you present this morning to see George Henry Wood duly executed, according to law?'*

Richard Turner: *'I was.'*

The Coroner: *'Was the prisoner hanged by the neck till he died?'*

Richard Turner: *'He was'*

The Coroner: *'Have you examined the body?'*

Richard Turner: *'I have examined the body. The neck was completely dislocated. You could pass your finger between the neck bones, more so than I ever saw before in any other case.'*

The Coroner: *'Was that the cause of death?'*

Richard Turner: *'Yes, that was the cause of death, and the death was instantaneous, and the rope did not break the skin.'*

The Coroner: *'Have you signed the usual certificate?'*

Richard Turner: *'I have.'*

At this stage, George Henry Wood's alleged epilepsy was once again raised by the Foreman.

He said, *'I would like to know if he was in his right mind and free from epilepsy at the time of his death?'*

The Coroner: *'That is a matter we have no jurisdiction to question, but the doctor may answer if he so wishes.'*

Richard Turner: *'He was perfectly sound in his mind.'*

This statement marked the end of the evidence. Without pausing for any deliberation, the jury judged death by judicial hanging and declared that the execution had been adequately carried out. After the jury was thanked and dismissed for their duties, the Under-Sheriff, Governor, and Reverend Wilkinson completed the death notices. A few moments later, the senior warder walked out of the prison and attached the three notices to the prison gates as prescribed by the Execution Act of 1877.

A telegram was sent to the Wood family at Rock Street, Brighton, to inform them that the execution had been carried out. They had waited eagerly for news about their son and, despite being told that a reprieve had been denied, had continually prayed for their son to be saved. However, when it finally came, they were understandably devastated but were relieved that their son was at peace.

Telegrams were also sent to the Treasury and the Office for Home Affairs. The message stated that the execution had successfully been carried out. They also said that George Henry Wood had not suffered from any type of fit before his death, much to the relief of the authorities. A few days after George Henry Wood's death, an unknown author wrote a further broadside ballad following George Henry Wood's execution. Its lyrics are as follows:

The man who did the Brighton murder,
And outraged the poor little child,
They have sent him from the world forever,
To a murderer's grave, he is consigned,
The hangman now has done his duty,
Within the dismal Sussex Gaol,
For his victim, full of childish beauty,
All feeling people did bewail.

Wood that killed the child at Brighton
To eternity has just been hurled.
The law has justly punished the right one,
For his crime, I'm sure disgraced the world.

The little girl you well remember,
With her brother was shopping in the town,
She had hardly seen five mid-summers,
Ere by this villain, she was struck down.
Her murderer held a good position,
Working on a railway line,
But 'tis said that in a drunken condition,

All thought or care did he resign.

By the magistrates committed,
At Lewes Assizes, he was tried,
I am not guilty there he pleaded,
But his guilt he could not hide.

Tho' defended by clever counsel,
Useless it soon proved to be,
He was sentenced to die upon the scaffold,
And now he is in eternity.

His innocence he still protested,
Although he was condemned to die,
A petition for him was presented,
Though we can't tell the reason why,
How could he expect a pardon,
For doing his unnatural crime,
He hid her body in the garden,
But her blood was on him all the time.

They bound him on the Tuesday morning,
And left him forth to meet his death,
The sun the heavens were adorning,
The gaolers hardly drew a breath,
The chaplain read the burial service,
And the last prayer for him did give,
The hangman touched the fatal lever,
And the Brighton murderer ceased to live.

Chapter 30: The Aftermath

After George Henry Wood's death, things slowly settled down for the traumatised Wood family. George Wood Senior continued working at the Belgrave Street Chapel for many years. Margery Wood continued to battle heart disease until she finally succumbed to the condition in December 1907.

George Wood Senior continued to work at the Belgrave Street Chapel and received support from his other children. On the 22nd of May 1894, a lengthy article appeared in the Mid Sussex Times, which detailed the wedding of James Wood, George Henry Wood's eldest brother, to Mary Ann Wickham at the Belgrave Street Chapel.

The occasion appears to have been a successful and happy one. Moreover, the article contains various family members' names and addresses, suggesting that the shame they experienced during George Henry Wood's trial reduced over time. This is reinforced by the fact that George Wood Senior remained at Rock Street until he died in 1911.

Meanwhile, the houses surrounding the field where Edith's body was found did not find the murder easy to overcome. Perturbed by the nature and infamy of the murder, residents in the vicinity demanded that the barn be demolished and launched a petition to that effect. The petition is as follows:

'We, the undersigned owners of property and residents in the neighbourhood of Chichester Place, do hereby make a united petition to the trustees of the field adjoining Chichester Place to the following effect, viz, that the barn in which such an awful crime has so recently been committed be pulled down. We respectfully beg to draw the attention of the trustees to the fact that the barn, for a very long period, has been a nuisance and a detriment to the inhabitants of

the district, a resort for tramps and others both by day and night. Therefore, we humbly petition that a place which affords such as shelter for nuisance and crime be cleared away as soon as possible.'

The petition received over twenty signatures and was delivered to St Mary's Hall's trustees, who permitted the barn to be demolished after the Assizes. T. Griffith, Builder and Contractor of 106 St George's Road, Kemp Town, was commissioned to carry out the work. After clearing the barn, he erected a small shed to hold a few tools.

In Manitoba, Reverend William Goulding continued to work at Manitoba Penitentiary, tending to the prisoners. However, in 1898, a memorandum was sent to the Canadian Minister of Justice, which questioned the Reverend's conduct. The message states that Arthur William Goulding had habitually neglected the duties required by the penitentiary regulations.

In addition, the note says that he did not possess the relevant qualifications for the post, questioned his conduct, and said he was objectionable in other particulars. No further details are given in the archives, but shortly after, he was dismissed.

Mr Russell Day, the Treasury's Prosecutor, continued working for the Office of Public Prosecutions. On at least two further occasions, he prosecuted men who used epilepsy as a defence and successfully argued for the death penalty. Many years would pass before epileptic sufferers were afforded more compassion and understanding by society. Many still suffer from the stigma today.

Doctor Saunders continued to work at the Sussex County Lunatic Asylum until he retired. In May 1892, he gave an interview to the Mid Sussex Times, warning of the perils of drunkenness. He still had a lot of sympathy for George Henry Wood and continued to believe he was irresponsible for Edith's murder. The article is as follows:

'Doctor Saunders, Medical Superintendent of the County Asylum, Haywards Heath, who gave evidence at the recent trial of Wood, the Brighton murderer, as to his mental state, especially relating to epilepsy, says:-

Sir, Before the tragedy associated with the name George Henry Wood passes into oblivion and the sooner it is dismissed from memory for the better, permit me to refer, by way of warning to one important incident in the case, viz., that Wood's drunken state on the 10th of December was due to the mischievous habit of having been given a drink by way of a 'tip.' To use the man's words to me, 'I never spent a penny of my own money. It (the drinks) was given to me.'

Two men exposed, as carmen, postmen at Christmas, and many others are, to the temptation of tipping at other people's expense, this case should serve as an awful warning, as it out also to do to those persons who are guilty of the practice of bestowing their gifts in this harmful way.'

Harry Edward Ayres, of Prince and Ayres Legal Offices, Middle Street, Brighton, continued practising law after the trial but began abusing alcohol. On the 15th of December, 1895, he appeared at the Marlborough police court, charged with being drunk and disorderly. A police constable showed evidence that he had encountered Mr Ayres and a cabman in an altercation in Old Bond Street, London.

Mr Ayres refused to leave the area. The police constable noticed he was drunk and arrested him. Mr Ayres said to the court, *'I may say I have been treated brutally and cowardly. They kept me for eight hours in the police cell!'* The Judge fined Mr Ayres 10s and advised him to contact the commissioner of the police. On the 17th of December 1899, he died.

James Terry, Chief Constable of the Brighton Police Constabulary, continued until he retired in 1894. He died on the 26th of September 1906 and is buried a small distance from Edith Jeal's grave on the grounds of the Extra Mural Cemetery.

Bibliography:

Files used at East Sussex Records Office:

ACC 3421/3/853, ACC 3609, ACC 5611/2/611, BTNRP_BH600439, COR 3/2/1907/150, ESC 28/1, PAR 232/36/1, PAR 277/2/22/23, PAR 311/25/3/1, PTS/2/2/2, QN/145, QR/968, QSB/1/5, QSB/1/5, R/A 2/516/30, R/E 35/1, R/L 24/2, SMH/14/3/1, SPA/3/1/9, SxMOA1/5/9/37/A/2, XC 37.

Files used at the National Archives:

PCO 8/208, HO 324/2, HO 144/242/A53544

Images
From the James Gray Collection, with permission from the Regency Society, Brighton:
From the British Library with permission

Newspapers:

Aberdeen Evening Express, The
Argus, The
Armagh Standard, The
Ballymena Observer, The
Banbury Advertiser, The
Belfast Telegraph, The
Berwickshire News and General Advertiser
Bicester Herald, The
Bognor Regis Observer, The
Brighton Gazette, The
Brighton Guardian, The
Brighton Herald, The
Bristol Mercury, The
Cheltenham Chronicle, The
Croydon Observer, The
Dublin Evening Telegraph, The
Dundee Advertiser, The
Dundee Courier, The
Eastbourne Chronicle, The

Eastbourne Gazette, The
Eastern Daily Press, The
English Lakes Visitor, The
Falkirk Herald, The
Farringdon Adviser and the Vale of the White Horse Gazette, The
Folkestone Express, Sandgate, Shorncliffe & Hythe Advertiser, The
Gentlewoman, The
Graphic, The
Hastings and St Leonards Observer, The
Herts Guardian, Agricultural Journal and General Advertiser, The
Horsham, Petworth, Midhurst and Steyning Express, The
Huddersfield Chronicle, The
Illustrated Police News, The
Islington Gazette, The
Kirkintilloch Herald, The
Lancashire Evening Post, The
Lancaster Gazette, The
Leeds Mercury, The
Leeds Times, The
Leicester Chronicle, The
Liverpool Mercury, The
Lloyd's Weekly Newspaper, The
Ludlow Advertiser, The
Mid-Sussex Times, The
Norfolk News, The
North Devon Gazette, The
Northern Constitution, The
Nottingham Journal, The
Paisley & Renfrewshire Gazette, The
Pall Mall Gazette, The
People, The
Reading Gazette, The
Royal Cornwall Gazette, The
Scotsman, The
Sheffield Daily Telegraph, The
Sheffield Evening Telegraph, The
Shields Daily Gazette, The
South Wales Daily News, The

Southern Echo, The
Sphere, The
Sphere, The
Sunderland Daily Echo, The
Sussex Advertiser, The
Sussex Agricultural Express, The
Sussex Daily News, The
Swindon Advertiser and North Wilts Chronical, The
Tamworth Herald, The
Tatler, The
Toronto Daily Mail, The
Walsall Free Press and General Advertiser, The
Warwick and Warwickshire Advertiser, The
West Sussex County Times, The
Woolwich Gazette, The
Worthing Gazette, The
Wrexham Advertiser, The
York Herald, The
Minnedosa Tribune, The
Portage la Prairie Weekly, The
Brandon Mail, The

Printed in Great Britain
by Amazon